SWINDOLL
LEADERSHIP
LIBRARY

SALVATION

EARL D. RADMACHER

CHARLES R. SWINDOLL, *General Editor*

ROY B. ZUCK, *Managing Editor*

WORD PUBLISHING

NASHVILLE

A Thomas Nelson Company

SALVATION
Swindoll Leadership Library

Unless otherwise indicated, Scripture quotations used in this book are from
the *New King James Version* (NKJV), copyright © 1979, 1980, 1982
by Thomas Nelson, Inc. Used by permission.

Scripture quotations identified KJV are from the *King James Version* of the Bible.

Scripture quotations identified NASB are from the *New American Standard Bible,*
copyright © 1960, 1962, 1963, 1971, 1972, 1973, 1975, 1977, 1999
by the Lockman Foundation. Used by permission.

Scripture quotations identified NLT are from the *Holy Bible: New Living Translation,*
copyright © 1996 by Tyndale House Publishers.

Published in association with Dallas Theological Seminary (DTS):

General Editor: Charles R. Swindoll
Managing Editor: Roy B. Zuck

The theological opinions expressed by the authors are not necessarily the official
position of Dallas Theological Seminary.

Library of Congress Cataloging in Publication Data:

Radmacher, Earl D.
Salvation/ Earl D. Radmacher ; Charles R. Swindoll, general editor;
Roy B. Zuck, managing editor
p.   cm.—(Swindoll Leadership Library)
Includes bibliographical references and indexes.

ISBN 0-8499-1374-8

1. Salvation. I. Swindoll, Charles R. II. Zuck, Roy B. III. Title.

BT751.2.R33 2000   99-048664
234–dc21   CIP

Printed in the United States of America
00 01 02 03 04 05 06 BVG 9 8 7 6 5 4 3 2 1

To my wife, Ruth,
whose love and encouragement
have been so strategic
in completing this work

CONTENTS

FOREWORD

A bestseller on the habits of successful people has recently swept through the business world and then the general public. One of the habits the book advocates is "putting first things first." If family time is deemed important, the author advises placing it on the calendar as a regularly scheduled event, much like a business appointment or meeting. If physical exercise is a high value for a reader, it should be labeled a "first thing" and treated as such. You get the point. Top-priority matters deserve top-priority attention.

Now even more books have come out on the subject of putting first things first. Computer screen savers blink, "First Things First . . . First Things First." The motto shows up everywhere.

Some people, however, have some fuzzy thinking about first things. One man, who was sure one of his "first things" was bicycling, sheepishly admitted he hadn't actually bicycled in more than two years! Some "first thing"! His real "first things" had become, without his realizing it, computer software classes and navigating rush-hour traffic patterns.

The Bible, a book of top-priority matters, is not at all fuzzy about first things. Throughout Scripture the theme of salvation rises above all other issues. It is a divinely appointed "first thing." The Cross is central to God's priorities. Remember Paul's succinct statement, "For I delivered to you as of *first importance* what I also received, that Christ died for our sins according to the Sciptures, and that He was buried, and that He was raised on the third day according to the Sciptures" (1 Cor. 15:3–4, italics added).

Salvation is *the* theme of the Bible. That's why I'm so pleased to add the book you're holding in your hands to our series. My longtime friend, Dr. Earl Radmacher, eminently qualified to write on this topic, discusses in detail the many facets of our salvation.

This book is no man-centered philosophical treatise. Rather, Radmacher heads straight to the appropriate Scripture passages and mines from them the gold concerning God's good news. All the crucial topics are included: sin, grace, faith, regeneration, redemption, propitiation, justification, adoption, sanctification, spiritual gifts, and glorification. Also included are sections on the critical areas of the believer's security and assurance.

If you're wondering about "first things" in the Bible you need search no further than the pages of this book. Truths set forth here concern issues that were settled "before the creation of the world," but that remain as relevant and urgent as today's top news story, in fact, more so. No other issue deserves our time and attention more than this one. This book provides information that is of primary importance. If you are anxious to put "first things first," this is the book for you.

—CHARLES R. SWINDOLL
General Editor

ACKNOWLEDGMENTS

On occasion someone will ask me, "Who discipled you?" That creates frustration for me because there are many people to whom I owe a debt of gratitude because of the contribution they have made to my initial and continuing salvation. I am repeatedly amazed at the networking in God's wonderful family of grace.

I have similar feelings now because, in such a short space, I cannot possibly name all the people who have influenced this book. I am encouraged, however, by the knowledge that the God who will reward the one who gives even "a cup of cold water" (Matt. 10:42) doesn't overlook anyone; thus one day He Himself will make up for my faltering memory.

Theologically I am indebted to Charles C. Ryrie, who led me in my earliest training by setting the example of giving priority to the inspired teachings of the biblical writers over the interpreters of those writings. As an interpreter himself, however, he was a master at taking difficult concepts and simplifying them for "the man on the street."

Exegetically I am indebted to the exegetical expertise and hermeneutical care of Zane Hodges, whose humility before the Word of God and untiring diligence continues to be a model for me of "a worker who does not need to be ashamed, rightly dividing the word of truth" (2 Tim. 2:15).

There have been times when I questioned his conclusions, but further investigation usually demonstrated his superior wisdom.

Practically I am indebted to my wife of forty-six years, who not only believes in me but also gently encourages me to "keep on keeping on" in the task of writing. Many were the times when she has set aside her pleasures to make it possible for me to keep at this work.

Editorially I am indebted to Dr. Roy B. Zuck, managing editor of this series, for his painstaking and tedious work in editing this manuscript. His attention to detail and his insightful suggestions have helped me communicate this valuable doctrine more clearly.

I am most deeply indebted to my Lord Jesus Christ and the God of all grace, who not only has rescued me from eternal damnation but has patiently moved me along in sanctification salvation and created within me the intense desire to be a part of that great throng that shall "cast their crowns before the throne, saying: 'You are worthy, O Lord, to receive glory and honor and power; for You created all things, and by Your will they exist and were created'" (Rev. 4:10–11).

INTRODUCTION

In introducing salvation, the grandest theme in the Scriptures, my esteemed professor Charles C. Ryrie writes, "The doctrine of salvation ... embraces all of time as well as eternity past and future. It relates in one way or another to all of mankind, without exception. It even has ramifications in the sphere of the angels. It is the theme of both the Old and the New Testaments. It is personal, national, and cosmic. And it centers on the greatest Person, our Lord Jesus Christ."[1]

When I think of the impact of that, it takes my breath away. But then I realize that humanity, in its desperate situation, needs a mighty rescue program equally far-reaching. My son Dan has written a hymn that speaks vividly of God's rescuing us from sin.

He Rescued Me

I never knew love, I was God's enemy
Until Jesus came along—and rescued me;
Surrendered His life, put away enmity
He gave me peace with God, and so He rescued me.

Chorus: He rescued me, oh, He rescued me;
I was sinking deep in sin, and I thought I knew peace within.
He rescued me, oh, He rescued me
When Jesus gave His life for me on Calvary.

For me He was bruised, beaten, and scorned;
He suffered the shame, He took the blame to rescue me.
Crucified, and come Easter morn
He rose from the grave, oh, praise His name, to rescue me.

Chorus: He rescued me, oh, He rescued me;
I was sinking deep in sin, and I needed His peace within.
He rescued me, oh, He rescued me
When Jesus gave His life for me on Calvary.

Sin had blinded me, stripped my health;
I was dying, trying to please myself.
Jesus offered to pay the price;
He exchanged my wrong for His righteous life by grace.

Chorus: He rescued me, oh, He rescued me;
I was sinking deep in sin, but now I know peace within.
He rescued me, oh, He rescued me
When Jesus gave His life for me on Calvary.

"Amazing grace, how sweet the sound"
When I put my faith in Jesus' name to rescue me.
"Once I was lost, but now I'm found;"
Once I was blind, but now I see since He rescued me.

Chorus: He rescued me, oh, He rescued me;
I was sinking deep in sin, but now I know peace within.
He rescued me, oh, He rescued me
When Jesus gave His life for me on Calvary.

Little wonder that the writer to the Hebrew Christians warned, "How shall we escape if we neglect so great a salvation" (Heb. 2:3)? The apostle Paul, writing to believers in Philippi, said, "Work out your own salvation with fear and trembling, for it is God who works in you both to will and to do for His good pleasure" (Phil. 2:12–13).

Strabo (63 B.C.–A.D. 24) told about the once-famous silver mines in Spain. In referring to the "working out" of those mines, he used the same word Paul used here. Strabo meant, of course, that the Romans were operating, exploiting, and getting the utmost value out of what was already theirs. Such is the apostle's meaning of "work out": I am to mine what is already mine.[3] We want to do just that in this study—to probe all the dimensions of this marvelous truth of salvation through faith in the Lord Jesus Christ.

PART ONE
God's Provision of Salvation

CHAPTER 1

What Does Salvation Mean?

Have you ever said something to a friend only to discover later that while he heard what you said he missed your meaning? This often happens when we read the Bible. How easy it is to bring a meaning to a Bible passage that was not what the writer had in mind. When we do that, we have missed the mind of God and are in serious danger of following the enemy of our souls. To protect ourselves from that danger we need to study the meaning of words and how they are used in their contexts. And this is especially true of the word *salvation*.

THE MEANING OF THE WORD *SALVATION*

The Vocabulary

The word *salvation* has its roots in the Hebrew word *yāšāʿ*, "to be wide or roomy" in contrast to "narrow or restricted." Thus words such as *liberation, emancipation, preservation, protection,* and *security* grow out of it. It refers to delivering a person or group of people from distress or danger, from a "restricted" condition in which they are unable to help themselves. John Hartley aptly states, "That which is wide connotes freedom from distress and the ability to pursue one's own objectives. To move from *distress to safety* requires deliverance. Generally the deliverance must come from somewhere outside the party oppressed."[1]

Yāšâ and words derived from it are used over three hundred fifty times in the Old Testament. It is first used in Exodus 14:30 to speak of Israel's mighty deliverance from the Egyptian bondage: "So the LORD saved [that is, delivered] Israel that day out of the hand of the Egyptians, and Israel saw the Egyptians dead on the seashore." As a testimony to this dramatic rescue from certain destruction, Moses wrote a song of great praise to the Lord, recorded in Exodus 15:1–18. This great deliverance—the Exodus— became the focal point of all God's saving acts in the Old Testament. In his last words of blessing to the nation, Moses said, "Happy are you, O Israel! Who is like you, a people saved [delivered] by the LORD, the shield of your help and the sword of your majesty!" (Deut. 33:29). Most important, however, *yāšâ* pointed forward to our great Deliverer, our Savior Jesus Christ. The Hebrew word for "Savior" comes from *yāšâ*, "to save."

In the New Testament the verb *sōzō* ("to save") and the nouns *sōtēr* ("Savior") and *sōtēria* ("salvation") parallel the Hebrew word and its derivatives. Thus the Old Testament concept of deliverance is carried over to the New Testament.

A number of times, however, *sōtēria* translates *šālôm* ("peace" or "wholeness"), which broadens the idea of rescue or deliverance to include recovery, safety, and preservation. There is a progression in these concepts: (a) rescue from imminent and life-threatening danger to (b) a place of safety and security and (c) a position of wholeness and soundness. The narrowness and restriction created by danger is replaced by the "breadth" of liberation in salvation.

Visualize a person on the *Titanic* facing the imminent expectation of drowning and death, but then being placed in a lifeboat. That is *rescue*. Then picture the person now in the lifeboat removed from danger and death. That is *safety*. Now picture an ocean liner coming alongside the lifeboat and hoisting it and its passengers aboard ship. Now they enjoy *security* and *soundness* of mind. All three ideas are included in the biblical concept of salvation.

The word *salvation* is used in a variety of ways. Failure to recognize this can lead to serious mistakes of interpretation. For example, in Matthew

4

24:13 Christ Jesus taught that the one who "endures to the end shall be saved." Is the "end" here referring to a period of time in history or to the end of a person's life? Does the "enduring" refer to physical endurance or spiritual endurance? To answer these questions the context must be examined carefully.

The Physical Meaning

Often the words *save* and *salvation* refer to physical not spiritual deliverance. This is especially true in the Old Testament. People were "saved" (rescued or delivered) from enemies on the battlefield (Deut. 20:4), from the lion's mouth (Dan. 6:20), and from the wicked (Pss. 7:11; 59:2).

When the New Testament uses *save* and *salvation* to refer to physical deliverance, those instances are more individual than national. Also the New Testament occurrences suggest not only rescue but also remedy and recovery. A graphic example of rescue from imminent death is God's sparing Paul's life in the shipwreck on his way to Rome (Acts 27:20, 31, 34). This case is of special interest in that God promised deliverance in advance (27:23–24), and Paul confidently moved ahead on those promises (27:25, 34). In a physical sense salvation refers to being taken from danger to safety (Phil. 1:19), from disease to health (James 5:15), and from death to life (5:20).

The Spiritual Meaning

Salvation, in the spiritual sense, is the most exciting and promising deliverance available to human beings. It reaches to the depths of our need and lifts us to the highest grandeur imaginable. Spiritual salvation involves three tenses—past, present, and future. Doctrinally these are expressed as justification, sanctification, and glorification, but each one is part of the broad scope of salvation. At the moment a person places his or her faith in the finished work of Christ, that individual is saved from the death-dealing *penalty* for sin and is declared righteous (Gen.15:6; Ps. 103:12; Rom. 4:1–5; Titus 3:5). Then in this present life the believer in Christ is also *being* saved from the *power* of sin (Rom. 5:10; Heb. 7:25; James 1:21). And he or she *will be* saved from the *presence* of sin forever in heaven (Rom. 13:11; 1 Pet. 1:9). These three aspects of salvation may be viewed this way:

Past	Penalty of Sin	Justification
Present	Power of Sin	Sanctification
Future	Presence of Sin	Glorification

As seen in the following diagram,[2] justification is a free gift, sanctification involves a process, and glorification will include reward for the sanctification process.

SO GREAT SALVATION

Free Gift	Process	Evaluation
as a result of trusting Christ for salvation (John 3:16; Rom. 3:24; Rev. 22:17)	of abundant growth/maturity (John 10:10; Phil. 2:12; 2 Pet. 1:5–9)	to determine reward (Matt. 16:24–27; 1 Cor. 4:5; 2 Cor. 5:10; Col. 3:23–25; Rev. 3:21; 22:12)
Theological: Justification	Theological: Sanctification	Theological: Glorification
Offer: Whoever	Offer: Christ's disciples	Offer: All believers
Basis: Faith alone in Christ	Basis: Faith resulting in obedience	Basis: Faithful obedience
Description: Free gift	Description: Works, deeds, degrees	Description: Various
How often: One time	How often: Lifetime process	How often: One time (judgment seat of Christ)

SALVATION IS A NECESSARY WORK

In Romans 5:12 Paul wrote of the initial act of rebellion in human history: "Sin entered the world, and death through sin,... because all sinned."

He did not say, "because all sin" (though that is also true, as we shall see) but "because all sinned." Here God lets us in on something we would not otherwise know. Because the human race is a unit, we are all somehow involved in Adam's one sin (Gen. 2:7; 3:19). We were all "in Adam" and so we experience the problem of Adam's situation. Everyone then is "under sin" (Rom. 3:9).

Writing to the Corinthians about this problem, Paul presented God's cure: "For since by man came death, by Man also came the resurrection of the dead. For as in Adam all die, even so in Christ all shall be made alive" (1 Cor. 15:21–22). How many are in Adam? Everyone who has been born. How many people are in Christ? Everyone who has been born from above (John 1:12; 3:16; 5:24). Release from being "under sin" comes only by salvation, that is, by being spiritually delivered into a new position. And that new position is "in Christ." "But now in Christ Jesus you who once were far off have been brought near by the blood of Christ" (Eph. 2:13). Paul summarized the two spiritual conditions this way: "For as by one man's disobedience many were made sinners, so also by one Man's obedience many will be made righteous" (Rom. 5:19).

Because the human race is "in Adam," everyone is spiritually dead, and, if this is not corrected, the ultimate result is eternal death. David spoke of spiritual death this way: "Behold, I was brought forth in iniquity, and in sin my mother conceived me" (Ps. 51:5). David was not speaking about the condition of his mother but about his natural position by birth. Like David, we are all born dead in sin (Eph. 2:1). Being "dead" naturally requires a new birth, which gives the believer a new nature and spiritual life. Probably no one is more able to reflect on that transformation than Paul, who called himself the "chief" of sinners (1 Tim. 1:15). "If anyone is in Christ, he is a new creation; old things have passed away; behold, all things have become new" (2 Cor. 5:17). In the clause "he is a new creation," the words "he is" do not occur in the original. The verse is actually a strong exclamation. Literally, it reads, "If anyone is in Christ—new creation!" Believers see things differently; they have a new mind and heart.

Because everyone is born dead in sin and without spiritual life, all of a person's thoughts, attitudes, and actions stem from his or her sin nature.

That person is energized not by God but by self, Satan, and the world system. Jeremiah spoke pointedly of the unregenerate heart: "The heart is deceitful above all things, and desperately wicked; who can know it?" (Jer. 17:9). Quoting the words of David and Solomon, Paul declared, "As it is written: 'There is none righteous, no, not one; there is none who understands; there is none who seeks after God. They have all turned aside; they have together become unprofitable; there is none who does good, no, not one'" (Rom. 3:10–12).

While unbelievers may carry out benevolent and altruistic acts, those actions have no ultimate value before God because they do not have His glory as their goal. Even the best actions of a non-Christian are self-oriented. Every person is a sinner, not only by birth but also by choice. He practices sin because of his sin nature and his slavery to Satan.

Some people argue that people are born not with a sinful nature but with a good nature. If that is true, why doesn't at least one person go through life without sinning? If people are good, why is it that everyone sins? I have never heard of anyone taking a class to learn how to sin. We are capable of doing that without any effort at all. It just comes naturally!

In practice every unregenerate person demonstrates his or her situation under sin in Adam. Thus without a change in nature and a new source of power no one can enter heaven. A person with a sin nature in heaven would be as out of place as a fish on land. Heaven would be hell to a person outside of Christ.

To enjoy fellowship with God, one must have a divine nature (1 Cor. 2:14). It would be as foolish to give the unregenerate person lessons on doing good as to try giving a drowning person swimming lessons. The unsaved don't need lessons. They need rescue! And only one person, Jesus Christ, is capable of meeting that need.

SALVATION IS EXCLUSIVELY A WORK OF GOD

Seeing the desperate plight of those who are spiritually dead, it becomes obvious that they must have outside help. W. Robert Cook asks, "Who can forgive his own sin? Impart eternal life to himself? Clothe himself in God's righteousness? Write his name in heaven?"[3] No one. So someone else must do it, and only God is equal to the task. But He is perfectly holy and cannot look approvingly on sin or sinners. Yet in His infinite wisdom God found a way—and that was by His marvelous *grace*. A well-known acrostic of "grace" is God's Riches At Christ's Expense. What we could not possibly do, God Himself accomplishes. The value of His divine provision is so great that no one could possibly pay for it. It must be received as a gift (Rom. 3:23–24). And no one has put this rescue operation more strikingly than Isaiah: "Surely He has borne our griefs and carried our sorrows; yet we esteemed Him stricken, smitten by God, and afflicted. But He was wounded for our transgressions, He was bruised for our iniquities; the chastisement for our peace was upon Him, and by His stripes we are healed. All we like sheep have gone astray; we have turned, everyone, to his own way; and the LORD has laid on Him the iniquity of us all" (Isa. 53:4–6). Paul described this monumental decision within the Godhead in 2 Corinthians 5:21: "He made Him who knew no sin to be sin for us, that we might become the righteousness of God in Him."

On His way to the cross to make the infinite payment for all our sins, Jesus spoke these words to the Father: "Father, the hour has come. Glorify Your Son, that Your Son also may glorify You, as You have given Him authority over all flesh, that He should give eternal life to as many as You have given Him. And this is eternal life, that they may know You, the only true God, and Jesus Christ whom You have sent" (John 17:1–3).

From beginning to end, therefore, "Salvation is of the LORD" (Jon. 2:9). It is a work of God, by God, for God, to God. It is not our work for God; it is God's work for us. Nothing we can do in mind, attitude, or action can add anything to God's provision of salvation. Over two hundred years ago the Anglican minister Augustus M. Toplady clearly caught the thrust of this truth in the well-known hymn "Rock of Ages."

> Rock of Ages, cleft for me, let me hide myself in Thee;
> Let the water and the blood, from Thy wounded side which flowed,
> Be of sin the double cure, save from wrath and make me pure.
>
> Not the labors of my hands can fulfill Thy law's demands;
> Could my zeal no respite know, could my tears forever flow,
> All for sin could not atone; Thou must save and Thou alone.

Nothing in my hand I bring, simply to Thy cross I cling;

Naked, come to Thee for dress, helpless, look to Thee for grace;

Foul, I to the fountain fly, wash me, Savior, or I die!

While I draw this fleeting breath, when my eyes shall close in death,

When I soar to worlds unknown, see Thee on Thy judgment throne,

Rock of Ages, cleft for me, let me hide myself in Thee.

A lost person cannot contribute to his rescue in any way. How could a finite person possibly contribute anything to the infinite provision of Almighty God?

Salvation Is a Complete Work

Few things are as satisfying in life as seeing someone persevere through great difficulties to finish a task. Providing our salvation was a far greater task for God than creating the universe, but what God starts He finishes. He did not begin this mighty rescue operation of humankind and then drop it. Jesus' last words in the Bible are graphic: "I am the Alpha and the Omega, the Beginning and the End, the First and the Last" (Rev. 22:13). Earlier we saw that salvation in the believer's life may be viewed in three tenses: past, present, and future. God not only rescues us from the devastating *penalty* of sin. He also takes us through the process of deliverance from the *power* of sin, and on to complete victory from the *presence* of sin forever in heaven. He doesn't lose any along the way, as Paul stated in Romans 8:29–30: "For whom He foreknew, He also predestined to be conformed to the image of His Son.... Moreover whom He predestined, these He also called; whom He called, these He also justified; and whom He justified, these He also glorified." Notice that there is no slippage. God finishes with 100 percent of those with whom He starts.

Many Christians are excited (and rightly so) about being rescued from eternal condemnation, but they forget that God's work of salvation involves much more. He is now "saving" believers by giving them victory over the power of sin. In that sense they are *being* saved. If more of the saved (from the penalty of sin) would go on being saved (from the power and dominance of sin), we would have far less trouble in getting the lost saved. Isn't that what Christ said to the disciples in the Upper Room before His passion week: "By this all will know that you are My disciples, if you have love for one another [that is, if you go on being saved from the power of sin]" (John 13:35)? We call this sanctification, which is discussed in chapters 11–14.

THE MOTIVES FOR SALVATION

Years ago Donald Grey Barnhouse, renowned pastor of Tenth Presbyterian Church in Philadelphia, wrote an article entitled "Why God Saved You." In the article he made this simple statement: "And so God planned to save you because He wished to demonstrate to all the universe what He could do with a piece of dirt, that in the coming ages, He might show the immeasurable riches of His grace."[4] By speaking of us as dirt, he was referring, of course, to God's forming man from dust and breathing into him so that he became a living soul (Gen. 2:7). That is our origin, and if we feel that we have any claims on God, then we need to look back to our roots—from dust!

Some might ask, "Did God *need* to save us? Did He *need* to rescue His creation that had rebelled against Him?" No, He was not compelled to do so. As Ryrie asked, "Why should God want to save sinners? Why should He bear the pain of giving His only begotten Son to die for people who had rebelled against His goodness? What could it possibly mean to God to have a family of human beings?"[5] The Scriptures reveal that He had several reasons or motives for providing salvation.

To Satisfy His Infinite Love for the Lost

The first motive God had in saving us was to satisfy His infinite love for the lost. This particular motive is stated repeatedly in the Scriptures, but no verse is more familiar and loved than John 3:16: "For God so loved the world that He gave His only begotten Son, that whoever believes in Him should not perish but have everlasting life." Paul emphasized that God loves sinners: "But God demonstrates His own love toward us, in that while we were still sinners, Christ died for us" (Rom. 5:8). Lewis Sperry Chafer, founder and first president of Dallas Theological Seminary, wrote that God "does all that His infinite love dictates."[6] Chafer argues that the "greatest of all motives which actuates God in the exercise of His saving grace is the satisfying of His own infinite love for those ruined by sin. In this may be seen the truth that the salvation of a soul means infinitely more to God than it could ever mean to the one who is saved, regardless of the glorious realities which constitute that salvation."[7]

To Deliver from Condemnation and Give Eternal Life

A second motivation behind God's work of salvation is to deliver those who believe from condemnation and to give them eternal life. The last words of John 3:16 state the motivation succinctly: "that whoever believes in Him should not perish but have everlasting life." The word "life" (Greek, *zōē*) means more than simply being alive. It is "life as a principle, life in the absolute sense, life as God has it, that which the Father has in Himself, and which He gave to the Incarnate Son to have in Himself, John 5:26, and which the Son manifested in the world, 1 John 1:2."[8] In John 10:10 Jesus said, "I have come that they may have life [*zōē*]; and that they may have it more abundantly," and in verse 11 He stated, "I am the good shepherd. The good shepherd gives His life [*psychē*] for the sheep." Verse 10 refers to a quality of life that can be enjoyed now. In other words God has not simply given us life extensively but life intensively. In verse 11 *psychē* refers to Jesus' incarnate breath of life. He gave that up in death, but He could not give up *zōē* for that is what He is essentially.

To Secure Good Works from the Saved

Paul wrote that believers are "His workmanship, created in Christ Jesus for good works, which God prepared beforehand that we should walk in them" (Eph. 2:10). Besides being interested in doing something *for* us—giving us salvation—the Lord is also interested in receiving something *from* us. A believer receives the gift[9] of salvation not by what he or she did but by what *God* did. Believers then become stewards with the possibility and opportunity of doing good works—not to become saved, but because we are saved.

To Display the Riches of His Grace for All Eternity

A fourth motivation God has in saving those who believe is stated in Ephesians 2:7: "that in the ages to come He might show the exceeding riches of His grace in His kindness toward us in Christ Jesus." In eternity He will use what He has done in us as a teaching tool for all of creation. That is, all believers, rescued by God's grace from condemnation to hell, will be a showpiece for all eternity to all created beings. "The principalities and powers in the heavenly places," that is, angels, are observing the wisdom of God in those who are being saved (3:8–12). The angels are learning something about the grace and love of God as they see what He is doing in our lives.

Many Christians have a difficult time understanding why God doesn't save more people. Others wonder why our loving God would let anyone be condemned to hell. The angels in heaven, however, don't have a problem with that at all. Their problem is how a righteous God could save *any* hell-deserving sinner. To them, that seems to be a compromise of the character of God. They are God-focused and we are self-focused. Yet God's salvation demonstrates to angels the richness and wonder of divine grace. Chafer captures this thought well. "There was that in God which no angel had ever seen. They had observed His wisdom and power displayed in the creation and upholding of all things. They had beheld His glory, but they had not seen His grace. There could be no manifestation of divine grace until there were sinful creatures who were objects of grace... The thought transcends all comprehension, that even one from this fallen sinful race will be so changed by divine power that he will be satisfying to God as an exhibition of His infinite grace, and, though the vast spaces of heaven be thronged with such, the demonstration is not enhanced by multiplied representations, for each individual will be the expression of God's superlative grace."[10]

One of the reasons God allows sin is so that He might have this specific opportunity to manifest His grace. And this can be extended only to hell-deserving sinners. So God's giving us salvation manifests by infinite wisdom His grace and love, without compromising His holiness and righteousness.

5 To Bring Praise to His Glory

God's greatest motivation, however, in saving believing sinners is that His glory might be praised for all eternity. God is "blessed" because He "chose us in Him before the foundation of the world" (Eph. 1:3–4). Three times in this same chapter the apostle wrote that believers are to praise His glory: "to the praise of the glory of His grace" (1:6), "that we who first trusted in Christ should be to the praise of His glory" (1:12), and "until the redemption of the purchased possession, to the praise of His glory" (1:14). To praise His glory means to honor, magnify, and display His attributes, and only sinners saved by grace can do that. So God's highest motivation for saving sinners is that they glorify Him. Everything we do should be motivated by the desire to exalt His glory.

A review of these five motives reveals that in salvation God is doing something *for* us, *from* us, *on* us, *in* us, and *through* us. Salvation is not simply for our benefit, but it is also for God's benefit.

CHAPTER 2
Who Can Provide Salvation?

In the fall of 1942, Field Marshal Bernard Law Montgomery took command of the British Eighth Army in North Africa and changed it from an army that couldn't win a battle to one that couldn't lose a battle. He led it on a six-month, six-thousand-mile victory march that drove Germany's Afrika Korps under Field Marshal Erwin Rommel out of Africa. When later asked what his secret was, Montgomery stated simply, "Having only a plan for victory and showing concern for the troops." He showed concern for his troops by being "a man among the men" and by appearing in field uniform rather than dress uniform with medals and ribbon. By doing this, he followed the model of our Savior, who voluntarily gave up the insignia of His majesty and became one with the people He came to save.

It was God's plan to deal with our problem personally. Thus He identified with us by becoming one with us (John 1:1–14). You can trust a person only to the extent you know him or her. And you can trust God only to the extent you know Him. When our Lord Jesus spoke to the Father in John 17:3, He said, "And this is eternal life, that they may know You, the only true God, and Jesus Christ whom You have sent." Earlier He taught His disciples, "If you had known Me, you would have known My Father also; and from now on you know Him and have seen Him" (14:7).

We need to be well acquainted with the person of our salvation.[1] A person may know the doctrine of salvation fully and yet never really know Jesus well enough to trust Him. J. I. Packer stresses that there is a distinct difference between knowing about God and knowing God.[2] And there is no shortcut to the process of knowing a person. That is true not only between human beings but also between us and God. Many of our struggles in the Christian life stem from the fact that we know about Christ but have not gotten to know Him intimately.

Interestingly, when Paul was nearing the end of his life as a veteran missionary, church planter, teacher, theologian, writer of Scripture, and prisoner for Christ, he said his supreme desire was to know Christ (Phil. 3:10). When we ask someone, "When did you come to know Christ?" we are referring to the day when that individual responded to the gospel. However, for Paul, knowing Christ was also an ongoing, lifelong process. Being born again happens in a split second of time; but coming to know Christ is a lifetime of learning of Him, walking with Him, and being made like Him. "But we all, with unveiled face, beholding as in a mirror the glory of the Lord, are being transformed into the same image from glory to glory, just as by the Spirit of the Lord" (2 Cor. 3:18). All of us should share that ambition—to know our Savior more intimately and personally.

Jesus Christ is the capstone of all Scripture. Everything before Christ's coming to earth was preparatory for Him, and everything after Christ is explanatory of Him. Thus the writer of Hebrews stated, "God, who at various times and in various ways spoke in time past to the fathers by the prophets, has in these last days spoken to us by His Son, whom He has appointed heir of all things, through whom also He made the world" (Heb. 1:1–2). And Jesus made this point to the disciples on the road to Emmaus: "And beginning at Moses and all the Prophets, He expounded to them in all the Scriptures the things concerning Himself" (Luke 24:27). The Gospels are the apex of God's revelation through Christ, and this is why the Old Testament looked forward to that period of revelation and why the New Testament after the Gospels looks back to it.

All the New Testament writers direct us back to the incarnate life of Christ. In 1 John 2:3–5 the apostle John stressed that an intimate knowledge of God leads believers to keep His commandments and also to experience perfect love. Then he added, "He who says he abides in Him ought himself also to walk [live] just as He walked [lived]" (2:6). How Jesus walked (lived) is seen only in the Gospels.

After discussing how to handle suffering, Peter pointed us to Christ's example: "For to this you were called, because Christ also suffered for us, leaving us an example, that you should follow His steps" (1 Pet. 2:21). We know "His steps" only through the Gospels.[3] The word "leaving" (*hypolimpanō*, used only here in the New Testament) is literally "leaving behind" or "leaving under." Believers are to follow Christ's example; He is our model.

After the writer of Hebrews wrote in the "Hall of Faith" (Heb. 11) about those who had gone before us, he encouraged believers to run the race that is set before us, "looking unto Jesus, the author and finisher of our faith" (12:2). The Greek word rendered "looking" (*aphoraō*) means "to look away from everything to something else." Then we are told to "consider Him who endured" (12:3). "Consider" (*analogizomai*) is used of an accountant carefully comparing the various columns of a balance sheet. Thus, as Paul, Peter, and John did, so too the writer to the Hebrews spoke of Jesus' incarnate life as our crowning example for life. We are to look only to Him and to consider His example carefully. Right living is a direct result of right thinking, and right thinking starts by thinking correctly about Jesus Christ. To see how He exemplifies and models biblical principles, we must go to the Gospels. It should not surprise us, therefore, that Satan, the enemy of our souls, has attacked the Gospels. Probably no part of God's Word has received such intensive and continual attack by unbelievers as the Gospels. History reminds us, however, that many are the hammers that have beat on the anvil of the Word of God, but the hammer heads are on the ground and the anvil still stands.

THE ENTRANCE OF THE GOD-MAN

After the entrance of sin and death into the world, resulting in our estrangement from God, He gave the initial announcement of His plan for victory. Addressing Satan, God said, "And I will put enmity between you and the woman, and between your seed and her Seed; He shall bruise your head, and you shall bruise His heel" (Gen. 3:15). This statement is sometimes called the *protevangelium* (literally, "first gospel") because in embryonic form it predicts the coming Savior. At the cross Satan would inflict a serious injury on Christ, the Seed of the woman, but a mortal blow would be dealt to Satan on that same cross (John 12:31; 16:11). He is a defeated foe, living as it were on borrowed time (Rev. 20:10).

When God told Moses he was to be the one to lead the Israelites out of Egypt, Moses asked the Lord a significant question: "Indeed, when I come to the children of Israel and say to them, 'The God of your fathers has sent me to you,' and they say to me, 'What is His name?' What shall I say to them?" (Exod. 3:13). God answered, "Thus you shall say to the children of Israel, 'I AM has sent me to you'" (3:14). God added, "Thus you shall say to the children of Israel: 'The LORD God of your fathers, the God of Abraham, the God of Isaac, and the God of Jacob, has sent me to you. This is My name forever, and this is My memorial to all generations'" (3:15).

God's memorial name, "I AM," from the verb "to be," speaks of His timeless existence. This name "I AM" is likely the source of the word *Yahweh,* though many translations render it "LORD." The name *Yahweh* speaks of His absolute eternal existence, but it also suggests His relationship with His people: "I have come down to deliver" (3:8). How did God come down to them? He came in the person of Moses, whom God used to rescue the Israelites from the Egyptians.

Fourteen centuries later, an angel told Joseph he was to give Mary's son the name "JESUS, for He will save His people from their sins" (Matt. 1:21). The word "Jesus" is a transliteration of the Greek form of the Hebrew "Joshua," which means "Yahweh is salvation." Yahweh came down in the person of Moses to the Israelites, but here Yahweh Himself came down in the incarnate Jesus, who is fully God and completely man, united in one person forever. The God whom no one has seen at any time is now seen in Jesus, who manifests God the Father perfectly (John 1:18). This is why Jesus could say, "He who has seen Me has seen the Father" (14:9). In His confrontation with the Pharisees, Jesus took to Himself the designation "I AM." "Most assuredly, I say to you, before Abraham was, I AM" (8:58). By the words "I AM" Jesus was identifying Himself with Yahweh of the Old Testament.

John recorded a classic statement of the eternal God entering into history and taking on Himself a human nature: "And the Word became flesh and dwelt among us, and we beheld His glory, the glory as of the only begotten of the Father, full of grace and truth" (1:14). The "Word" was introduced in 1:1 as being *eternal* ("In the beginning was the Word"),[4] *distinct* from God the Father but in intimate relationship with Him ("the Word was with God"),[5] and of the very *same essence* as God the Father ("the Word was God"). This verse is one of the strongest New Testament statements on the deity of Jesus Christ.

Jehovah's Witnesses, who deny His deity, try to undercut the obvious force of this verse by saying that the third clause, "the Word was God," should be rendered "the Word was a god." They have failed to acknowledge, however, that the Greek grammar of this clause emphasizes quality, thus stressing that the "Word" and "God" are of the same nature.[6] If John had written "the word was *the* God," he would have declared that the Word and the Father are one and the same, and this would have denied the very distinction of the two, as stated in the second clause, "the Word was with God." The Greek wording in John 1:1 is the best way to express the equality of the Son of God with God the Father as well as the Son's distinction from the Father. Jesus Christ, who possesses full deity as the Son of God, is the One who came to bring salvation to all who believe. If He were not fully God, He could not be our Savior.

THE PERSON OF THE GOD-MAN

Paul's classic statement in Philippians 2:5–7 addresses the great mystery of the relationship of the divine and the human in the person of Jesus Christ: "Let this mind be in you which was also in Christ Jesus, who, being in the form of God, did not consider it robbery to be equal with God, but made Himself of no reputation, taking the form of a bondservant, and coming in the likeness of men."

After the apostle expressed his elation over the all-sufficiency of Jesus Christ even in the midst of his suffering (1:12–14, 18–26), he turned to a practical admonition to unity through humility (1:27–2:4). He placed a searching challenge before the Philippians: "Let nothing be done through selfish ambition or conceit, but in lowliness of mind let each esteem others better than himself. Let each of you look out not only for his own interests, but also for the interests of others" (2:3–4). Many Christians today tend to be so self-centered, especially in our individualistic society, that we have a difficult time being more concerned about others than we are about ourselves. To put others first seems so unnatural. The natural approach is frequently expressed in the slogan, "If you don't look out for yourself, no one else will."

The fact is that when we accept God's way, we have all the resources of heaven behind us. Thus at the end of this letter Paul could say to the Philippians, who had given generously out of their poverty, "My God shall supply all your need according to His riches in glory by Christ Jesus" (4:19).[7] This verse is not simply a blank check to be filled in by anyone. This is a missionary speaking to a church that had accepted the challenge and had given liberally to Paul out of its poverty. So now he could say to them, "Who will meet your needs? My God will meet your needs. And He will do so out of the abundance of Jesus' riches in glory."

This is a critical principle of the way the family of God operates in serving one another. There is something therapeutic about it. Actually most of us could get our needs met by looking out for ourselves. But that would pander to our selfishness and immaturity and leave us in the nursery spiritually. As we all seek to meet each other's needs, we cultivate the qualities of goodness, kindness, and humility that reveal Christ in us and that glorify our Father in heaven.

After this searching, practical exhortation, Paul then presented the greatest example of such a self-sacrificing regard for the interests of others, namely, the condescension of Christ in His incarnation. In other words, do you want to be able to respond to Paul's exhortation in 2:3–4? Then, look to Jesus! If we look to Him to see who He was, how He thought, and what He did, we will find resources for our own thinking that will produce the kind of action He is asking us to perform. What we think about deeply is the raw material of our actions.[8] This is why Paul wrote, "Let this mind be in you which was also in Christ Jesus" (2:5). If we exercise humility as He did, this selfless attitude will result in our being united and loving.

In 2:6–8 Paul presented several marvelous facts about who our Lord is and what He did in His condescension. First, Christ exists "in the form of God," that is, He is deity, fully God. The Greek participle translated "existing" denotes Christ's preincarnate existence in heaven and His continued existence afterward. From all eternity He has existed in the very essence of the Godhead and He continues to be the same forever. In the Incarnation His deity was not diminished or changed in any way.

Second, Christ did not consider it "robbery" (*harpagmon*) to be equal with God. Though this Greek word is difficult to translate, the idea is that He did not consider it something to be clung to compulsively. What did Christ feel was unnecessary for Him to hang on to? As Jacobus J. Mueller suggests, the verse refers to "existence in a *manner* equal to God."[9] Understood this way, the expression "equality with God," describes His *manner of existence* as God. J. B. Phillips captures this meaning well in this paraphrase: "He [Jesus Christ] who had always been God by nature, did not cling to His prerogatives as God's equal, but stripped Himself of all privilege."[10] In other words, Christ stripped Himself not of His deity (equality of essence) but of the *manner* in which He existed. He left heaven's glory to live on the earth with humanity that He came to save. Though He left His royal position in heaven with all its privileges, He remained "in the form of God."

Third, He "emptied Himself" (2:7, NASB). What does this mean? Did He lose or set aside some attributes of deity, after all? The words "made Himself of no reputation" (NKJV) translate the verb "emptied" (*ekenōsen*). Some have taught from this passage that Christ, in His incarnation, laid aside some or all of His attributes. The idea has even crept into some fine hymns such as "And Can It Be?" by Charles Wesley. The second stanza of that hymn includes the words "Emptied Himself of all but love."[11] But the Son of God did not empty Himself of *any* attribute of deity. He could not do so, because immutability is of the very essence of God. God cannot change! "Jesus Christ is the same yesterday, today, and forever" (Heb. 13:8). Further, this would contradict the statements in Philippians 2:6 that Christ has always existed in the form of God and continues to exist in that form. However, Christ could relinquish His prerogatives or His privileges, and that is precisely what He did. When He was about to complete His earthly mission, He prayed to the Father, "I have glorified You on the earth. I have finished the work which You have given Me to do. And now, O Father, glorify Me together with Yourself, with the glory which I had with You before the world was" (John 17:4–5).

The *thinking* of Christ in Philippians 2:6, then, is the cause for His *action* recorded in verse 7. In contrast ("but") to the appropriateness of enjoying the prerogatives and privileges of His person as God, He emptied Himself in the Incarnation. This verse carefully explains the *how* of His emptying. Actually the verse does not answer the question, "Of *what* did Christ empty Himself?" Instead it answers *how* He did so, namely, by taking "the form of a bondservant." Mueller carefully notes: "Nothing is mentioned of any abandonment of divine attributes, the divine nature or the form of God, but only a divine paradox is stated here: He emptied Himself by taking something to Himself, namely, the manner of being, the nature or form of a servant or slave. At His incarnation He remained 'in the form of God' and as such He was Lord and Ruler over all, but He also accepted the nature of a servant as part of His humanity. He was not revealing Himself on earth in glorious or glorified human form, but in the humble form of a servant."[12]

Christ also emptied Himself by "becoming in the likeness of men." This denotes the human manner of existence which He took in contrast to the "existence in a manner equal to God" which He left in heaven. He who was God took on Himself the likeness of humanity and became the God-Man, not a man-God. To do this He had to take off the royal robes of heaven and identify with the people He came to save. In His incarnation God the Son added to Himself a true and complete human nature and in doing that He had to give up the existence He enjoyed in the counsel of the triune God before His incarnation.

The Results of the God-Man

For centuries biblical scholars have sought to state accurately the results of this central fact of history, the Incarnation. Simply stated, in one person are joined two natures—undiminished deity with true and complete humanity—without confusing the natures or dividing the person. There is no loss of separate identity for each of His natures. Yet there is a communication of all the attributes of each of His two natures to His person. That is, some things are true of His human nature, but His whole person is in view. For example, when He said "I am thirsty" (John 19:28, NIV), His thirst was true of His human nature, and yet the God-Man was thirsty. We cannot say that only part of Christ was thirsty. On the other hand, "He knew what was in man" (2:25). Omniscience is an attribute of deity, but it was the person of Christ who knew, not simply His divine nature. Ryrie summarizes this well: "Practically speaking, it is the basis for Christ being seen to be weak, yet omnipotent; ignorant, yet omniscient; limited, yet infinite."[13] Christ is not humanized deity or deified humanity. Thus when you look at Jesus, you see what God is like, and at the same time in Him you see true humanity apart from sin. What a wonderful contrast to the weird pagan concepts of Greek mythology in Paul's day. How great is the wisdom of God!

This doctrine stretches our thinking. For example, the helpless infant being held in Mary's arms was at the same time the eternal God sustaining Mary. Again, as we think of the temptations of Christ, which were intense beyond anything any other human beings have ever encountered, we dare not separate the humanity from the deity. Was He tempted? Yes, severely! Could He have sinned? No, not without creating a rift between the two natures. God cannot sin!

As Christ walked on earth, He voluntarily relinquished the independent use of His divine attributes. He veiled His majesty. He emptied Himself not by laying aside His powers but by refusing to use them independently from the will of the Father in accomplishing the mission for which He came. Addison Leitch gives a practical illustration we can all identify with:

When a man plays with his boy and is hoping to train him, in baseball for example, while he is playing with him, he will have to play with the boy on the boy's level. He will throw at the speed and at the distance the boy can manage; he will hit easy grounders, he will run just fast enough to make the play interesting. In doing all of this he will lose none of his own powers. While involved in the game with his boy he can think of his wife, make up his mind about a business deal, turn aside to answer the phone call from another adult, or perhaps protect the boy from a dog or a bully by reasserting his full powers. For the sake of the boy, however, he "empties" himself of his full powers, which powers he never really loses.[14]

An example of Christ's refusal to use His powers independently is seen at the time of His arrest. Hundreds of soldiers and others who were brandishing swords and clubs laid hold of Jesus. Suddenly Peter rose to the occasion, drew his sword, and struck the servant of the high priest. Telling Peter to sheathe his sword, Jesus asked him, "Do you think that I cannot now pray to My Father, and He will provide Me with more than twelve legions of angels?" (Matt. 26:53). Jesus was not simply talking about power; He was also helping Peter understand something about His veiled majesty. If Peter had been really thinking just minutes before—when the soldiers who came to take Him fell to the ground as dead when He simply uttered His memorial name I AM (Yahweh)—he would never have taken out his sword. Yes, there were moments when Jesus Christ unveiled the insignia of His majesty in the will of the Father for the purpose of mentoring His disciples. The same lessons speak volumes to us.

The Reason for the God-Man

Why was it necessary for the eternal Son of God to leave His glory and "come down" and take to Himself a human nature? The answer takes us back to where we started in chapter 1: our desperate dilemma under the curse of sin with no way out. We need a Savior, but no human being is uncontaminated with the curse of sin. And even if a perfect individual could be found, he could not provide a sacrifice for more than one person. The Savior needed to be uncontaminated by sin and also infinite in order to atone for all the sin of the world. Furthermore, because the penalty for sin is death, the person would have to be human in order to be able to die.

Only one person qualifies to be the Savior from sin: Jesus Christ! Only the God-Man can bring us salvation. As stated earlier, the name "Jesus" means "Yahweh is salvation." An angel told Joseph, "And she [Mary] will bring forth a Son, and you shall call His name JESUS, for He will save His people from their sins" (Matt. 1:21). The angel then quoted Isaiah's prophecy given seven centuries before, "'Behold, the virgin shall be with child, and bear a Son, and they shall call His name Immanuel,' which is translated, 'God with us'" (1:23). John the Baptist introduced Him by exclaiming, "Behold! The Lamb of God who takes away the sin of the world" (John 1:29). Jesus Himself said that "the Son of Man has come to seek and to save that which was lost" (Luke 19:10). And in one voice with all the prophets before him, Paul said the only answer is Jesus, the God-Man: "For He [God the Father] made Him [Christ the Son] who knew no sin to be sin for us, that we might become the righteousness of God in Him" (2 Cor. 5:21).

But there is much more! The ministry of the God-Man did not cease with His earthly sojourn. He is not only our sinless Sin-Bearer; He is also our faithful High Priest. The God-Man is at the right hand of the Father representing believers consistently because He understands God and He understands us. And that will be true for all eternity.

CHAPTER 3

Salvation—From Eternity to Eternity

Having examined the breadth and depth of meaning in the word *salvation*, God's motives in providing such a magnificent rescue operation for those with such desperate need, and then the mighty act of God in providing the God-Man as our Savior, we now turn to the accomplishments of that salvation, beginning even before creation and moving from eternity to eternity.

SALVATION IN ETERNITY PAST

Salvation in the Plan and Purpose of God

Before the creation of the world and of humanity, before the entrance of sin into the angelic world or the human race, before there was ever the need of a Savior, God had already planned for our salvation. In fact, not one thing happens in history that is not known to God from all eternity, including especially the provision of our Savior. When Peter exclaimed that we are redeemed "with the precious blood of Christ, as of a lamb without blemish and without spot," he reached back to that eternal purpose of God: "He indeed was foreordained before the foundation of the world, but was manifest in these last times for you who through Him believe in God" (1 Pet. 1:19–21). Before the creation of the world, Jesus was the Lamb to be slain. Our rescue was not an afterthought when sin entered the world; we were in the mind of God from all eternity. What marvelous grace!

Along a similar line Paul wrote that we have been "predestined according to the purpose of Him who works all things according to the counsel of His will" (Eph.1:11).

Special Words of Salvation in God's Plan

Election. The word "elect" (*eklegō*) simply means "to pick out or choose." The New Testament usually uses a Greek verbal form that means "to pick out or choose for oneself." Thus Paul declared concerning those who have believed and become the recipients of saving grace: "He [God] chose us in Him [Christ] before the foundation of the world" (Eph. 1:4). Election is God's sovereign, gracious plan before creation to save those who believe, not because of any foreseen merit in them, but only because of His good pleasure. This is a *sovereign* plan because God was under no obligation to elect anyone, and it is an act of *grace* because the recipients are totally undeserving.

Being omniscient, God knows not only all actual things but also all possible things. And He is holy, righteous, loving, and good. So the decree or "design"[1] of God must be the best of all possibilities.

To contemplate that God chose us to be His heirs for all eternity is awesome. Yet this doctrine of election has been a source of fear down through the centuries because of a failure to see its scriptural focus.[2] The Scriptures use the term only in a positive sense and only of the regenerate. If someone reading this is fearful of not being among the elect, he simply needs to follow Paul's instruction to the Philippian jailer and fear no longer: "Believe on the Lord Jesus Christ and you will be saved" (Acts 16:31). Those who have believed and thus are saved can rejoice in God's electing grace. God gave us this beautiful truth to give us encouragement (Rom. 8:29–30), not fear, and to lead us to praise Him (Eph. 1:5–6).

The illustration has often been given of a person entering heaven through a door with a sign "Whosoever will may come." Then when the person goes through the door and looks back, he sees another sign: "Chosen in Him from before the foundation of the world." The first sign speaks of the availability of salvation and the second addresses the fact of God's choosing. Both are true. For if God had not elected, none would have believed.

Foreknowledge. Proginōskō, the Greek word for foreknowledge, sometimes means, as in English, "to know beforehand," as in Acts 26:5 and 2 Peter 3:17. But often it means to have a conscious relationship of love. As Paul wrote, "And we know that all things work together for good to those who love God, to those who are the called according to His purpose. For whom He foreknew [*proginōskō*], He also predestined to be conformed to the image of His Son,[3] that He might be the firstborn among many brethren" (Rom. 8:28–30).[4]

A common view of the words "whom He foreknew" is that by foresight God saw the faith by which some would believe. The problem with this view is that the object of foreknowledge in Romans 8:29 is not a person's faith but is a person ("whom"). That is, God foreknew the person, not something he or she would do. This is also consistent with the determining action in the other links in the chain right on to glorification. God, not man, is the active Agent from beginning to end. Those whom God elected, He engaged in a conscious, loving relationship (Rom. 8:28).

Predestination. The Greek word rendered "predestination" means "to mark off with a boundary beforehand"; it logically follows election and foreknowledge. God preplanned a great destiny for those whom He chose for Himself and with whom He established a loving relationship. This destiny is that they "be conformed to the image of His Son" (Rom. 8:29). Paul reinforced this later when he declared that we have been "predestined according to the purpose of Him who works all things according to the counsel of His will" (Eph. 1:11). And as John wrote, "When He is revealed, we shall be like Him, for we shall see Him as He is" (1 John 3:2).

SALVATION IN HISTORY

When I was in college, I spent the summers helping build houses. It was always exciting to look at a brand-new set of plans to see what the owner had envisioned, but it was even more exciting to be involved in bringing the plans into reality. Even more exciting is to see how God unfolds His plan of redemption in history.

The Old Testament is the grand picture book of Scripture. It is replete with types and symbols, feasts and sacrifices, laws and prophecies that speak vividly of the Lord and His gracious plan of redemption through the coming Messiah. In the midst of the pictures, pageantry, and legal system, however, some people in biblical times lost sight of the Messiah and God's unchanging gospel of grace. Jesus was constrained, therefore, to confront the Jewish leaders who were seeking to kill Him: "You search the Scriptures, for in them you think you have eternal life; and these are they which testify of Me. But you are not willing to come to Me that you may have life" (John 5:39–40). After His resurrection, when Jesus confronted the two discouraged disciples on the road to Emmaus, He chided them: "O foolish ones, and slow of heart to believe in all that the prophets have spoken! Ought not the Christ to have suffered these things and to enter into His glory?" (Luke 24:25–26). Jesus then "expounded to them in all the Scriptures the things concerning Himself" (24:27), all the way from the books of Moses through the Old Testament prophets. The Old Testament portrayed the Messiah in various ways, and salvation was always by God's grace.

The Elements of Salvation

Throughout history salvation has always involved three elements: a *basis*, a *channel*, and an *object*. The *basis* has always been death. Because of sin, people die (Gen. 2:17; Rom. 3:23; 5:12). But by sacrifices that involve the death of animals, sin was atoned for. This was true of the animals that died when God provided skin coverings for Adam and Eve after they sinned (Gen. 3:21). It was true of animals that were sacrificed by Israelites in the Old Testament Levitical system. This truth of sacrifice for the sins of humankind is portrayed vividly in Isaiah's words about the suffering Servant. "But He [Jesus Christ] was wounded for our transgressions, He was bruised for our iniquities; the chastisement for our peace was upon Him, and by His stripes we are healed. All we like sheep have gone astray; we have turned, every one, to his own way; and the LORD has laid on Him the iniquity of us all" (Isa. 53:5–6).

Jesus was the Lamb whom God the Father had planned from before the foundation of the world to be slain (1 Pet. 1:18–20). As the Lamb of God He bore the sins of the world (John 1:29); and in eternity future, He will be the Lamb seated on a throne (Rev. 5:6–12). Jesus is the focal point of all history. All revelation prior to Him was preparatory for Him and all revelation after Him was explanatory of Him. Speaking to the disciples on the road to Emmaus after His resurrection, Jesus explained, "These are the words which I spoke to you while I was still with you, that all things must be fulfilled which were written in the Law of Moses and the Prophets and the Psalms concerning Me" (Luke 24:44). Every time a Jewish believer offered an animal sacrifice, it was typifying Christ, the final Sacrifice. Thus when John the Baptist introduced Jesus, he was summarizing the entire Old Testament sacrificial system in one concise statement: "Behold! The Lamb of God who takes away the sin of the world!" (John 1:29).

Throughout Scripture the *channel* of salvation is always faith alone, apart from any works. Paul made this clear in discussing Abraham's salvation: "What then shall we say that Abraham our father has found according to the flesh? For if Abraham was justified by works, he has something to boast about, but not before God. For what does the Scripture say? Abraham believed God and it was accounted to him for righteousness. Now to him who works, the wages are not counted as grace but as debt" (Rom. 4:1–4). In other words, before the Cross people were saved by faith apart from works. What was true of one man—Abraham—was true of a whole nation. When the Israelites "saw the great work which the LORD had done in Egypt; . . . [they] believed the LORD" (Exod. 14:31). Interestingly the words "believed the LORD" are the same as Abraham's words in Genesis 15:6, which were later quoted by Paul in Romans 4:22.

The *object* of our salvation is Christ. Eternal salvation comes only through Him. "This is the testimony: that God has given us eternal life, and this life is in His Son" (1 John 5:11). Salvation is available through no one else (Acts 4:12).

The faith of the believers has always been in the *promises* of God for redemption. Under Old Testament revelation believers obviously did not know as much about the *Person* of their redemption as we know through later revelation; however, they believed that God would deliver His people even as He had promised immediately after the Fall. Speaking of the ultimate victory of our Redeemer, the Son of God, over the serpent, Satan, God said, "And I will put enmity between you and the woman, and between your seed and her Seed; He shall bruise your head, and you shall bruise His heel" (Gen. 3:15).

Later Abraham believed that God was able to do what seemed impossible. "And not being weak in faith, he did not consider his own body, already dead (since he was about a hundred years old), and the deadness of Sarah's womb. He did not waver at the *promise* of God through unbelief, but was strengthened in faith, giving glory to God, and being fully convinced that what He had *promised* He was also able to perform" (Rom. 4:19–21 [italics added]). Consequently, God "accounted it to him for righteousness" (Gen. 15:6).

Still later, as already noted, the nation Israel, an entire "people group," believed the Lord (Exod 14:31).

A number of theologians today are advancing the view that some people who have never heard of Christ can still be saved if they have "implicit faith" in God. Space does not permit discussion of this issue, but see endnote 5 for books that defend this view that salvation is available only through faith in Christ.[5]

The Pattern of Salvation

Abraham is a wonderful example of a person who was saved by faith. The Lord called Abram, a middle-aged, prosperous, and pagan man, out of Ur of the Chaldeans, and gave him some astounding promises (Gen. 12:1–3). On the basis of these promises, Abram and Sarai left with their many belongings to the place of God's calling. The trip to Canaan involved famine, warfare, and family problems along the way, but through it all Abram had faith in the Lord who had promised. The king of Sodom would have made him rich, but Abram focused instead on the "Lord,[6] God Most High, the Possessor of heaven and earth" (14:22). After that, the Lord appeared to Abram a third time (12:7; 13:14–17; 15:1) and directed him to "count the stars if you are able to number them" (15:5), thus assuring him that though he was still childless, his descendants would be innumerable like the stars. Then Scripture records that "he believed in the LORD and He accounted it to him for righteousness" (15:6). The Hebrew word rendered "accounted" has commercial connotations, that is, Abram's faith was computed or tallied as a credit for righteousness.

In Genesis 15 all three elements of salvation—the basis, the channel, the object—are present. The *basis* of his salvation was death. Abram brought sacrifices—three animals and two birds—to the Lord, sacrifices that involved death (15:9). The *channel* of Abram's salvation was his faith, as noted in 15:6. And the *object* of his faith was the Lord, who stated, "I am the LORD, who brought you out of Ur of the Chaldeans, to give you this land to inherit it" (15:7).[7] Before the events in Genesis 15, Abram had already exercised faith in the Lord. But 15:6 pinpoints the fact that his salvation, like ours, is available only by faith in the Lord's promise. Abraham, then, became a pattern of faith for everyone after him. "But to him who does not work but believes on Him who justifies the ungodly, his faith is accounted for righteousness" (Rom. 4:5).

The Sufferings of the Savior

In chapter 2 we looked at the condescension of the eternal Son of God in voluntarily emptying Himself of the resplendent glory that was His in order to identify thoroughly with humanity (John 1:1–14; Phil. 2:5–8). The humiliation did not stop there, however, for it continued downward through suffering and death. No one has expressed that humiliation in verse and music better than William E. Booth-Clibborn in his hymn "Down from His Glory":[8]

> Down from His glory, ever living story,
> My God and Savior came, and Jesus was His name.
> Born in a manger, to His own a stranger,
> A man of sorrows, tears and agony.
>
> What condescension, bringing us redemption;
> That in the dead of night, not one faith hope in sight,

God, gracious, tender, laid aside His splendor,
Stooping to woo, to win, to save my soul.

Without reluctance, flesh and blood His substance,
He took the form of man, revealed the hidden plan.
O glorious myst'ry, Sacrifice of Calvary,
And now I know Thou art the great 'I Am.'

O how I love Him! How I adore Him!
My breath, my sunshine, my all in all!
The great Creator became my Savior,
And all God's fullness dwelleth in Him.

His suffering in life.[9] As we consider Jesus' sufferings, it is important to distinguish His sufferings in life from His sufferings in death. His sufferings in life were nonatoning, whereas His sufferings in death atoned for our sins. Scripture is clear in teaching that "without the shedding of blood there is no remission of sins" (Heb. 9:22); thus His sufferings in His pre–Cross days on earth were in no way vicarious or atoning. The substitutionary work of Christ relates only to His death on the cross.

Though Christ's sufferings in life did not provide atonement for sin, they were of value for three reasons. First, His sufferings equipped Him to be our High Priest, as the writer to the Hebrews affirmed several times. "For it was fitting for Him, for whom are all things and by whom are all things, in bringing many sons to glory, to make the captain of their salvation perfect through sufferings" (2:10). "In all things He had to be made like His brethren, that He might be a merciful and faithful High Priest in things pertaining to God" (2:17). "Though He was a Son, yet He learned obedience by the things which He suffered. And having been perfected, He became the author of eternal salvation to all who obey Him" (5:8–9). "For the law appoints as high priests men who have weakness, but the word of the oath, which came after the law, appoints the Son who has been perfected forever" (7:28).

These several references to our sinless Savior being made perfect may pose a problem for some people. But the problem disappears if we realize that the idea of the verb *teleioō* is not to correct some fault but to bring something to completion.[10] It was important that the "captain" (*archēgos*, literally, "pioneer or originator") of our salvation (2:10) should be made fully qualified to be our High Priest by passing through suffering. Thus not only has He experienced the sufferings we go through, but He has also endured them and triumphed over sin, death, and Satan through them. Therefore He is able to function as the believers' "merciful" (sympathetic) and "faithful" (trustworthy) High Priest (2:17).

Second, Christ's life sufferings also provide an example for us to follow. One of the themes of 1 Peter is that the suffering of Christians is a natural part of a life dedicated to Christ. Suffering is one of God's tools to shape godly character in us; thus Peter reminded his readers of Jesus' example in suffering: "For to this you were called, because Christ also suffered for us, leaving us an example, that you should follow His steps: 'Who committed no sin, nor was deceit found in His mouth'; who, when He was reviled, did not revile in return; when He suffered, He did not threaten, but committed Himself to Him who judges righteously; who Himself bore our sins in His own body on the tree, that we, having died to sins, might live for righteousness—by whose stripes you were healed" (1 Pet. 2:21–24).

These verses refer to Jesus' life-sufferings, which provide a pattern (2:21–23), and to His sufferings in death, which paid the price for sin (2:24). People to whom we look today as examples or models often fail us. They all have feet of clay. But "looking unto Jesus" (Heb. 12:2) will never disappoint us because He is perfect. We can feel confident in planting our feet solidly in "His steps." Although no secular writer of His day wrote about His life, our heavenly Father saw to it that four believers (Matthew, Mark, Luke, and John) recorded it without error so that the story of the greatest life ever lived could be known by every generation to come.[11]

Third, the life-sufferings of Jesus encourage believers because they teach us there are great rewards for endurance. Jesus endured the cross because it was en route to the crown: "Let us run with endurance the race that is set before us, looking unto Jesus, the author and finisher of our faith, who for the joy that was set before Him endured the cross, despising the shame, and has sat down at the right hand of the throne of God. For consider

Him who endured such hostility from sinners against Himself, lest you become weary and discouraged in your souls" (Heb. 12:1–3).

Early in His ministry Jesus told His disciples about the eternal value of endurance through persecution: "Blessed are you when they revile and persecute you, and say all kinds of evil against you falsely for My sake. Rejoice and be exceedingly glad, for great is your reward in heaven" (Matt. 5:11–12). Later Jesus told them about the eternal reward they would receive in return for having invested their lives for Him (19:28–29).

After His ascension and exaltation to the right hand of the Father, Jesus made a magnificent offer to believers: "To Him who overcomes I will grant to sit with Me on My throne, as I also overcame and sat down with My Father on His throne. He who has an ear, let him hear what the Spirit says to the churches" (Rev. 3:21–22). And in His last words in the final chapter of the Bible He reminded us, "And behold, I am coming quickly, and My reward is with Me, to give to everyone according to his work'" (22:12).

So the life sufferings of Christ have eternal value for believers. Realizing that value, let us look at them more specifically.

The Passover feast is the only one of Israel's seven feasts that is specifically called a type of Christ (1 Cor. 5:7), though other feasts were called "a shadow of things to come" (Col. 2:16–17). For the Passover —which commemorated the night in which the Lord delivered Israel out of Egypt— each household on the tenth day of Nisan (our March–April) was to bring a lamb, a male of the first year without blemish. They were to keep it for four days to prove that it had no physical defects. Then every household was to kill their lamb at twilight and apply some of the blood to the two doorposts and the lintel of the house where they ate (Exod. 12:1–14; Deut. 16:1–8). This procedure pictured the sufferings of Christ in both life and death. Like the lamb which was examined for four days, Jesus' life sufferings demonstrated His sinless character.[12] Thus Peter spoke of Jesus "as a lamb without blemish and without spot" (1 Pet. 1:19). And the author of Hebrews declared that He "was in all points tempted as we are, yet without sin" (Heb. 4:15). John wrote, "In Him there is no sin" (1 John 3:5). Paul said that God "made Him who knew no sin to be sin for us" (2 Cor. 5:21). Jesus Himself asked the Pharisees, "Which of you convicts Me of sin?" (John 8:46). Though tested often and in every way, He remained the sinless, spotless Savior.

Since Christ did not suffer for His own sins, what was the source of His suffering? First, He suffered because of His *holy character*. Can you picture what it must have been like for Jesus Christ, who was absolutely holy, to live in the midst of sin? Try to think of the most horrendous crimes and sins, and picture yourself having to be immersed in that kind of environment. Abraham's nephew, Lot, who was a righteous man, faced that problem. He was troubled because of the filthy conduct of the wicked (2 Pet. 2:7–8). Also Jesus was hated by the wicked onlookers because of His purity and righteousness (John 15:18–25).

Second, Jesus suffered in life because of His *infinite compassion*. When Jesus saw the unbelief of Jerusalem, He wept over the peace it was missing. And He suffered because the Jews rejected Him as their Messiah. When people were troubled, He wept with them. When Lazarus died, Jesus wept with Mary and Martha. He feels for us as no one else could possibly feel, because His compassion is infinite.

Third, Jesus suffered in life because of His *omniscient anticipation*. Think of Christ's kindness to Peter in the Upper Room when he knew Peter would deny Him that very night. Instead of a scorching rebuke, He gave comfort: "Simon, Simon! Indeed, Satan has asked for you, that he may sift you as wheat. But I have prayed for you, that your faith should not fail; and when you have returned to Me, strengthen your brethren" (Luke 22:31–32). In the Garden of Gethsemane, knowing He would soon be crucified, Jesus said to His disciples, "My soul is exceedingly sorrowful, even to death" (Matt. 26:38). Then He went a little farther and fell on His face and prayed, "O My Father, if it is possible, let this cup pass from Me; nevertheless, not as I will, but as You will" (26:39). In the intensity of this anticipation, an angel came and strengthened Him and Luke, a medical doctor, added, "And being in agony, He prayed more earnestly. Then His sweat became like great drops of blood falling down to the ground" (Luke 22:44).[13] Then He told them they should be on their way, because His betrayer was coming (Matt. 26:45–46).

His holy character, His infinite compassion, and His omniscient anticipation all added to the suffering Christ endured in His earthly life before the Cross.

His sufferings in temptation. The battle of the ages was predicted in Genesis 3:15, and the two contestants were the Lord Jesus Christ and Satan. Throughout history Satan has sought to destroy the people of God and to corrupt the line of the promised Savior. Immediately after Jesus was baptized, He was led by the Holy Spirit into the wilderness, where He was severely tempted by Satan for forty days and nights. The Greek word for "tempt" can mean to solicit to evil (Gal. 6:1; James 1:13) or to test or demonstrate (John 6:6; Heb. 11:17). Both ideas are true of Jesus' temptation: Satan solicited Jesus to evil, whereas God proved through the testing that Jesus is indeed the sinless Son of God, who "was manifested that He might destroy the works of the devil" (1 John 3:8). Louis Barbieri points out the similarities of Satan's tests throughout history: "Interestingly Satan's temptations of Eve in the Garden of Eden correspond to those of Jesus in the desert. Satan appealed to the physical appetite (Gen. 3:1–3; Matt. 4:3), the desire for personal gain (Gen. 3:4–5; Matt. 4:6), and an easy path to glory (Gen. 3:5–6; Matt. 4:8–9). And in such cases Satan altered God's Word (Gen. 3:4; Matt. 4:6). Satan's temptations of people today often fall into the same three categories (cf. 1 John 2:16)."[14]

This was intensive testing, but it was not over. It got worse. Luke recorded, "Now when the devil had ended every temptation, he departed from Him until an opportune time" (Luke 4:13). One such opportunity came right after Peter made his glowing confession, "You are the Christ, the Son of the Living God" (Matt. 16:16), and Jesus told His disciples about His coming death and resurrection (16:21). Satan used Peter to try to keep Jesus from the cross (16:22), but Jesus fired the same salvo at Peter that He had given in the wilderness temptation, "Get behind Me, Satan!" (16:23; see 4:10). And later Satan entered Judas (John 13:27), who betrayed Him to His enemies with a kiss (Matt. 26:48–49). But the peak of Jesus' testing came not in His physical pain and deprivation nor in betrayal and broken relationships, but as He, the holy Son of God, took on Himself the sin of the world, becoming a curse for us (Gal. 3:13).

Because the Captain of our salvation was made "perfect through suffering," Jesus can sympathize in depth with all our weaknesses. He "was in all points tempted as we are, yet without sin" (Heb. 4:15). But how could Jesus be tempted as we are? Since He is God, He has infinite power to resist temptation, power we don't have. Addison Leitch addresses this problem this way: "For the sake of men and their redemption he emptied himself by laying aside, not the powers, but the right to use them independently. He must do what man has failed to do; he must obey God in human flesh. He must, therefore, seek the will of God, wait for the power of God, be obedient even unto death. He never lost the powers; he gave up, we repeat, their *independent* exercise.'"[15]

Leitch added,

I am never tempted to turn stones to bread or launch a campaign for my ministry by diving off the pinnacle of the temple, assuming I could climb it in the first place. How then is Jesus tempted as I am tempted? He is tempted to use his powers (as I am tempted to use such powers as I have) in some selfish manner, apart from the will of God, apart from the word of God. Notice that Jesus has the power. He can turn stones to bread and he can cast himself off the pinnacle of the temple. To do so, however, is to destroy what he came to do redemptively. If he is able to "throw his weight around," then he will have advantage in his human experience which we do not have. To that extent and in that way he will not fulfill all righteousness in the flesh as humanity had not been able to before. His victories must be human victories over human temptations.[16]

In the first major encounter, Satan tempted Jesus to assert His independence from the Father by turning stones to bread—which Satan knew He was fully able to do—to satisfy His hunger. "Though He was hungry, and it was right to eat, yet He would not eat independently of the Father's will. Satan had tempted Him not away from spiritual bread but away from the Father and toward literal bread, gained independently of the Father's will."[17]

No one has ever experienced the intensity and degree of testing Jesus experienced. All of us have fallen short of 100 percent testing, so to speak, because we all sin. Only Jesus has taken the full pressure; thus He is the only one fully able to feel the depth and intensity of our problems. Granted, He did not have a sin nature, so the essence of the temptation had to be in the power of the solicitation to evil, not in the inner susceptibility to respond. The temptation came because of His human nature and was external rather than internal; but that does not lessen the external pressure of Satan's solicitation to evil. If anything, the pressure was more real because of His holy character.

Another question related to Satan's temptation of Jesus is this: Could Jesus have sinned and, if not, was He truly human? One author wrote, "To deny that Jesus could have sinned is to deny His humanity and to fall into the error of Docetism, which maintains that His humanity was only an appearance and not actually real."[18] The proper response to this is to start with facts, the things we know for sure, on the authority of God's Word. Scripture teaches us that Jesus Christ is both fully God (John 1:1; 8:58; Phil. 2:6) and fully man (Luke 2:52; John 19:28). In His human nature He was temptable (Heb. 4:15), but in His divine nature He was neither temptable nor capable of sinning (James 1:13). If Jesus could have sinned while He was on earth, this means He could sin now in heaven. Obviously this issue is not insignificant or inconsequential.

We tend to judge Jesus' temptation by our own temptability. However, we have a sin nature and we tend to make that synonymous with being human. But before there was ever sin, there was humanity. When Adam was created, he was fully human but he did not have a sin nature. Yet he was temptable and able to sin.

Like Adam, Jesus had a full human nature but, unlike Adam, He had a divine nature; therefore he cannot be compared with Adam or with us. Paul Enns noted that "for sin to take place, there must be an *inner* response to the *outward* temptation. Since Jesus did not possess a sin nature, there was nothing within Him to respond to the temptation. People sin because there is an inner response to the outer temptation."[19]

Sin is not essential to being human, for Adam was human before he was a sinner. But sin is contrary to being divine. Thus because Jesus was *both* human and divine inseparably united, He could not sin. As Chafer has said, "Should His humanity sin, God would sin."[20]

During my seminary days I had a job drilling and tapping holes in grid bars—six-foot-long heavy steel bars that go in cotton gins. We had a huge machine for putting pressure on them to straighten them ever so slightly. You couldn't take that grid bar and put it over your knee and bend it, but you could easily bend a piece of wire. If I were to weld the wire to the grid bar, however, I would no longer be able to bend the wire—not because of the strength of the wire but because of the strength of the steel bar to which it was attached.

Because Jesus Christ is the same yesterday, today, and forever (Heb. 13:8), whatever attributes were true of Him in His incarnate state are also true in His present state of glory. We have a sinless Savior who was tempted to the fullest extent, and He knows precisely how to sympathize with us in all of our tests. Thus He will never allow us to be tempted beyond what we can endure (1 Cor. 10:13).

The Sacrifice of the Savior

We now approach that event which was the most heinous crime and also the most sublime sacrifice in all of history—the death[21] of the God-Man. In this single most important event in history, Jesus Christ triumphed over sin, Satan, and death.

The pictures of His death. The Old Testament has scores of prophecies about Christ that were fulfilled in His first coming.[22] Prophecy is *verbally* predictive of something or someone in the future, whereas a type[23] is *pictorially* predictive. Like a picture book, the Old Testament gives numerous portraits of the death of Christ.

The Book of Hebrews, for example, makes sense only if you grasp something of the Old Testament pictures of the death of Christ in typology. For example, the writer of Hebrews wrote, "Therefore, brethren, having boldness to enter the Holiest by the blood of Jesus, by a new and living way which He consecrated for us, through the veil, that is, His flesh, and having a High Priest over the house of God, let us draw near with a true heart in full assurance of faith, having our hearts sprinkled from an evil conscience and our bodies washed with pure water" (10:19–22). Interestingly the writer had made a similar statement in 4:16: "Let us therefore come boldly to the throne of grace, that we may obtain mercy and find grace to help in time of need." Hebrews 10:19 picks up where 4:16 left off. This invitation for those Jewish believers to come boldly to the throne of grace was drastically different from what they and their ancestors knew was the penalty for approaching God wrongly.

"Approach to God," Leon Morris explains, "was a tricky business in the days of Moses and Aaron. On the one hand it was the greatest of blessings and no one wanted to be without God's promised presence. . . . But on the other hand God was awe-inspiring and powerful. To approach him in the wrong way might be disaster."[24] A sobering reminder of this is when Aaron's two sons died because they "offered unauthorized fire before the LORD" (Lev. 10:1, NIV).

One of the most significant types in the Old Testament was the annual Day of Atonement, the most holy day of the year (Exod. 30:10; Lev. 16:1–34; Num. 29:7–11). It was a day of fasting rather than feasting, of solemnity rather than rejoicing. On the tenth day of the seventh month the high priest, after undergoing meticulous ceremonial washings and making extensive sacrifices for himself and for the people, entered the inner sanctuary of the tabernacle by himself and sprinkled blood on the mercy seat (Lev. 16:14–16; Heb. 9:7). If anyone else were to attempt it, he would be stricken dead (Lev. 16:2). According to Jewish tradition, priests used to tie a rope to the foot of the high priest when he went in. The rabbis thought, "If he dies while he is in there, who will go in to get him out?" They could picture dead bodies (like Nadab and Abihu) at the entrance to the Most Holy Place. So they tied a rope to his leg so they could pull him out. This tradition says something about the seriousness of approaching the presence of God.

Imagine how strange it must have seemed to the recipients of the Book of Hebrews to read that they could "enter the Holiest" boldly. For more than fourteen hundred years the Jews knew that to enter the presence of God in the tabernacle or temple would result in their death. What brought about the change? John the Baptist answered this in one sentence: "Behold! The Lamb of God who takes away the sin of the world!" (John 1:29). Millions of lambs had been offered on Jewish altars, none of which took away even one sin. But each of those lambs typified the one Lamb who was to come. Now believers can enter God's presence "by the blood of Jesus, by a new and living way which He consecrated for us, through the veil" (Heb. 10:19–20). The Day of Atonement covered Israel's sin for a year, but Jesus, as John said, took them away. And His death atoned for the sins of the world, not just Israel's sins.

When Jesus offered His last cry from the cross, "It is finished" (John

19:30), the Father in heaven responded by tearing the temple veil in two from the top to the bottom,[25] picturing for all to see that "because Christ's blood was shed, all who believe in Him have access into the very holiest of all."[26] By faith in the finished work of Jesus Christ, God's Messiah, individuals are now priests before God, and by His grace they can come with boldness (not brashness) into His presence. And they can come not on a single day, the Day of Atonement, in a single place on earth, the tabernacle, but as often as they desire without any mediator other than Jesus Christ. This glimpse at the Day of Atonement is only one of many types of Christ presented in the Old Testament.[27]

The pain of His death. When my oldest son was in art school, he made a clay sculpture of my head that sits on a shelf above my study desk. Several years later a student of mine, working in landscaping, came across a Christ Thorn tree and carefully wove some of the branches into a crown of thorns that sits on the sculpture my son made. The long thorns are not only very sharp but seem to create infection. It serves to remind me that on the cross Jesus wore that kind of "crown" for me. When He was on trial, people mocked Him, spat on Him, beat Him with their hands, and hit Him on the head with a rod. In addition, to placate the raging mob, Pilate had Him flogged. The whip was made of leather thongs with bits of metal and bone attached, which ripped open the flesh. Jesus' body was then thrown over the crossbeams on the ground and affixed to it with spikes driven through His flesh. The cross was hoisted up and dropped into a hole in the ground.

In the Roman Empire crucifixion was considered the most painful and degrading form of capital punishment. It was so horrible that it was administered only to slaves and the lowest types of criminals, and not to Roman citizens. At any moment Jesus could have called a halt to this mockery of illegal trials and inhuman treatment. But He willingly endured the pain of the cross because of divine love. "Therefore My Father loves Me, because I lay down My life that I may take it again. No one takes it from Me, but I lay it down of Myself. I have power to lay it down, and I have power to take it again" (John 10:17–18).

This physical mistreatment was humiliatingly shameful and excruciatingly painful. But it did not begin to compare with the mental and spiritual anguish of His taking on Himself the sin of the world. When He "bore our sins in His own body on the tree" (1 Pet. 2:24), He was shaken to the very center of His being. But beyond that was the pain of becoming a curse for us (Gal. 3:10) and experiencing the wrath of God the Father that had to be unveiled against sin. To be deserted by all the disciples while He was paying the price for their sin was wrenching enough, but to be abandoned by the heavenly Father brought forth His cry, "My God, My God, why have You forsaken Me?" (Matt. 27:46). As Max Lucado noted, "He withstood the beatings and remained strong at the mock trials. He watched in silence as those he loved ran away. He did not retaliate when the insults were hurled nor did he scream when the nails pierced his wrists. But when God turned his head, that was more than he could handle."[28]

Never has there been anyone more *alone*. One-third of all Americans admit to frequent periods of loneliness, and a recent Gallup survey discovered that loneliness is the key factor in the high suicide rate for the elderly. But no one ever suffered loneliness more than Jesus Christ. He suffered on the cross all alone. Writing about Jesus' cry of abandonment; Lucado says, "I keep thinking of all the despairing people who cast despairing eyes toward the dark heavens and cry 'Why?' And I imagine him. I imagine him listening. I picture his eyes misting and a pierced hand brushing away a tear. And although he may offer no answer, although he may solve no dilemma, although the question may freeze painfully in mid-air, he who also once was alone, understands."[29]

Wayne Grudem warns us not to misunderstand Christ's cry of abandonment: "The question ['Why have You forsaken Me?'] does not mean, 'Why have you left me forever?' for Jesus knew that he was leaving the world, that he was going to the Father (John 14:28; 16:10, 17). Jesus knew that he would rise again (John 2:19; Luke 18:33; Mark 9:31, et al.). . . . This cry of desolation is not a cry of total despair. Furthermore, 'Why have you forsaken me?' does not imply that Jesus wondered why he was dying. . . . Jesus knew that he was dying for our sins."[30]

The words of William R. Newell in the gospel song "At Calvary" are penetrating:

> Oh, the love that drew salvation's plan!
> Oh, the grace that brought it down to man!
> Oh, the mighty gulf that God did span at Calvary!

The participants in His death. In Jesus' death we see both the enormity of man's guilt for a vicious criminal act and the immensity of God's love to rescue His enemies (Rom. 5:8–10). On the one hand the Cross was a great tragedy, but on the other it was a mighty triumph.

Who was responsible for the death of Jesus on the cross? As noted already, Jesus Himself was responsible. He said, "I lay down My life that I may take it again. No one takes it from Me, but I lay it down of Myself. I have power to lay it down, and I have power to take it again" (John 10:17–18). Also God the Father was involved. Isaiah wrote, "And the LORD laid on Him the iniquity of us all. . . . Yet it pleased the LORD to bruise Him; He has put Him to grief" (Isa. 53:6, 10). In Peter's sermon on the Day of Pentecost he declared that Jesus was "delivered by the determined purpose and foreknowledge of God" (Acts 2:23). And Peter and John, in praying to the Lord, said that the human perpetrators were gathered together "to do whatever Your hand and Your purpose determined before to be done" (4:28). Later Paul wrote that God the Father "made Him [Jesus] who knew no sin to be sin for us, that we might become the righteousness of God in Him" (2 Cor. 5:21). Because of the voluntary act of the Son of God, the Father is freed to work on behalf of the sinner. "It was necessary," as Chafer pointed out, "in the light of His holy character and government, that the price of redemption should be required at the hand of the offender or at the hand of a substitute who would die in the offender's place. By the death of Christ for sinners, the moral restraint is removed and the love of God is free to act in behalf of those who will receive His grace and blessing."[31]

Satan was active in the Crucifixion as well. As the "god of this age" (2 Cor. 4:4) and "the prince of the power of the air" (Eph. 2:2), he was seeking to keep Jesus from the cross, which would spell doom for the devil and all the minions of hell.

Also a number of individuals were responsible for Jesus' death. Speaking prophetically, a psalmist graphically described the assault by the kings and the nations which occurred in its most dramatic form at the cross: "Why do the nations rage, and the people plot a vain thing? The kings of the earth set themselves, and the rulers take counsel together against the LORD and against His Anointed, saying, 'Let us break their bonds in pieces and cast away their cords from us'" (Ps. 2:1–3). What insanity that the puny "kings of the earth" would try to withstand the King of the universe. Peter addressed Israel, the nation that God had favored above all the nations of the earth, charging them, "Jesus of Nazareth, a Man attested by God to you . . . you have taken by lawless hands, have crucified, and put to death" (Acts 2:22–23). After Peter was released from prison, he acknowledged to the Lord in prayer that several were involved in putting Jesus to death: "For truly against Your holy Servant Jesus, whom You anointed, both Herod and Pontius Pilate, with the Gentiles and the people of Israel, were gathered together" (4:27). Each of these had his own agenda, but in the wickedness of their hearts they lashed out against the very One who loved them enough to die for them.

The proof of His death. According to Jewish law it was necessary to remove the bodies of executed criminals before sunset (Deut. 21:23). Therefore to avoid breaking the law the Jews requested that the legs of the condemned be broken to hasten their death. With broken legs the victims could no longer lift their bodies to breathe and would soon suffocate. The soldiers broke the legs of the other two, but when they came to Jesus, they saw that He was already dead. So they pierced His side with a spear, and blood and water came out, indicating He was dead. The apostle John testified that he was an eyewitness to this (John 19:34–35).

Joseph of Arimathea, a rich man who was a prominent member of the Sanhedrin, had not agreed with the decision to crucify Jesus, for he was a good and righteous man, and a secret disciple of Jesus. He received permission from Pilate to take away the body of Jesus (Matt. 27:57; Luke 23:50–52). Nicodemus, another Sanhedrin member,[32] also a secret disciple, brought a mixture of myrrh and aloes, about seventy-five pounds, and the two men put the spices between strips of linen cloth and wound them around the body of Jesus (Matt. 27:59; John 19:39). Mary Magdalene and another Mary sat opposite the tomb, watching the preparation and planning to return later with additional spices. Joseph and Nicodemus then laid the body in a new tomb hewn out of the rock by Joseph, a tomb in which no one had been laid. This fulfilled the Scripture, "And they made His grave with the wicked—but with the rich at His death" (Isa. 53:9).

Sometimes people refer to the gospel as "the death, burial, and resurrection of Jesus Christ." However, the burial of Jesus is not a part of the gospel as such. Rather, it is the proof of the death of Christ. It may be seen as follows, based on Paul's words about the gospel in 1 Corinthians 15:1–8:

Death
according to the Scriptures (biblical proof)
burial (physical proof)

Resurrection
according to the Scriptures (biblical proof)
appeared to many (physical proof)

I am stressing this because a more balanced statement of the gospel needs to be made, not only by laypersons but also by pastors and theologians. In a seminary class I was making quite an impassioned presentation on the value of the death of Christ. A student (now a missions professor) interrupted by raising his hand and asking, "Don't you believe in the resurrection of Christ?" I responded, "Certainly I believe in the resurrection of Christ. Why would you ask such a question?" "Well," he said, "there seems to be such a neglect on the Resurrection in our books and teaching; whereas, when I turn to all the evangelistic messages in the Book of Acts, the emphasis is on the Resurrection. The death of Christ without the Resurrection would be no gospel at all. It would simply be a tragedy." How right he was! With that in mind now, we turn from the low point of sorrow and gloom to the greatest joy in history, the resurrection of Jesus Christ. Indeed, He is alive!

The Satisfaction with the Savior

Have you ever cheered at an endurance race for someone whom you love very much and who had been overcoming obstacle after obstacle and finally crossed the finish line? All of your pent-up emotion turns loose with tears and cheers. What ecstasy! I believe that is a small picture of what must have filled the heart of God the Father when Jesus, having obeyed every command of the Father and fulfilled every prophecy of Scripture about His death, gave His victory cry, "It is finished" (John 19:30),[33] and then said, "Father, into Your hands I commit My spirit" (Luke 23:46). The Father's instant response brought reverberations in heaven and on earth.

The rending of the veil. Jesus was on the cross for three hours in the daylight (from nine in the morning until noon), and then for the first three hours of the afternoon God the Father brought a supernatural darkness over the whole land (Mark 15:33), undoubtedly as a cosmic sign of His judgment on human sin which He placed on Jesus (Isa. 53:6, 10; 2 Cor. 5:21). Then when Jesus noted that He had completed His redemptive work, "the veil of the temple was torn in two from top to bottom" (Matt. 27:51). By splitting the veil "from top to bottom" God the Father dramatically showed His complete satisfaction with the Son's work on the cross. This showed that believers may now "enter the Holiest by the blood of Jesus, by a new and living way which He consecrated for us, through the veil, that is, His flesh" (Heb. 10:19–20).

The resurrection of Jesus Christ. We come now to that happy and exalting truth which was the central message of the early Christians.[34] Like the rending of the veil in the temple, the resurrection of Jesus was confirmation of the satisfaction of the Father with the completed work on the cross. Because Jesus was raised, God brings justification to everyone who believes (Rom. 4:25). Justification is provided because the Resurrection proves that God accepted Jesus' sacrifice.

The Resurrection, as George Ladd explains, "is not merely a question of the integrity and historical trustworthiness of a few resurrection stories. The entire New Testament was written from the perspective of the resurrection. Indeed, the resurrection may be called the major premise of the early Christian faith."[35] Ladd also writes, "Our churches have developed the custom of celebrating this event once a year on Easter Sunday, thus making its observance a seasonal matter. Seldom is a sermon on the resurrection heard at other times. This limitation of remembrance is not in the least the New Testament pattern."[36]

Luke wrote that Jesus "presented Himself alive after His suffering by many infallible proofs, being seen by them during forty days" (Acts 1:3). Interestingly, though Luke didn't list these "many infallible proofs," he did write that Peter said in Cornelius's house, "Him God raised up on the third day, and showed Him openly, not to all the people, but to witnesses chosen before by God, even to us who ate and drank with Him after He arose from the dead" (10:40–41). Later Paul mentioned some of those who saw Jesus in His resurrected state (1 Cor. 15:5–8). These witnesses attest to the reality of the resurrection of the One who said, "I am the resurrection and the life" (John 11:25).

PART TWO
God's Accomplishments in Salvation

CHAPTER 4

What Does Jesus Do for Sinners?

When Jesus gave the cry of victory, "It is finished," from the cross, what was finished? What had been accomplished at the cross? Some things were accomplished at the cross for sinners (the subject of this chapter), and other things were accomplished for saints, those who believe in Christ (the subject of chapter 5).

The Lord Jesus accomplished four marvelous acts on behalf of the unregenerate: substitution, redemption, propitiation, and reconciliation. His death as a Substitute for sinners is the heart of the Atonement, and the basis of the other three.

SUBSTITUTION FOR SINNERS

Many New Testament verses state that Jesus Christ died *for* sinners. For example, He was made "sin for us" (2 Cor. 5:21), He became "a curse for us" (Gal. 3:13), and He "suffered once for sins" (1 Pet. 3:18).

Two Greek prepositions translated "for" denote substitution. The stronger of these is *anti*, "in place of." We see this in the word "Antichrist," who, as a counterfeit, will present himself in place of or instead of Christ. The meaning of "in place of" is seen in Matthew 2:22 ("Archelaus was reigning over Judea *instead of* his father Herod"), 5:38 ("an eye *for* an eye or a

53

tooth *for* a tooth"), Romans 12:17 ("Repay no one evil *for* evil"), and Matthew 20:28 ("Just as the Son of Man did not come to be served, but to serve, and to give His life a ransom *for* many").

The other preposition is *hyper*, whose basic idea is "on behalf of" or "for the benefit of." Jesus said, "Pray *for* those who spitefully use you" (Matt. 5:44). Peter said to the Lord, "I will lay down my life *for* your sake" (John 13:37). However, as H. Riesenfeld noted, "Often 'on behalf of' carries an implication of 'in place of,' 'in the name of.' It is hard to avoid this sense in 1 Cor. 15:29, and this is the obvious meaning in Philemon 13. In 2 Cor. 5:14–15 Paul plays on the double sense of *hyper*. Christ's death is first 'in our place,' but it is then 'on our behalf' or 'for our sake.'"[1] An example of *hyper* meaning both "in place of" and "on behalf of" is Philemon 13, in which Paul expressed his desire that Onesimus minister to the apostle's needs in place of Philemon. Robert Lightner makes this point: "If *hyper* has the meaning of substitution in a context totally unrelated to salvation, then it can also have that meaning when it is used in relation to the redemptive work of Christ. Therefore, we conclude that while *anti* only connotes substitution, *hyper* connotes both the idea of 'in behalf of' another and also the idea of substitution."[2]

The meaning of "in place of" can be seen in Hebrews 2:9 (Jesus tasted "death for [*hyper*] everyone." In 2 Corinthians 5:21 ("For He made Him who knew no sin to be sin *for* us, that we might become the righteousness of God in Him") and 1 Timothy 2:5–6 ("Christ Jesus . . . gave Himself a ransom *for* all"). *Hyper* may carry either meaning "on behalf of" or "in place of," or perhaps both.

Why place such emphasis on these prepositions? Two reasons: Jesus' substitutionary death is without a doubt His most important accomplishment and it has been the subject of much erroneous teaching over the centuries. About two hundred years after the church began, Origen (184–254), a church father in Alexandria, Egypt, suggested the view that the death of Christ was a ransom paid to Satan. That theory gained such a hold on the church that it was believed for about one thousand years. Other explanations of the Atonement developed later, including the "moral influence" view of Abelard (1079–1142) and the "example" theory of Socinius (1539–1604). However, since human beings have a death sentence over them because of their sins, they need more than a mere moral influence as an example of martyrdom or obedience.[3] They need someone to pay their penalty. As Paul wrote, the curse of the Law was precariously hanging over us and Christ came under it and took the curse Himself (Gal. 3:13).

REDEMPTION FROM SIN

The Exodus was God's mighty act of redemption from the oppressive burdens the Egyptians had placed on Israel. Moses appealed to Pharaoh to let his people go and Pharaoh's insolent reply was, "Who is the LORD that I should obey His voice to let Israel go? I do not know the LORD, nor will I let Israel go" (Exod. 5:2). When Moses returned to the Lord, He said to Moses, "Now you shall see what I will do to Pharaoh. For with a strong hand he will let them go, and with a strong hand he will drive them out of his land. . . . I am the LORD; I will bring you out from under the burdens of the Egyptians, I will rescue you from their bondage, and I will redeem you with an outstretched arm and with great judgments" (6:1, 6).

The verb "redeem" (gā'al) may be rendered "to redeem, avenge, revenge, ransom, do the part of a kinsman."[4] It conveys the idea of buying back or purchasing something lost by paying a price. God promised to be the Redeemer (gō'ēl). The Lord brought ten plagues on Egypt, each of which was directed against a particular Egyptian deity.[5] The last plague was the death of the firstborn in each Egyptian family. But the Israelites were preserved from this plague by sacrificing a lamb and sprinkling its blood on their doorposts and lintels. This was called the Passover because God said, "When I see the blood, I will pass over you; and the plague shall not be on you to destroy you when I strike the land of Egypt" (12:13).

This day of redemption, the Passover, was to be celebrated in perpetuity by this nation that had been redeemed by the blood of lambs. "So this day shall be to you a memorial; and you shall keep it as a feast to the LORD throughout your generations" (12:14). The Passover, the first of the feasts of the Jewish calendar year, was celebrated on the fourteenth day of the first month (Nisan).

This historic event provides two pictures (types) of Christ. First, the blemish-less lamb was a type of our sinless Savior, our Passover Lamb, who was sacrificed for (*hyper*) us. This portrays His substitutionary death. Second, the blood of the Passover lambs is a type of Christ's blood, which speaks of the ransom, the price that was paid for our redemption. Thus, as Paul wrote, believers in Christ are "justified freely [literally, 'without cost'] by His grace through the redemption that is in Christ Jesus" (Rom. 3:24).

The Book of Ruth presents a beautiful portrayal of Christ, our Kinsman-Redeemer. The love story between the widow Ruth, a Moabitess who forsook her pagan heritage, and Boaz, the kinsman-redeemer, gives us a vivid picture of the redemption that takes place between the believer and Jesus. As noted earlier, the verb *gāʾal* means to buy back or redeem. If a person were to buy back or redeem something or someone as a kinsman-redeemer (*gōʾēl*), he had to meet five qualifications.[6] First, he must be a blood relative of the one he redeems (Deut. 25:5; Ruth 3:9). This is the requirement that brought the Son of God from heaven to earth to become man (John 1:14; Phil. 2:5–8). Second, the *gōʾēl* must be able to redeem (Ruth 2:1). Christ alone could pay the price of our redemption (Acts 20:28; 1 Pet. 1:18–19). Third, the *gōʾēl* must be willing to redeem (Ruth 3:11). Christ voluntarily left heaven (Phil. 2:5–6) to provide a ransom for us (Matt. 20:28). Fourth, the *gōʾēl* must be free from the calamity that had happened to the one to be redeemed. Christ had no sin nature for He is God and He never sinned (2 Cor. 5:21). Fifth, the *gōʾēl* must act to redeem by paying the price. Jesus did this in His death on the cross.

Gāʾal can also mean "to require blood, to avenge bloodshed." If a person intentionally killed another, the Mosaic law allowed a *gōʾēl* to avenge that death by slaying the murderer (Num. 35:19). Satan was a murderer from the beginning (John 8:44) and humans have no one to take vengeance on him. Vernon McGee explained, "This aspect of the meaning of the *gōʾēl* was wonderfully fulfilled in Christ. Sin and Satan have killed man and are therefore murderers. Satan is called a murderer in the Scripture, and man is his victim. In the Garden of Eden he led man to eat of that which brought death to the human family . . . but the One was promised who would be an enemy of Satan and his destroyer: "And I will put enmity between you and the woman, and between your seed and her Seed; He shall bruise your head, and you shall bruise His heel" (Gen. 3:15). In the fullness of time, the avenger of blood came."[7] "Inasmuch then as the children have partaken of flesh and blood, He Himself likewise shared in the same, that through death He might destroy him who had the power of death, that is, the devil, and release those who through fear of death were all their lifetime subject to bondage" (Heb. 2:14–15).

In light of the reality of this bondage, it is not difficult to see how Origen's "ransom to Satan" view of the atonement captured the thinking of the church. But no ransom was to be paid to Satan, for he was a usurper of what did not belong to him and had no right to demand payment. It was God who exacted payment; yet the Bible does not speak of a ransom being paid to God the Father for He did not hold us in bondage.

Three Greek verbs, virtually synonyms, emphasize different aspects of redemption. The first verb is *agorazō*, "to purchase in the marketplace." It is used thirty-one times in the New Testament. This verb was used of men in the Roman world purchasing slaves in the market (*agora*). The verb speaks of Christ paying the price to purchase those who are slaves of sin and Satan. Twice Paul reminded the saints in Corinth that they were "bought [from *agorazō*] at a price" (1 Cor. 6:20; 7:23), and therefore they needed to let that price affect how they lived. Looking to the future, John envisioned the choir of twenty-four elders and four living creatures falling down before the Lamb with harps in hand, singing a "new song." "You are worthy to take the scroll, and to open its seals; for You were slain, and have redeemed [from *agorazō*] us to God by Your blood out of every tribe and tongue and people and nation" (Rev. 5:9).

Almost fifty years ago, in my earliest ministerial assignment, I told a Child Evangelism class a story on redemption called "Twice Bought." A little boy lost his boat that he had made. Then one day he saw it in the window of a pawn shop. It was for sale, and the only way he could get it was to buy it back. So the boat was twice his: He created it, and he bought it. Every believer in Christ is a twice-owned person. We are God's both by creation and by redemption.

The second verb, similar to the first, is *exagorazō*. The prefix *ex* emphasizes separation of what has been purchased from the slave market altogether. *Exagorazō* is used two times to stress that believers have been set free from bondage to the Law and its condemnation (Gal. 3:13; 4:5).

This adds the idea of being taken *out of* the slave market. Twice this word refers to "buying back" time (Eph. 5:16; Col. 4:5).

The third verb is *lytroō*. Related to the verb "to loose" (*luō*), it carries the fullest meaning of redemption, namely, "to set free by the payment of a ransom." Peter spoke of Jesus' death as the redemption price that sets us free and motivates us to live for Him. "Conduct yourselves throughout the time of your stay here in fear; knowing that you were not redeemed [*lytroō*] with corruptible things, like silver or gold, from your aimless conduct received by tradition from your fathers, but with the precious blood of Christ, as of a lamb without blemish and without spot" (1 Pet. 1:17–19).

In a similar vein the apostle Paul stressed to Titus that our lifestyle needs to be motivated by the anticipation of the coming of "our great God and Savior Jesus Christ, who gave Himself for [*hyper*] us, that He might redeem [*lytroō*] us from every lawless deed and purify for Himself His own special people, zealous for good works" (Titus 2:13–14).

A related noun is *apolytrōsis*, the act of buying back a slave so that he is free. When a person believes in Christ, he or she is freed from slavery to sin. This word is rendered "redemption" in Romans 3:24; 8:23; 1 Corinthians 1:30; Ephesians 1:7, 14; 4:30; Colossians 1:14; and Hebrews 9:15.

This truth of our freedom in Christ is beautifully expressed in the song "My Redeemer."

> I will sing of my Redeemer
> And His wondrous love to me;
> On the cruel cross he suffered
> From the curse to set me free.
> Sing, oh, sing of my Redeemer,
> With His blood He purchased me;
> On the cross He sealed my pardon,
> Paid the debt and made me free.[8]

PROPITIATION TOWARD GOD

Whereas redemption is God's work on the cross in reference to sin, propitiation is His work on the cross in relation to Himself. Christ's death propitiated (satisfied, appeased) the righteous wrath of God.

Paul wrote that believers are "justified freely by His grace through the redemption that is in Christ Jesus, whom God set forth as a propitiation by His blood, through faith, to demonstrate His righteousness" (Rom. 3:24–25).

Sin violates God's righteousness and thus brings His wrath against the sinner. People today have a difficult time accepting the idea of God's wrath; they prefer to think of God's love to the exclusion of His righteousness and wrath. Leon Morris wrote, "The wrath of God is a conception which cannot be eradicated from the Old Testament without irreparable loss. It is not the monopoly of one or two writers, but pervades the entire corpus so that there is no important section of which it can be said 'Here the wrath of God is unknown!' The ubiquity of the concept must be stressed, because of the tendency in some circles today to overlook it or explain it away."[9]

The concept of wrath stresses the seriousness of sin. Thus Morris continued: "Sin is not just a mere peccadillo which a kindly, benevolent God will regard as no consequence. On the contrary, the God of the Old Testament is One who loves righteousness (Pss. xxxiii. 5, xlviii. 10, etc.), and whose attitude to unrighteousness can be described as hatred. . . . Modern men find a difficulty with this aspect of the Old Testament teaching, in part at least because they have so well learned that God is love. But it is important to notice that this was a truth known and valued by men of Old Testament times, and they apparently did not find it insuperably difficult to combine ideas that God loved them and that He hated all that is evil and would punish it severely."[10]

How can we reconcile God's attributes of love and wrath? His wrath, as Morris explains, is not "an uncontrollable outburst of passion." Instead it "is the reverse side of a holy love, a flame which sears but purifies . . . always exercised with a certain tenderness, for even when He is angry with man's sin God loves man and is concerned for his well-being in the fullest sense."[11]

How can God reach out to us in love without compromising His holiness? The answer is seen in the link between "propitiation" and "by His blood" in Romans 3:25. The verb "to propitiate" is used in pagan religions of human efforts to appease their capricious gods.[12] But the Bible never describes people as appeasing God. Rather, God Himself provides the propitiation in Christ.

Amazingly the Greek word for propitiation, *hilastērion*, is translated "mercy seat" (literally, "place of propitiation") in Hebrews 9:5. Why is that?

Behind the second veil, in the Most Holy Place of the tabernacle, was located the ark of the covenant. The ark of the covenant was a highly decorated and beautifully fashioned rectangular chest about four feet long, two feet high, and two feet wide, overlaid with pure gold. In the box were the two stone tables with the Ten Commandments, along with other symbols of God's mercy. The lid, a slab of pure gold, was called the mercy seat. Two cherubim, made of hammered gold and with wings stretched out and facing each other, covered the mercy seat.

Once a year on the Day of Atonement the high priest entered the Most Holy Place with "a censer full of burning coals of fire" so that a cloud of incense would cover the mercy seat. On the mercy seat he sprinkled blood of a sacrificial bull and the blood of a sacrificial goat (Lev. 16:12–15). Year after year, century after century, the high priest did this; yet this never took away even one sin. Instead, it enabled God's wrath against us to be propitiated or satisfied until Jesus Christ came as our Great High Priest and offered on the cross the only acceptable sacrifice—Himself (Heb. 9:11–28)! Christ then became our "propitiation" by "His blood" (Rom. 3:25). God's wrath against sin is held back when a sinner, through faith, comes to Christ. Just as the mercy seat was the place of propitiation because of shed blood, so Christ became "the propitiation [*hilasmos*] for our sins" (1 John 2:2) by His death on the cross. With His righteous wrath against sin satisfied, God could act in mercy and grace toward sinners, all of whom deserve eternal damnation.

RECONCILIATION TOWARD GOD AND MAN

Reconciliation means the removal of alienation between God and humankind. The Greek word for "reconcile" (*katallassō*) means to exchange enmity for friendship, hostility for peace. This is necessary because Adam and Eve's sin plunged the entire human race into separation from God and enmity against Him. Sinners are called "enemies" of God (Rom. 5:10; Col. 1:21). Does this mean that sinners feel enmity toward God or that God feels enmity toward sinners? Stated differently, does a believing sinner reconcile himself to God or does God do the reconciling? The Scriptures make it clear that only God can do the reconciling. And Paul wrote, "We were reconciled to God through the death of His Son" (Rom. 5:10), and "you who once were alienated and enemies in your mind by wicked works, yet now He has reconciled in the body of His flesh through death" (Col. 1:21–22).

Passages that speak of reconciliation between humans help illustrate this great truth. One is Matthew 5:23–24: "Therefore if you bring your gift to the altar, and there remember that your brother has something against you, leave your gift there before the altar, and go your way. First be reconciled to your brother and then come and offer your gift." Here an offender needs to go to the one he offended and do something to release the hostility or anger his offended brother has against him. The offender is responsible to take the initiative in bringing about a changed relationship. A second example is in 1 Corinthians 7:10–11. "Now to the married I command, yet not I but the Lord: A wife is not to depart from her husband. But even if she does depart, let her remain unmarried or be reconciled to her husband." Here a wife is to seek to remove enmity between herself and her husband, presumably because of some offense on her part against him.

In these two examples the offender is to take the initiative in seeking to remove the enmity. But this cannot be done in reference to salvation! A sinner, the offender, is incapable of removing his offense between himself and God, the offended One. So God did for people what they could never do for themselves. What man ought to do he can't. But because Christ propitiated God's wrath, God is now free to take the initiative to reach out to sinners and reconcile them to Himself. That is why Paul wrote that God "reconciled us to Himself through Jesus Christ" and "God was in Christ reconciling the world to Himself" (2 Cor. 5:18–19).

Roger Nicole makes a helpful observation about this doctrine: "Conservatives have always stressed the love of the Triune God as basic to reconciliation: this love is the moving cause rather than the effect or product of Christ's atoning work. This reconciliation, however, is not accomplished in defiance of the eternal perfections of God—His justice, holiness, immutability, sovereignty; rather the fact that these, as well as divine love, are seen in their most challenging expression at the Cross is what constitutes the triumph of the resourcefulness of grace."[13]

Reconciliation with God is available to all who in simple faith trust in the finished work of Jesus Christ on the cross.

CHAPTER 5
What Does Jesus Do for Saints?

W hat spiritual benefits accrue to the person who by faith receives
Christ as his or her Savior? This chapter selects a few of the many
results that stem from receiving salvation, several relating specifically to
our daily living.

ESTABLISHED IN GRACE AS THE RULE OF LIFE

Everyone who trusts in Jesus Christ for salvation is "justified freely by His
grace" (Rom. 3:24; see also Titus 3:7), is saved by grace (Eph. 2:5, 8), and
has redemption and forgiveness "according to the riches of His grace"
(Eph. 1:7). As a result we "are not under law but under grace" (Rom. 6:14).
We "stand" (that is, we are positioned spiritually before God) in a position of grace (5:2).

Yet many Christians seem to think they are obligated to keep the Law.
Even some theological writers suggest this idea. Let me cite some statements from several authors: "The law is a rule of life for believers, reminding
them of their duties and leading them in the way of life and salvation."[1]
"Christ does not free us from the law as a rule of life."[2] "Christians should
recite the commandments (as their creeds) to keep in memory what they
must do to enter into life."[3] "The law is a declaration of the will of God for

man's salvation."[4] "Though Christ has redeemed us from the curse of the law he has not freed us from the obligation to it."[5]

How can these statements be correlated with Paul's words in Romans 10:4 that "Christ is the end of the law for righteousness to everyone who believes"? Does this mean something was wrong with the Law? No, there was nothing wrong with the Law (Rom. 7:12; 1 Tim. 1:8), but Israel was wrong in trying to attain righteousness through the Law (Rom. 10:3). Paul told the Galatians that was a foolish approach: "O foolish Galatians! Who has bewitched you?... Did you receive the Spirit by the works of the law, or by the hearing of faith? Are you so foolish? Having begun in the Spirit, are you now being made perfect by the flesh?" (Gal. 3:1–3).

Why are people confused about the relationship between law and grace? One reason is the failure to realize that the Bible uses the word *law* in several different ways, most of which pertain either to moral law (Matt. 22:37–40) or to the Mosaic Law. The latter included moral laws, ceremonial laws, civil laws, criminal laws, sanitary laws, and governmental laws. The moral law consists of the eternal principles of righteousness, which reflect the character of God. The moral law of God, which existed before Moses and continues after the Cross, is the essence of God's will for everyone in every generation under all conditions.

On the other hand, the Mosaic Law is a set of regulations covering many areas of life for the nation Israel. "What purpose then does the law serve? It was added because of transgressions, till the Seed [Christ] should come" (Gal. 3:19). The Law, Paul wrote, was like a tutor to correct and instruct the Israelites in God's ways until Christ was revealed and the tutor was no longer needed (3:23–25). Thus the Mosaic Law was for a particular people for a particular purpose over a particular time period. Paul's statement, "Christ is the end of the law" (Rom. 10:4), does not mean Christ abolished all law. Instead it means that Christ is the end of the code of laws in the Mosaic Covenant. Christ lived under them and fulfilled them to the letter (Matt. 5:18).

The fact that Christians are under grace and not the Law (6:14), that is, the Mosaic Law, does not mean they have no laws to follow. Lawlessness or anarchy is the essence of sin (1 John 3:4). Paul encouraged believers to fulfill the "law of Christ" (Gal. 6:2) and James spoke of "the perfect law of liberty" (James 1:25). To be "under grace" means we are living under a new administration from God, with a new set of principles with grace as its focus. Ryrie illustrates this well: "As children mature, different codes are instituted by their parents. Some of the same commandments may appear in those different codes. But when the new code becomes operative, the old one is done away."[6] Through the centuries God established different administrations or dispensations in which God's children were to demonstrate their obedience. None of those administrations for believers was ever a means of attaining righteousness. Eternal life has always been available only by grace through faith in the Lord.

Although the Mosaic Law is often divided into three parts—ceremonial, civil, and moral—the writers of Scripture did not recognize such a division. The Mosaic Law was always viewed as a unit. According to Jewish tradition the Mosaic Law has 613 commandments. Yet the word *law* is normally singular in the New Testament. For example, James wrote, "For whoever shall keep the whole law, and yet stumble in one point, he is guilty of all" (James 2:10). And Paul said, "For as many as are of the works of the law are under the curse; for it is written, 'Cursed is everyone who does not continue in all things which are written in the book of the law, to do them'" (Gal. 3:10). Yet many people want to try to follow one part of the Law of Moses and not another. But it doesn't work that way because it is a unit. For example, those who want to keep the law pertaining to the Sabbath need to note the penalty for picking up sticks on the Sabbath (Num. 15:32–36). And if we are to keep the Mosaic Law, we will need an Aaronic priest, for we must bring animal sacrifices to a tabernacle, and we need to be part of a nation that is a theocracy. Christ is a priest not after the Aaronic order but after the order of Melchizedek (Heb. 7:17, 21). Therefore He does not administer the Mosaic Law. Since "the priesthood [is] changed, of necessity there is also a change of the law" (7:12). So believers cannot have both Christ and the Law of Moses.

The Mosaic Law was given to Israel, not to believers today in the church age. "These are the statutes and judgments and laws which the LORD made between Himself and the children of Israel on Mount Sinai by the hand of Moses" (Lev. 26:46). The nation Israel was governed by God on earth. That nation is still under the disciplinary hand of God in an exclusive relationship, and, in the future, when its people return to the Lord, He will gather them from all the nations where He has scattered them (Deut. 30:1–6) in keeping with His laws of blessing and cursing. So it is wrong to apply to Christians today promises given to Israel.

Some laws in the Mosaic Covenant, such as nine of the Ten Commandments, are repeated in the New Testament and are valid today. This is because they are rooted in God's essential character, not because they are in the Decalogue. However, the fourth commandment (to keep the Sabbath) is not repeated in the New Testament and is therefore no longer binding on believers. It was the sign of a covenant between God and Israel (Exod. 31:13, 17), a covenant that is no longer in effect, and Christians are not bound to observe days (Rom. 14:5–6).

The Law of Moses was not a means of deliverance from the penalty of sin. The Law was given that mankind might have a vivid picture of the character of God and how far short we fall. The Law, though it was "glorious" (2 Cor. 3:8, 11), was a means of making sin known. "For if there had been a law given which could have given life, truly righteousness would have been by the law. But the Scripture has confined all under sin, that the promise by faith in Jesus Christ might be given to those who believe" (Gal. 3:21–22). The Greek verb translated "confined" has the idea of being locked up together, or shut in on all sides so that there is no possibility of escape. The Law leaves us condemned, so that the only escape from sin is faith in Christ. Because we are under grace and not the Law, we can rejoice with Philip Bliss in his song, "Once for All":

> Free from the law—O happy condition!
> Jesus has bled, and there is remission;
> Cursed by the law and bruised by the fall,
> Grace has redeemed us once for all.

FREEDOM FROM SIN'S CAPTIVITY

As a result of Adam's sin and our participation in that sin, we were all constituted sinners and death was the result. However, even though death reigned from Adam to Moses, it was not until the Law was given through

Moses that what was inherently wrong previously became explicitly and exceedingly obvious. Yet "where sin abounded" because the Law did its work of condemnation, "grace abounded much more [literally, 'superabounded']" (Rom. 5:20). This superabounding grace raises the question, Why not then sin so that grace may abound? (see 6:1). The apostle responded in shock with the strongest kind of negation, which might be rendered, "Perish the thought" (6:2). This would be to deny the tremendous results believers receive because of their identification with Christ's work on the cross. One of the major purposes of Jesus' death was to deal with our sin nature. Paul wrote that at the cross "our old man was crucified with Him, that the body of sin might be done away with, that we should no longer be slaves to sin" (6:6). The verb "done away with" is *katargeō*, which is used in the epistles twenty-six times, six of which are in Romans (3:3, 31; 4:14; 6:6; 7:2, 6). In these six verses in Romans it is rendered "without effect" (3:3), "make void" (3:31), "made of no effect" (4:14), "done away with" (6:6), "released" (7:2), and "delivered from" (7:6).

The sin nature, then, was not removed; it was nullified or rendered inoperative. Our "old man," or the other man, was "crucified with Him." The "old man" is what we were in our depraved, unregenerate state without the life of God.[7] That person is gone forever, crucified with Christ. But the "body of sin" was not crucified; it was "made of no effect." It has lost its power in our lives.

This word *katargeō* is also used of Satan in Hebrews 2:14: Christ died to "destroy . . . the devil." Of course, Satan has not been annihilated, but his tyranny over us has been broken. The New Living Translation conveys this idea by translating Hebrews 2:14, "only by dying could he [Christ] break the power of the Devil." Similarly the "body of sin" (which Paul personified in Romans 7:20 as "the sin that dwells in me") has not been annihilated, but it has been nullified. And this is because Satan's tyranny (the power that energizes sin) has been nullified. As a result, "we should no longer be slaves of sin" (6:6). The power of the sin nature and our slavery to Satan were made void, rendered of no effect, and we were released from their demands. John didn't hesitate to admonish us, "My little children, these things I write to you, so that you may not sin" (1 John 2:1). Believers are released from slavery to sin and its energizer, Satan, by the finished work of Christ. He has triumphed!

A person in Christ is a new person. He or she is not simply the old person worked over. That's why Paul wrote, "If anyone is in Christ, he is a new creation; old things have passed away; behold, all things have become new" (2 Cor. 5:17). Think of the miracle God performs at the moment a person exercises faith in Christ. The believer has an entirely new power source and new possibilities. The tyranny of Satan has been destroyed and the slavery to sin is broken.

A key passage on our identification with Christ's death and resurrection is Romans 6:1–11.

> What shall we say then? Shall we continue in sin that grace may abound? Certainly not! How shall we who died to sin live any longer in it? Or do you not know that as many of us as were baptized into Christ Jesus were baptized into His death? Therefore we were buried with Him through baptism into death, that just as Christ was raised from the dead by the glory of the Father, even so we also should walk in newness of life. For if we have been united together in the likeness of His death, certainly we also shall be in the likeness of His resurrection, knowing this, that our old man was crucified with Him, that the body of sin might be done away with, that we should no longer be slaves of sin. For he who has died has been freed from sin. Now if we died with Christ, we believe that we shall also live with Him, knowing that Christ, having been raised from the dead, dies no more. Death no longer has dominion over Him. For the death that He died, He died to sin once for all; but the life that He lives, He lives to God. Likewise you also, reckon yourselves to be dead indeed to sin, but alive to God in Christ Jesus our Lord.

When Paul wrote in verse 2 that we have "died to sin," he was not saying our sin nature has been extinguished or that we are sinless. Instead, as already noted, the phrase means that the tyranny of sin has been broken and that Satan's dominion or right to rule has been disannulled.

Is this contradicted, however, by the statement in verse 7, "he who has died has been freed from sin"? No, because the word "freed" is *diakaioō*, "to justify." Only here is it rendered "freed" because at the point of justification the believer is set free from bondage to the old master. Before sinners trust Christ, they are by nature children of wrath, with Satan as their master, and the sin nature, their capacity for sinning, is energized by that deceiver (Eph. 2:1–3). But when a sinner trusts Christ, he or she becomes a new creation (2 Cor. 5:17), partakes of God's divine nature, and is indwelt by the Holy Spirit. Now the new person and the flesh are bidding for control of one's life. No longer is the individual obligated to sin; he doesn't "have" to sin. Although the devil appeals in devious and subtle ways for believers to follow him and to give in to their sinful desires, God gives assurance that the One who is resident in us, that is, the Holy Spirit, is greater than the one who is in the world, that is, the devil (1 John 4:4).

What did Paul mean when he said believers are "baptized" into Christ's death (Rom. 6:3)? The words "baptized" and "baptism" would be familiar to Paul's readers because people who expressed faith in Christ were baptized in water (Matt. 28:19; Acts 2:41). Water baptism outwardly pictures the inner reality of our being identified with Christ in His death and resurrection. Just as He died and was resurrected to new life, so individuals, at the moment of salvation, died to (were separated from) the tyranny of sin and were resurrected to a new life (6:4), and our bodies will be resurrected when He returns (6:5, 8–9). In his hymn "O for a Thousand Tongues to Sing" Charles Wesley put it this way: "He breaks the pow'r of canceled sin, he sets the pris'ner free; His blood can make the foulest clean, His blood availed for me."

In light of these wonderful truths that we "know" (6:3), Paul urged us to "reckon yourselves to be dead indeed to sin, but alive to God" (6:11). One summer when I was a boy I heard a farmer repeatedly saying, while chewing on a piece of straw, "I reckon." To me this seemed meaningless. But later when I looked up the word *reckon* in a dictionary, I found that it means to "count, estimate, compute, regard or think of as, consider, think, suppose." And this is exactly the meaning of *logizomai,* the Greek word for "reckon." This was an accounting term. So Paul was urging believers to enter in our ledgers the fact of our being dead to sin and alive to God. In other words, we should recognize these truths and live in light of them. Paul did not say we are to behave *as if* we are dead to sin but to lead godly lives *because* we died to sin.

Also the reckoning is not simply negative. Like a good battery, it has a positive as well as a negative pole. Besides being dead, we are alive (6:11)!

And in verse 5, Paul stated, "For if we have been united together in the likeness of His death, certainly we also shall be in the likeness of His resurrection." Because Christ is alive we are too. Therefore we are to walk in "newness of life" (6:4). Each believer is a new creation, with God's life in him or her, so that each Christian is a "new man." We "have put off the old man with his deeds, and have put on the new man who is renewed in knowledge according to the image of Him who created him" (Col. 3:9–10).

The following diagram illustrates the three scriptural resources that believers have for obtaining spiritual victory and the three opponents that seek to pull believers toward sin.

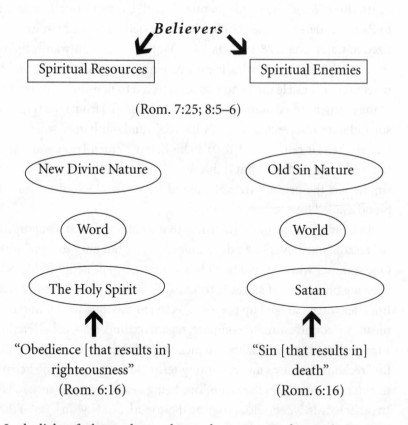

In the light of what we know about who we are, Paul wrote in Romans 6:12–14: "Therefore do not let sin reign in your mortal body, that you should obey it in its lusts and do not present your members [that is, parts of your body] as instruments of unrighteousness to sin, but present yourselves to God as being alive from the dead, and your members as instruments of righteousness to God. For sin shall not have dominion over you, for you are not under law but under grace." The command "do not present your members . . . to sin" could literally be rendered, "Stop presenting your members . . . to sin." But why is this command even necessary? If our bondage to sin has been broken, why do we still sin? The answer, as stated before, is that our sin nature, or our capacity for sin, has not been eradicated. God has made us new creations so that we have the opportunity of choice. This period of testing, then, is our opportunity to develop faithfulness as good stewards, to be obedient to our Master, the Lord Jesus—by not yielding to sin.

FORGIVENESS AND CLEANSING FROM SIN

Because Christ has freed us from the tyrannical rule of Satan and captivity to our sinful ways, we have sufficient spiritual resources to keep from sinning. We need not sin, for, as the apostle John put it, "My little children, these things I write to you, so that you may not sin" (1 John 2:1). However, in the previous chapter he had said concerning the sin nature, "If we say that we have no sin, we deceive ourselves, and the truth is not in us" (1:8), and concerning personal sin, "If we say that we have not sinned, we make Him a liar, and His word is not in us" (1:10). A. T. Robertson made a pointed observation about these verses: "John has no patience with professional perfectionists (1:8–10), but he has still less with loose-livers like some of the Gnostics who went to all sorts of excesses without shame."[8] Unfortunately, because our "disarmed" enemy is still clever and subtle, we often succumb to his tactics. But the provisions our Lord makes for His children are more than adequate.

As much as John wished his readers would not commit sin (2:1), he knew those who deny the fact of sin (1:8, 10) are likely to be deceived and to fall into sin. So he assured them, "And if anyone sins, we have an Advocate with the Father, Jesus Christ the righteous" (2:1). Four times John used the word "Advocate" (*paraklētos*, "one called alongside") to refer to the Holy Spirit (John 14:16, 26; 15:26; 16:7). And Christ Himself is our Advocate with God the Father against the charges of the devil, that "accuser of the brethren" (Rev. 12:10).

In rabbinic literature *paraklētos* meant "a friend of the accused person, called to speak to his character, or otherwise enlist sympathy in his favor."[5] In 1 John 2:1 Christ, our *paraklētos,* is our "counsel for the defense." In this verse John called the Son of God "Jesus Christ the righteous," and in 2:2 he added that "He Himself is the propitiation for our sins." The One who has satisfied the righteous demands of the holy God (as our propitiation) is presently at the right hand of the Father pleading our case.

No one could be more qualified to serve believers in this capacity, for "He always lives to make intercession for them. For such a High Priest was fitting for us, who is holy, harmless, undefiled, separate from sinners, and has become higher than the heavens" (Heb. 7:25–26). Paul, too, wrote of the ministry of Jesus as our Intercessor: "It is Christ who died, and furthermore is also risen, who is even at the right hand of God, who also makes intercession for us" (Rom. 8:34).

However, why must Christ engage in continuing intercessory work since He exclaimed on the cross, "It is finished"? Is His work not really complete, after all? Yes, His judicial substitutionary work on the cross *is* finished. The crucifixion made complete provision for redemption, propitiation, and reconciliation. And that completed work on the cross provides the *basis* for His continual intercessory work on behalf of believers. The *finished* work of Christ enables Him to carry on as our Advocate and Intercessor in heaven, where God the Father "seated Him at His right hand in the heavenly places," (Eph. 1:20). As our High Priest He "is seated at the right hand of the throne of the Majesty in the heavens" (Heb. 8:1; see also 1:3; 10:12). Jesus' present work relates to the believers' sanctification, which includes, among other things, forgiveness of sins and cleansing.

This work of Christ with respect to forgiveness and cleansing raises other questions: Didn't the atoning work of Christ cover the payment for all our sins? And doesn't that include past, present, and future sins? If all our sins are forgiven at the moment of salvation, why do believers need an Advocate, Jesus Christ the Righteous One, to plead their case before the Father's throne when they sin? Through the centuries people have given confusing and often contradictory answers to these questions. Some of the early church fathers believed that water baptism washed away sins. So, they reasoned, "If baptism washes away sins, what will happen to a believer who commits sins after baptism?" Not knowing what would remit those postbaptism sins, some early Christians delayed baptism as long as possible, thereby supposedly decreasing their chances of being lost.[10] Out of this grew the Roman Catholic teaching that some sins are mortal (serious) and others are venial (of lesser consequence). It is easy to see how people could begin to question whether a Christian could lose his salvation.

It is vital, therefore, to understand that God has provided for what may be called "initial judicial forgiveness" and also for "repetitive judicial forgiveness." The first provision—initial judicial forgiveness—is given when a person receives Christ as his or her Savior. This forgiveness of sins is available because of the death of Jesus Christ on the cross. He has "offered one sacrifice for sins forever" (Heb. 10:12) and that one offering "has perfected forever those who are being sanctified" (10:14). The second provision—repetitive judicial forgiveness—is given through Jesus Christ's continuing work as our Advocate. Each time believers sin, Christ the Advocate pleads their case, even when they are not repentant or have not realized their sin. This repetitive judicial work as their Advocate occurs even before believers confess sins they commit in their Christian living. Wendell Miller observed, "Obviously, in God's courtroom, where all statements by our advocate are absolutely righteous, He does not deny our sins, make excuses for us, plea bargain in our behalf, or try to have the case dismissed on the basis of technicalities. Instead of attempting to obtain a believer's release from the penalty of his sin by denying his guilt or by presenting supposedly mitigating circumstances, every time a believer sins, Jesus identifies that believer as His own and says, 'I paid for that sin on the cross, too.' To that defense there can be no other response but the one made possible by the cross. The Father answers, 'That's right. We will mark it paid in full. He is still judicially (*positionally*) perfect.'"[11]

 God forgives a believer's sin on the basis of Jesus' work as our Advocate (1 John 2:1); this forgiveness is unconditional.

But a question still remains. What about the confession John wrote about in 1 John 1:9: "If we confess our sins, He is faithful and just to forgive us our sins and to cleanse us from all unrighteousness"? This forgiveness refers to what may be called "conditional fellowship." God, who is light (1:5), wants to have fellowship with us, His children, but He cannot do that if we are walking in darkness (1:6). So He has provided a way whereby we can take care of the sin that interrupts that fellowship in God's family. This forgiveness is conditioned on a believer confessing his or her sin, so it differs from the initial judicial forgiveness a person receives at the moment of salvation and from the repetitive judicial forgiveness of sins committed thereafter.

God has provided for continual cleansing from the sin nature: "If we walk in the light as He is in the light, we have fellowship with one another, and the blood of Jesus Christ His Son cleanses [present tense] us from all sin. If we say that we have no sin, we deceive ourselves, and the truth is not in us" (1:7–8). In these verses the singular word "sin" refers to the sin principle within the believer. God's promise of continual cleansing from sin is a reminder of our continual need. John's use of the present-tense "cleanses" does not allow for any notion that we can do away with the old sin nature in this life.

How do we get that continual cleansing from the defilement of sin? We receive that by walking in the light as John wrote in 1:7. Our "new man" needs to be given continual exposure to the light so that the light will overcome the darkness. As Zane Hodges noted, "It is significant that John talked of walking *in* the light, rather than *according to* the light. To walk *according to* the light would require sinless perfection and would make fellowship with God impossible for sinful humans. To walk *in* it, however, suggests instead openness and responsiveness to the light."[12]

When I was a boy, several other guys and I were hiking when we were surprised by a sudden cloudburst. We crawled into a cave for shelter, but when the rain didn't stop, we decided to gather some sticks and start a fire to warm ourselves. Thankfully, the fire gave us light as well as heat. The light enabled us to see spiders and a snake, so we decided to leave the cave and venture back out in the rain. The same thing will happen when we walk with God, in whom is no darkness of evil or imperfection at all.

When we confess our sins, the estrangement and loss of fellowship with the Lord is restored. In 1:9 the plural word "sins" suggests that John was referring to acts of sin, not the sin principle, as in verses 7 and 8. The blood of Jesus Christ goes on cleansing us from sin as we walk in the light. But specific acts of sin are to be dealt with by confession and forgiveness. So this provision may be called "repetitive fellowship forgiveness."

The word "confess" means, literally, "to say the same thing." That is, we are to have the same attitude toward sin that God has. When God says in the Scriptures that something is sin, our immediate response should be, "That's right, Lord, that is sin. I renounce it. I agree with you about what it is and I am grateful for the blood of Jesus Christ that cleanses from all sins. And I thank you, Lord, that you are faithful and just in your dealings with me." Forgiveness of sin to maintain fellowship with the Lord depends on confession of sins, and cleansing of defilement from the sin nature depends on walking in the light.

The following summary of these forms of forgiveness is adapted from Wendell Miller.[13]

Four Kinds of God's Forgiveness of Sin

1. *Initial Judicial Forgiveness*
   Time: At the moment of belief in Christ
   Nature: Conditioned on faith alone
   Sins involved: All previous sins committed before justification
   Result: Eternal life

2. *Initial Fellowship Forgiveness*
   Time: At the moment of belief in Christ
   Nature: Removal of estrangement
   Sins involved: All previous sins committed before justification
   Result: Fellowship with God begun (1 John 1:7)

3. *Repetitive Judicial Forgiveness*
   Time: At the moment a Christian sins
   Means: Jesus' work as the believer's Advocate
   Nature: Immediate and unconditional
   Sins involved: Sins committed in a believer's life

4. *Repetitive Fellowship Forgiveness*
   Time: When a Christian confesses his sin
   Means: Jesus' ministry as the believer's High Priest
   Nature: Conditioned on confession
   Result: Fellowship with God restored (1 John 1:9)

PART THREE

God's Invitation to Salvation

CHAPTER 6
What Is Common Grace?

We learned in chapter four that God has not spared anything from His infinite resources in making provision for our salvation. The work of atonement on the Cross is an accomplished fact. Now the gracious invitation to salvation is going out worldwide. Among the last words of the Bible are these: "And the Spirit and the bride say, 'Come!' And let him who hears say, 'Come!' And let him who thirsts come. Whoever desires, let him take the water of life freely" (Rev. 22:17). We now turn to the application of that mighty reservoir of grace to the deep and desperate need of mankind.

THE MEANING OF COMMON GRACE

When we move to the work of the Holy Spirit, we are making a transition from the objective work of Christ to its subjective application. This is where God takes the initiative to reach out to us in grace. The word *grace* is used in a variety of ways, including, for example, a person's beauty or charm of movement. Or some people refer to a prayer before a meal as "saying grace." When we turn to grace in the Bible, however, we find it means *undeserved and unmerited favor*. Two dimensions of grace are common (or general) grace and special (or saving) grace.

"Common grace" refers to grace that is available to all humanity. Its benefits are experienced by all human beings without discrimination. It reaches out in a multitude of ways, promoting what is good and restraining what is evil. The Bible's first mention of grace is in Genesis 6:8: "Noah found grace in the eyes of the LORD." But God gave mankind a "grace period" of one hundred and twenty years, while Noah was building the ark. Apart from common grace God in His holy wrath would have destroyed them at their first act of rebellion. But His delay, as well as His sparing Noah and his family, revealed His common grace.

"Then the LORD saw that the wickedness of man was great in the earth, and that every intent of the thoughts of his heart was only evil continually" (6:5). So He said, "I will destroy man whom I have created from the face of the earth" (6:7).

THE NEED FOR COMMON GRACE

W. Robert Cook has stated the need for common grace in outline form. Contemplating these facts makes us realize the utter impossibility of society continuing to function apart from common grace.

1. The debasing effects of sin (Rom. 1:21–32)
   Otherwise [without common grace] men and situations would be ultimately self- and others-destructive.
2. The judicial effects of sin (Rom. 5:12–21)
   Otherwise guilt would be overwhelming.
3. The corrupting effects of sin (Rom. 3:10–18; Eph. 2:1–3)
   Otherwise moral decay would dominate society.
4. The deceiving effects of sin (Jer. 17:9)
   Otherwise rational thought and deed would be impossible.
5. The debilitating effects of sin (Jer. 17:9)
   Otherwise mankind would not be able to perform any (nonredemptive) good.
6. The blinding effects of sin (2 Cor. 4:4)
   Otherwise evil would never be recognized as such.[1]

When we think of the debasing, judicial, corrupting, deceiving, debilitating, and blinding effects of sin, we then realize how assuring it is that

God in His grace makes the sun shine on the just and the unjust. A nineteenth-century agnostic and antagonist of Christianity, Robert Ingersoll, is reported to have shaken his fist toward the heavens and demanded, "If there is a God, I defy You to strike me dead." Why did God allow him to continue to breathe? Because of His common grace. Common grace keeps the human race from displaying the fullest demonstration of its depravity.

L. Berkhof explains common grace by asking a series of probing questions:

> How can we explain the comparatively orderly life in the world, seeing that the whole world lies under the curse of sin? How is it that the earth yields precious fruit in rich abundance and does not simply bring forth thorns and thistles? How can we account for it that sinful man still "retains some knowledge of God, of natural things, and of the difference between good and evil, and shows some regard for virtue and good outward behavior"? What explanation can be given for the special gifts and talents with which the natural man is endowed, and of the development of science and art by those who are entirely devoid of the new life that is in Christ Jesus? How can we explain the religious aspirations of men everywhere, even of those who did not come in touch with the Christian religion? How can the unregenerate still speak the truth, do good to others, and lead outwardly virtuous lives?[2]

All these factors give evidence of God's common grace. Man is not manifestly as evil as he might be. In fact, many people give evidence of noble, gracious, and benevolent deeds.

THE CHANNELS OF COMMON GRACE

Some of the channels of common grace are direct, in which God takes immediate action, whereas other means are indirect. We call these indirect means of common grace divine providence.

Natural Revelation

The most basic means of divine common grace is the light of revelation that shines in nature and enlightens every person in the world (John 1:9) and holds him accountable. "For the wrath of God is revealed from heaven against all ungodliness and unrighteousness of men, who suppress the truth in unrighteousness, because what may be known of God is manifest in them, for God has shown it to them. For since the creation of the world His invisible attributes are clearly seen, being understood by the things that are made, even His eternal power and Godhead, so that they are without excuse" (Rom. 1:18–20).

There is not a person on earth who has not experienced this common grace of God through natural revelation. It is manifest *in them* and is shown *to them*; thus the attributes of God are clearly seen in human beings as well as in the created universe. In his book *Fearfully and Wonderfully Made*,[3] the famous surgeon Paul Brand testified to this truth of God's handiwork in creating the human body. And the internationally recognized physicist Walter Dyke did the same in *Biblicosm*[4] in examining the marvelous handiwork in God's created universe.

Viewing the starry universe caused the psalmist to exclaim, "The heavens declare the glory of God; and the firmament shows His handiwork. Day unto day utters speech, and night unto night reveals knowledge. There is no speech nor language where their voice is not heard. Their line has gone out through all the earth, and their words to the end of the world" (Ps. 19:1–4). The revelation of God in the material universe is so clear that it is like eloquent speech. Paul wrote of the power of revelation in nature: "So then faith comes by hearing, and hearing by the word of God. But I say, have they not heard? Yes indeed: 'Their sound has gone out to all the earth, and their words to the end of the world'" (Rom. 10:17–18). Here Paul quoted Psalm 19:4.

God holds humanity responsible for this light of revelation through their conscience because they "show the work of the law written in their hearts, their conscience also bearing witness, and between themselves their thoughts accusing or else excusing them" (2:15). Commenting on this verse, John Calvin said that such Gentiles "prove that there is imprinted on their hearts a discrimination and judgment by which they distinguish between what is just and unjust, between what is honest and dishonest."[5]

In what sense have people "heard" the voice of common grace in creation? Not in the sense of "special revelation," for not all have received it. As noted earlier, common grace is not saving grace. But can we say anything further about the value of common grace in nature? In Acts 8–10

Luke recorded how three men responded to the "light" they had and in each case God brought them, in unique ways, to the greater light of the gospel by which they were saved.

God called Philip to leave a successful evangelistic meeting to go to Gaza in the desert, where He encountered an Ethiopian official returning from Jerusalem (Acts 8:26–40). The Ethiopian was reading the prophecy in Isaiah 53 about the substitutionary death of the coming Redeemer, but he didn't understand it. When Philip explained the passage and gave him the gospel, the Ethiopian received Christ as his Savior. Common grace led him to read the Old Testament, and saving grace brought him to Christ. Common grace and saving grace met in Isaiah 53.

Saul of Tarsus, a religious zealot, a Pharisee of the Pharisees, was bent on destroying Christians and Christianity because of his strong belief that their teachings were blasphemous. He was sincerely committed to the Old Testament revelation as he had been taught. But he was completely mistaken about Jesus Christ. Though he was racing headlong in the wrong direction, God in His common grace spared his life. Then when God supernaturally stopped him, common grace and saving grace joined hands, caused him to do an about-face, and he was saved (9:1–23).

A Gentile by the name of Cornelius, a devout man who feared God, gave alms generously and prayed regularly, but he was not saved until Peter told him the good news of salvation (10:1–48). Common grace led him to be devout, but he needed saving grace.

These three each responded to the light they had.[6] When they responded, God brought each one to the greater light of the gospel whereby they could believe and be saved. Whatever importance we may place on these three unique conversions, the fact remains that there is no one in all the world who has not heard the powerful and unique voice of natural revelation. Everyone in the world, no matter how secluded, has received the benefits of general revelation.[7]

Sunshine, Rain, and Crops

A second aspect of God's common grace is His providing sunshine and rain so that crops will grow for the benefit of humanity. Paul said that God "did not leave Himself without a witness, in that He did good" for humankind by providing rain and giving food (Acts 14:17). Jesus said that God the Father sends sunshine and rain on both the saved and the unsaved (Matt. 5:45), and that "He is kind to the unthankful and evil" (Luke 6:35).

Human Government

A third means of common grace is human government. As the God of order, He has ordained that order should be maintained through human government, even through sinful and unregenerate humanity. Paul wrote, "Let every soul be subject to the governing authorities. For there is no authority except from God, and the authorities that exist are appointed by God. Therefore whoever resists the authority resists the ordinance of God, and those who resist will bring judgment on themselves" (Rom. 13:1–2).

It is striking to realize that the cruel emperor Nero, who later declared himself a god, was ruling the Roman Empire when Paul wrote that "the authorities that exist are appointed by God." Yet Nero was the one who, mourning that Rome had grown so haphazardly, dreamed of rebuilding it and renaming it Neropolis. Probably Nero was the one who arranged for the fire that was started on July 18, A.D. 64, and that burned for nine days and razed two-thirds of the city. Tacitus noted that Nero blamed the fire on the Christians and put many of them to death in cruel ways: "They were put to death with exquisite cruelty, and to their sufferings Nero added mockery and derision. Some were covered with skins of wild beasts, and left to be devoured by dogs; others were nailed to crosses; numbers of them were burned alive; many, covered with inflammable matter, were set on fire to serve as torches during the night. . . . At length the brutality of these measures filled every breast with pity. Humanity relented in favor of the Christians."[8] Ultimately in A.D. 68 Nero was driven from power by the Roman senate. Will Durant related Nero's efforts at suicide that ended with his driving a dagger into his own throat.[9]

Ultimately, human government in the Roman Empire prevailed, made corrections, and brought new and better order. Long before the Roman Empire, God had used pagan nations and their rulers to discipline His people. For example, Jeremiah had warned Judah for twenty-three years concerning their disobedient ways, but they mocked him, called him a false prophet, and would not heed his warnings. So God brought Nebuchadnezzar, king of Babylon, to Judah and he devastated the land and took the people captive (Jer. 25:8–11). But later, as God promised, the Babylonians would be destroyed (25:12).

God is Sovereign! He rules the nations through government. He used pagan Nebuchadnezzar to discipline His people, and then He punished Nebuchadnezzar with insanity for his iniquity (Dan. 4). When his sanity was restored, Nebuchadnezzar "blessed the Most High and praised and honored Him who lives forever" (4:34). This shows that in common grace God rules in human government in spite of people's wickedness.

God uses government to discipline and punish, but He also uses it to provide for our good. Besides government being "an avenger to execute wrath on him who practices evil" the government ruler is "God's minister . . . for good" (Rom. 13:4). When the people of Judah were taken into captivity to Babylon, Jeremiah told them, "Seek the peace of the city where I have caused you to be carried away captive, and pray to the LORD for it; for in its peace you will have peace" (Jer. 29:7). And Paul wrote, "Therefore I exhort first of all that supplications, prayers, intercessions, and giving of thanks be made for all men, for kings and all who are in authority, that we may lead a quiet and peaceable life in all godliness and reverence" (1 Tim. 2:1–2). God can use governments for our benefit, so He tells us to pray that our leaders will govern in such a way that we can enjoy peaceable lives. When that happens, we have greater opportunity to spread the gospel of "God our Savior, who desires all men to be saved and to come to the knowledge of the truth" (2:3–4).

After the devastating destruction of the Flood, sinful people planned to build a tower in Babel, and thereby to make a name for themselves (Gen. 11:1–4). The Lord responded, "Indeed the people are one and they all have one language. . . . Come, let Us go down and there confuse their language, that they may not understand one another's speech" (11:6–7). What terrible language barriers mankind faced. This communications problem lasted for thousands of years. Then at the appropriate time, soon before God was ready to introduce His Son to the world, He used a pagan, Alexander the Great, to give much of the then-known world a common language. In his conquest Alexander made Greek the world's *lingua franca.*

It was normal for a world conqueror to replace the language of the conquered with that of the conqueror. But when Rome conquered Greece, the Roman Empire retained the Greek language as the language of literature and used Latin only as the language of commerce. The Romans, however, made another significant contribution to a disordered world. They brought about the benefits of an advanced civilization and an era of peace and safety that came to be known as the *Pax Romana.*

> Today our highest labors seek to revive the *Pax Romana* for a disordered world. Within that unsurpassed framework Rome built a culture Greek in origin, Roman in application and result. She was too engrossed in government to create as bountifully in the realms of the mind as Greece had done; but she absorbed with appreciation, and preserved with tenacity, the technical, intellectual, and artistic heritage that she had received from Carthage and Egypt, Greece and the East. She made no advance in science, and no mechanical improvements in industry, but she enriched the world with a commerce moving over secure seas, and a network of enduring roads that became the arteries of a lusty life. Along these roads, and over a thousand handsome bridges, there passed to the medieval and modern worlds the ancient techniques of tillage, handicraft, and art, the science of monumental building, the processes of banking and investment, the organization of medicine and military hospitals, the sanitation of cities, and many varieties of fruit and nut trees, of agricultural or ornamental plants, brought from the East to take new roots in the West.[10]

What a beautiful example of God's providence. In His common grace the *Pax Romana* enabled the first-century missionaries of the church to travel safely, with the protection of the Roman army, over thirteen thousand miles of new roads and a thousand bridges.

In the fifteenth century Johannes Gutenberg invented movable type and the printing press. The press thus eliminated the tedious, slow process of copying documents by hand—a major barrier in communications. This, too, was a work of God's common grace. Of interest is the fact that the first book to be printed on Gutenberg's press was the Bible in 1456. "Many people feared that the new art of printing was a 'black' art that came from Satan. They could not understand how books could be produced so quickly, or how all copies could look exactly alike."[11] What a pity to attribute God's provision to Satan's activity! Yet this revolution in communications in 1456 is miniaturized by present-day computers and cyberspace. On March 28, 1998, the Associated Press announced, "Nanoelectronics: Scientists make electronic circuits using DNA." Technion, one of Israel's premier research institutes, has produced a wire that is one-thousandth the width of a hair, less than half the size of wires in use today. They hope to build a wire that is 250 times smaller than the existing ones. They say that a DNA-made microchip could store 100,000 times as much information as a current model. Their ultimate dream is to store all the texts of the Library of Congress— seventeen million books along five hundred miles of shelves—on a space the size of a speck of dust! And that is simply the common grace of God operating through sinners.

In 1949 Mao Tse-Tung, the former leader of communist China, commissioned the development of a much simpler Chinese language, minus the thousands of characters that complicated their printing presses before. He did this so that the communist principles in his *Little Red Book* could be more widely distributed. However, thirty years later Mao Tse-Tung was dead, and there was little interest in his book. But the language he commissioned was used in printing fifty thousand copies of the "little red book" of Jesus Christ, the New Testament! But God is in control of governments, and that was one of the means that He used to accomplish His purposes.

And as I sat at my computer typing this manuscript, I stopped to send a message by e-mail to a missionary friend in Spain and I received a reply within minutes. How thankful we can be to the Lord for His providence in common grace.

Christian Testimony

A fourth area of common grace is the testimony of believers. Christians, individually and together, can have an influence in the world like preserving salt and penetrating light. Jesus said, "You are the salt of the earth.... You are the light of the world.... Let your light so shine before men, that they may see your good works and glorify your Father in heaven" (Matt. 5:13–14, 16). In the same vein the apostle Paul wrote, "Walk in wisdom toward those who are outside, redeeming the time. Let your speech always be with grace, seasoned with salt, that you may know how you ought to answer each one" (Col. 4:5–6).

In my student days in seminary, I used to sell programs for football games at the Cotton Bowl in Dallas. "You can't know the players unless you have a program," was my regular line. The high point of the year emotionally was the October weekend of the Texas/Oklahoma game, when many football fans went wild on drinking frenzies. It was not a safe place to be the night before the game. Each year on the Friday before the game, a friend of mine went to one of the downtown hotels and rode up and down on an elevator. The people would walk into the elevator swearing and talking suggestively, and right at the beginning of the elevator trip he would mention Jesus Christ. Immediately the conversations changed! He would do that all night long. He literally changed the atmosphere by his talk in that small cubicle of humanity.

Years ago I served as a station chaplain at the Dallas Naval Air Station. Often chaplains serving with me came in all varieties spiritually and de-nominationally. One day as I returned to my office, I encountered a group of enlisted men huddled around a chaplain who was on hand for the weekend. He had just spoken the punch line of a dirty joke, and the group exploded in laughter until they saw me. Then they quickly dispersed in all directions. As they went by me, I heard them say, "Boy, that chaplain is really a neat guy." I thought to myself, "Yeah, and they think I'm a killjoy, someone who spoils their fun." At about that time my yeoman came into my office and said to me, "Chaplain, I know how you feel right now. But, let me tell you that when those guys get into trouble, they will not go to the other chaplain. They will be here in your office." Common grace broke up that little meeting.

The presence of even a silent Christian testimony can change a portion of society where we function.

The True, the Good, and the Beautiful

A fifth area of God's common grace is the presence of the true, the good, and the beautiful. Paul encouraged us to occupy our minds with "whatever things are true, whatever things are noble, . . . whatever things are pure, whatever things are lovely" (Phil. 4:8). Obviously both regenerate and unregenerate people possess talents and patience to produce works of art, music, and literature. Every human has been graced by God with the sense of sight, sound, touch, smell, and taste. Even though the world is under the curse of sin, it is replete with opportunities to enjoy viewing the power of Niagara Falls, the massive depth and colors of the Grand Canyon, or the quiet, fragile beauty of the Olympic National Rain Forest. How pleasant it is to enjoy the soft touch of a baby's hand. And who does not enjoy the aroma and taste of culinary delights? What joy it brings to spend an evening at the symphony or an afternoon strolling through an art museum enjoying the talents that have been patiently refined and put on canvas.

Even in a world under the curse of sin, humanity still enjoys and honors the faithfulness of a couple committed in loyal love to each other over a lifetime. And even though the Prentice-Hall surveys in *The Day America Told the Truth*[12] reveal startling figures of untruthfulness, everyone values the virtue of truth. We wrestle against lust and seek to extol love. And though we often rationalize our shading of the truth or telling outright lies, in our hearts we desire and deeply appreciate honesty. Yes, there is in our present world the common grace of God whereby humans enjoy the true, the good, and the beautiful. What a foretaste of what is yet to come for those who move beyond common grace, which does not save, to the saving grace of God in Jesus Christ.

THE DECLINE OF COMMON GRACE

The thrust of common grace is either negative in restraining evil or positive in encouraging good. God restrained Satan from doing all he wanted to do to Job (Job 1:12; 2:6).

The person behind the restraint of sin is the Holy Spirit. Second Thessalonians 2:6–12 addresses this subject of the restraint of evil: "And now you know what is restraining, that he may be revealed in his own time. For the mystery of lawlessness is already at work; only He who now restrains will do so until He is taken out of the way. And then the lawless one will be revealed, whom the Lord will consume with the breath of His mouth and destroy with the brightness of His coming. The coming of the lawless one is according to the working of Satan, with all power, signs, and lying wonders, and with all unrighteous deception among those who perish, because they did not receive the love of the truth, that they might be saved."

In this passage Paul gave us insight into a future time when the supernatural restraint of sin will be terminated and the dual forces of mankind's depravity and Satan's tyranny will be evident.

In the Tribulation the future world ruler, the Antichrist, who is here called "the lawless one," will set himself up as God in the temple and will demand worship. However, until that time lawlessness is now held back by the One who is restraining (2:7). Several suggestions have been made about the identity of the restrainer, but the only person who fits the requirements is the Holy Spirit. The Antichrist, called "the man of sin" and "the son of perdition" (2:3), will be energized by Satan "with all power, signs, and lying wonders" (2:9). And the only power greater than Satan is God.

Soon after the Rapture of the church, the Holy Spirit's ministry of restraining the Antichrist will cease, and the man of sin will carry out his work of deceit and destruction on the earth. At that time order and beauty, which we know today because of the Holy Spirit's work of common grace, will turn to utter chaos. This will be a time of trouble unparalleled in all of history (Dan. 12:1; Matt. 24:21).

Although 2 Thessalonians 2:6–12 does not specifically mention the removal of the church before the revelation of the man of sin, the removal of restraint and the Rapture of the church may coincide. With the removal of the church there will be the loss of a major avenue of common grace in the world.

CHAPTER 7

How Does God Convict Sinners of Their Sin?

THE OFFER OF SALVATION

In voicing God's universal call to salvation, the prophet Isaiah wrote, "Look to Me, and be saved, all you ends of the earth! For I am God, and there is no other" (Isa. 45:22). "Ho! Everyone who thirsts, come to the waters; and you who have no money, come, buy and eat. Yes, come, buy wine and milk without money and without price" (55:1). How appropriate that this universal offer of the gospel is also in the closing verses of the Bible: "'I, Jesus, have sent My angel to testify to you these things in the churches. I am the Root and the Offspring of David, the Bright and Morning Star.' And the Spirit and the bride say, 'Come!' And let him who hears say, 'Come!' And let him who thirsts come. Whoever desires, let him take the water of life freely" (Rev. 22:16–17).

This universal offer of life reminds us of Jesus' words: "If anyone thirsts, let him come to Me and drink" (John 7:37). And again, "Come to Me, all you who labor and are heavy laden, and I will give you rest" (Matt. 11:28). This is the same offer that Paul made. Speaking of the righteousness that comes by faith, he gave the gospel: "If you confess with your mouth the Lord Jesus and believe in your heart that God has raised Him from the dead, you will be saved. For with the heart one believes unto righteousness, and with the mouth confession is made unto salvation" (Rom. 10:9–10).[1]

Then Paul continued with a strong statement about God's universal offer of salvation: "For the Scripture says, 'Whoever believes on Him will not be put to shame.' For there is no distinction between Jew and Greek, for the same Lord over all is rich to all who call upon Him. For 'whoever calls on the name of the LORD shall be saved'" (10:11–13). This universal offer is also a genuine offer. The cross of Christ is broad enough and deep enough to cover all the sins of everyone who will come to Him.

This general call to salvation is a part of common grace. It may or may not lead to saving faith in the mighty work that Christ accomplished on the cross for the sinner's eternal salvation. Even though the offer of this great gift from God is genuine and available to all, many do not receive it by believing in Jesus Christ. "He [Jesus] came to His own, and His own did not receive Him. But as many as received Him, to them He gave the right to become children of God, to those who believe in His name" (John 1:11–12). "He who believes in Him is not condemned; but he who does not believe is condemned already, because he has not believed in the name of the only begotten Son of God. And this is the condemnation, that the light has come into the world, and men loved darkness rather than light, because their deeds were evil" (3:18–19).

When the Jewish leaders persecuted Jesus and sought to kill Him, He got to the heart of their problem: "But you are not willing to come to Me that you may have life" (5:40). The general call of the gospel becomes effective when it is joined with faith in the finished work of Jesus Christ: "He who believes in the Son of God has the witness in himself; he who does not believe God has made Him a liar, because he has not believed the testimony that God has given of His Son" (1 John 5:10).

THE CONVICTING WORK OF THE HOLY SPIRIT

God's convicting work of the Holy Spirit is another facet of common grace. The central passage of Scripture on this specific work of the Holy Spirit is John 16:7–11. "It is to your advantage that I go away; for if I do not go away, the Helper will not come to you; but if I depart, I will send Him to you. And when He has come, He will convict the world of sin, and of righteousness, and of judgment: of sin, because they do not believe in me; of righteousness, because I go to My Father and you see Me no more; of judgment, because the ruler of this world is judged."

The Origin of Conviction

The One who brings about conviction when the gospel is presented is the Holy Spirit. Jesus said the Holy Spirit is our Helper, a word that translates *paraklētos*, "one called alongside to help." Earlier we noted that Jesus Christ, our *paraklētos*, intercedes on our behalf before God the Father in response to Satan's accusations against us. The Spirit of God—also called "the Spirit of truth" in John 14:17 and 15:26—is the other *paraklētos*, the other One called alongside to help believers in making a foolproof case for Jesus Christ against the world. As Robertson observes, "So the Christian has Christ as his Paraclete with the Father, the Holy Spirit as the Father's Paraclete with us (John 14:16, 26; 15:26; 16:7; 1 John 2:1)."[2]

The Agency of Conviction

Though John 16:8 does not say that the Holy Spirit convicts unbelievers directly, it does say He convicts "the world." However, He uses believers as His "agents" of conviction. "If I do not go away, the Helper will not come to *you*; but if I depart, I will send Him to *you*" (John 16:7, italics added). Christ had already said that "the world cannot receive" the Spirit of truth "because it neither sees Him nor knows Him; but you know Him, for He dwells with you and will be in you" (14:17). Of course, the people Christ was addressing in the Upper Room Discourse were the apostles who, unlike us, were recipients of revelation. However, what the apostles began as "agents" of the Holy Spirit's convicting work, we are to continue. We see this in Jesus' prayer in the next chapter: "I have manifested Your name to the men whom You have given Me out of the world. . . . I do not pray for these alone, but also for those who will believe in Me through their word" (17:6, 20).

Christ prayed not just for the apostles; He prayed for all those who would come to Christ through their witness. Think of Jesus' very last words to the disciples before His ascension to heaven: "But you shall receive power when the Holy Spirit has come upon you; and you shall be witnesses to Me in Jerusalem, and in all Judea and Samaria, and to the end of the earth" (Acts 1:8). I often hear people today praying for "pentecostal power" and talking about "power evangelism," which in their minds is "signs and wonders and miracles." But the apostles exercised those powers even *before* the Day of Pentecost. Christ and the apostles healed all kinds of sicknesses and diseases and even raised the dead (Matt. 10:8). On the Day of Pentecost God did not introduce any greater power miracles. Instead, the new power Jesus was introducing to believers was *power as witnesses, in proclaiming the message of the gospel.* And they would receive this power from the Holy Spirit. In the Upper Room Jesus had told them about the birth of the church by means of the Holy Spirit: "And I will pray the Father, and He will give you another Helper, that He may abide with you forever—the Spirit of truth . . . you know Him, for He dwells with you and will be in you" (John 14:16–17).

The word "you" in these verses is plural and refers to the disciples. In fact, the three occurrences of "you" in verse 17 are each in the emphatic position in Greek. In other words, Jesus was saying that something significant would happen to them. Literally verse 17 reads, "With you He abides [timeless present tense] and in you He will be." Later, as they got closer to the event, Jesus told them not to leave Jerusalem but to wait for the promise of the Father because they would be baptized in (not "by") the Holy Spirit[3] in a few days. Later Peter explained that event: "And as I began to speak, the Holy Spirit fell upon them, as upon us at the beginning. Then I remembered the word of the Lord, how He said, 'John indeed baptized with [literally, in] water, but you [plural] shall be baptized with [literally, in] the Holy Spirit'" (Acts 11:15–16). The only event that could have been indicated by the words "the beginning" was the Day of Pentecost in Acts 2.

Paul wrote of that event in 1 Corinthians 12:12–13: "For as the body is one and has many members, but all the members of that one body, being many, are one body, so also is Christ. For by [literally, in] one Spirit we were all baptized into one body—whether Jews or Greeks, whether slaves or free—and have all been made to drink into one Spirit." In other words, on the Day of Pentecost, Jesus Christ, the ascended and exalted Head of the church, baptized Jews and Gentiles together into one new body, and placed them in the Holy Spirit for His care and safekeeping until the body would be complete and meet Jesus Christ face to face.

The big event on the Day of Pentecost, then, was not the coming of the Holy Spirit. He had been there all along (John 14:17). Rather, there was a fantastic celebration of a new birth. The church—a bride for the Bridegroom—was born. But in the sweep of history, what was to be the unique role of the church? The church was to be the one with the *power* of witnessing and outreach.

To accomplish that task of Acts 1:8, God assigned the Holy Spirit to a new role as *Paraclete* for the church, the One who would be the Advocate on earth for Jesus Christ through the preaching of the gospel by the church. In other words, we don't have to do the convincing and persuading. That is the work of the Holy Spirit. What we need to be sure about is that we make the gospel clear.

At the time of Christ there were approximately two hundred million people on the earth. Then in about 1850 the population reached one billion. The population doubled to two billion in eighty years, by 1930. Then in only forty-five years it doubled again, to four billion, in 1975. And this year (2000) an estimated six billion people are on the earth![4] We are living in the time of the greatest demographic explosion in history.

By noting some facts about the growth of the church we capture a little of what Christ had in mind when He said, "You shall receive power . . . and you shall be witnesses to Me." In the *Mission Frontiers Bulletin* Rick Wood wrote, "God's initiative since A.D. 100 displays determined and increasing activity to build His Church. Note: It took 18 centuries for evangelicals to go from 0 % of the world's population to 2.5% in 1900, only 70 years to go from 2.5% to 5% in 1970, and just the last 22 years to go from 5% to 10% of the world's population. *What this means is that now, for the first time in history, there is one evangelical for every 9 non-evangelicals world-wide.*"[5]

The disciples had become sorrowful not only because Jesus had said He would leave them (John 16:5–6), but also because He said they would be put out of the synagogues and people would consider they were doing God a service by putting them to death (16:2). But Jesus wanted them to see that this would be a great advantage for them, because if He did not depart, then the Advocate would not come to them (16:7). But when He departed, He would send the Holy Spirit. Obviously Jesus knew that their momentary sorrow would turn to joy when they experienced the power of the ministry of the Holy Spirit through them in their witnessing. Think of the fearless boldness of Peter and John in addressing the Sanhedrin (Acts 4) in contrast to the disciples' fear and sorrow in the Upper Room. The powerful witness of the disciples in the Book of Acts differs remarkably from their deserting the Lord just before He was crucified.

The Nature of the Conviction

What specifically does the Holy Spirit do as Advocate through believers? The Greek word for "convict" in John 17:8 is *elengkō*, sometimes also translated "convince," "reprove," or "rebuke." The word basically means "to bring to light, to expose," that is, to demonstrate something clearly beyond the fear of successful contradiction. Jesus used this word to the Pharisees when He asked, "Which of you convicts Me of sin?" (8:46). He was not asking, "Which one of you charges Me?" Or "Which one of you rebukes Me?" Instead, He asked, "Which one of you convinces Me?" That is, "Which of you can demonstrate beyond refutation that I am a sinner?" When the Holy Spirit convicts sinners, He is making the case stick, so to speak. The person being convicted in this way will know the truth of the matter in his or her heart. If he or she refuses the truth, it is because darkness is opposing the light brought by conviction.

What are the specific areas of truth about which the Holy Spirit will convict the world? We need to know this because, if the Spirit of God, the Agent of conviction, is to do His convicting work through believers, we need to be speaking words He can use. Thus Jesus said the specific areas of which the Holy Spirit will convict the world are sin, righteousness, and judgment (16:8).

Conviction of sin. The Holy Spirit convicts of sin (singular), not sins (plural). Often a believer witnessing for Christ starts with sins, but that is not what the Holy Spirit does when He is making a case for Jesus Christ.

We may help a man who is an alcoholic get over drinking, thus sparing him some physical and social problems, but he will not be any closer to heaven. We may help a drug addict get over his addiction, or a liar stop lying. But often reformation is of no more value than hooking good apples on a rotten apple tree or trying to put good bark on a dead tree. Because an unregenerate person's basic need is not to get rid of certain sins, the Spirit of God never convicts the sinner of sins, as such. Instead, He convicts sinners of the sin of not believing on Jesus Christ. Evangelist Larry Moyer explains the problem this way: "Why did Christ die on the cross? So that individuals might have their marriages mended? No! So that individuals might be fulfilled? No! These things have occurred when individuals have trusted Christ, but unhappy marriages and unfulfilled lives are simply symptoms of an even larger problem—separation from God. Christ died on the cross for one reason—to bring everyone who trusts Him into a right standing with God."[6]

Wherever we start, then, as a point of contact, using the common grace afforded us in the convicting ministry of the Holy Spirit, we should move steadily to the issue of belief in Christ and what he has done as a ransom for our sins. Getting people to put away their sins will not bring them to Christ. They need a spiritual rebirth, and that new nature is available only when they reckon with Jesus Christ Himself.

The first church I pastored was a small church in a rural town. In that town and the surrounding farming community there were a number of churches. To introduce myself to people in the community, the chairman of the deacon board and I called on each of the homes. After introducing myself to the man answering at the door of one home, I immediately received a verbal barrage as follows: "I know why you are here. They bring all the new pastors to my house when they come to town to tell me to quit smoking, quit cussing, quit drinking, quit beating my wife." After I gained my composure, I managed a smile and said, "I really didn't know you did all those things. As a new pastor in town I simply wanted to introduce myself and let you know that if I can ever be of help to you, contact me. And, by the way, keep your heart open to God. He may want to talk to you sometime." He seemed a little taken back, but pleasantly surprised.

A couple of months later I was nailing some siding on the outside of the church building. The man pulled up in his pickup and asked, "Can you use some help?" "Sure!" I replied, "Go get a hammer." The next Sunday, he and his wife and two children were in the morning service. I sensed that when I presented the gospel and gave opportunity to receive Christ that he wanted to do something about it, but he didn't. I learned from his wife later that he had been brought up quite legalistically and was taught that the way to accept Christ was to go forward in church. But being a proud, blustery man, that seemed too humiliating. The next Sunday at the invitation, I said to the congregation, "Now I don't have God in a box up here at the altar. You can believe on Christ and receive Him right in your seat where you are. But if you would like to talk with me about it, why don't you stop off in the room to your right as you exit, and I will meet you there." He did, and I had the opportunity of leading him to faith in Christ.

Sam (not his real name) became active as a helper. As the Christmas program approached, heavy rains came and the swollen river through town overflowed thousands of acres, and the children couldn't get to the program. Sam offered to bring his motorboat and go out with me and pick up people. As we were going out for a load, Sam said, "By the way, I stopped smoking." "Really?" I responded. "Why did you do that?" "I got to thinking about the fact that I spend twenty-five dollars a month on cigarettes [1955 prices], and we could sure put that money to better use in the church, so I decided to stop." He didn't go through any program; he simply had a new vision and new inner resources.

I have learned over the years that you can spend a lot of time picking leaves off of a tree, but if you wait until the sap stops flowing, the leaves will fall off by themselves. A missions professor told me of a tree in the Philippines that retains its leaves even after the sap stops flowing. The leaves don't drop until the new sap comes up in the branches and twigs and pushes the old leaves off. Instead of trying to force people to give up their sins, we need to confront them with the one sin of disbelief. Then when they come to Christ, their new life in Him urges them to drop off their old ways. The Holy Spirit convicts of *sin*.

Conviction of righteousness. The second area of conviction by the Holy Spirit, Jesus said, pertains to "righteousness, because I go to My Father and you see Me no more" (John 16:10). Apart from God's righteousness no one can be saved. The Mosaic Law presented a standard of righteousness, which Christ, and only Christ, kept perfectly (Matt. 5:17–18). The Law made sin evident (Rom. 5:13; 7:7), and Jesus Christ, in fulfilling the Law, became the perfect demonstration and standard of righteousness. Paul addressed this problem of our sin and the provision of Christ's righteousness: "For all have sinned and fall short of the glory of God, being justified freely by His grace through the redemption that is in Christ Jesus, whom God set forth as a propitiation by His blood, through faith, to demonstrate His righteousness" (Rom. 3:23–25).

God is freed to act graciously in love toward sinners because the blood of Christ, the "Righteous One" (see Acts 3:14; 7:52; 22:14), has satisfied the demands of His holy character. In the resurrection and ascension of Christ, then, God is demonstrating vividly His complete satisfaction with His sacrifice. Jesus Christ, who personifies that righteousness, is the only acceptable standard worthy of our belief. Any object of faith other than Christ will leave the person in his or her sin.

In His convicting work the Holy Spirit brings to light faulty views of the righteousness of Christ. Those who crucified Jesus had a faulty view of Him; therefore Peter charged them with having failed to assess Jesus Christ correctly: "Men of Israel, hear these words: Jesus of Nazareth, a Man attested by God to you by miracles, wonders, and signs which God did through Him in your midst, as you yourselves also know—Him, being delivered by the determined purpose and foreknowledge of God, you have taken by lawless hands, have crucified, and put to death; whom God raised up, having loosed the pains of death, because it was not possible that He should be held by it" (Acts 2:22–24). The convicting work of the Holy Spirit brought about a change of mind about Christ as the only righteous and worthy object of faith: "Therefore let all the house of Israel know assuredly that God has made this Jesus, whom you crucified, both Lord and Christ. Now when they heard this, they were cut to the heart, and said to Peter and the rest of the apostles, 'Men and brethren, what shall we do?'" (2:36–37).

Whenever there is a change of mind in the heart, the seat of reflection, there will always be a heartfelt need for change of action. They had now recognized, through the convicting work of the Holy Spirit, that Christ is indeed who He claimed to be.

Conviction of judgment. The third area of the convicting work of the Holy Spirit relates to the need for sinners to make a decision. They cannot ride the fence. They have to choose whom they will believe. Thus Jesus said the Holy Spirit convicts "of judgment, because the ruler of this world is judged" (John 16:11). To decide against the Spirit of God, by refusing to believe in Jesus Christ, is to decide for the devil, "the ruler of this world" (see Eph. 2:2). And to decide for the devil is to experience eternal condemnation in hell. One of the major accomplishments of the cross was Jesus' judgment of Satan. He is a defeated foe and his doom is sure, but he still parades around as a "roaring lion," seeking to deceive and to destroy (1 Pet. 5:8).

The fact that the Holy Spirit is making a case for Jesus Christ through the truth spoken by believers to sinners does not mean the devil has folded his hands and backed off. Not at all! In fact, if anything, he has picked up steam and the battle for people's souls has intensified. Satan desires to hide the truth. Jesus told the Pharisees, "You are of your father the devil, and the desires of your father you want to do. He was a murderer from the beginning, and does not stand in the truth, because there is no truth in him. When he speaks a lie, he speaks from his own resources, for he is a liar and the father of it" (John 8:44).

The apostle Paul spoke of the devil's tremendous deceptive powers, which seem so right to unbelievers but are the way of death: "But even if our gospel is veiled, it is veiled to those who are perishing, whose minds the god of this age has blinded, who do not believe, lest the light of the gospel of the glory of Christ, who is the image of God, should shine on them" (2 Cor. 4:3–4). Zane Hodges observes, "Evidently Satan does not subscribe to the notion that man is inherently incapable of believing. He would be wasting his time blinding man if man is already hopelessly blind!"[7] In Jesus' parable of the sower He spoke of birds that devour the seed that is sown (Luke 8:5), and then explained that this pictures Satan's work: "Those by the wayside are the ones who hear; then the devil comes and takes away the word out of their hearts, lest they should believe and be saved" (8:12).

In the light of Satan's craftiness and deceitfulness—remember the Garden of Eden—we need to be sure that in conveying the gospel we are providing content that the Holy Spirit can use in defeating Satan and lifting the veil that blinds unbelievers.[8] In the light of this great need to present the gospel clearly, is it any wonder that Paul contended so strongly in the conflict over the young church in Antioch (Acts 13:44–48), in the Jerusalem Council (Acts 15), and in an entire letter to the Galatians in which he blamed Peter and Barnabas because "they were not straightforward about the truth of the gospel" (Gal. 1:14)? Again, Hodges gives a penetrating thought for those who would be used of God in this battle: "To the extent that human beings present the gospel falsely or in garbled form, they serve well the aims of Satan, who is *actively* blinding the minds of the unsaved. But to the extent that we give people the gospel in all its clarity and simplicity, we can become instruments whom God uses to focus His light on darkened human hearts."[9] Ultimately everyone must express commitment to either Christ or Satan. And we are called to have a vital part in enabling people to make that choice.

Thinking of these three areas of the convicting ministry of the Holy Spirit, we see that we as believers can partner in team ministry with God the Holy Spirit (John 15:26–27). In bringing sinners to Christ, the Spirit of God prepares them through His convicting work and through believers speaking words about sin, righteousness, and judgment. When we speak these truths, the Holy Spirit attests the truth of what we say in the hearts of sinners. In essence the Holy Spirit says, "What he is saying is true. You had better believe it."

The Method of Conviction

In His convicting work the Holy Spirit uses believers' witnesses by word of mouth and by their conduct, by their talk and their walk. Paul put these two together in Philippians 2:14–16: "Do all things without complaining and disputing, that you may become blameless and harmless, children of God without fault in the midst of a crooked and perverse generation, among whom you shine as lights in the world, holding fast the word of life, so that I may rejoice in the day of Christ that I have not run in vain or labored in vain."

Some Christians say they don't believe in talking about religion. They say they believe in "living it." Suppose we are still in the Vietnam War and I have a son in Vietnam and another son about to be drafted. And suppose my neighbor's son is also to be drafted soon. Let's say I receive a message from the commanding general's office, telling me he has good news. "The war is over. Your son is coming home!" I would be overjoyed at the news! Suppose I look out the window and see my neighbor working among the flowers in his yard. He looks terribly sad because he is expecting that his son will soon be leaving for Vietnam. And I think, "I must go and share the good news." I run over to his yard and greet him joyously. And he says to me, "What are you so happy about?" Suppose I just smile and say, "Oh, I don't believe in talking about it, I just believe in living it."

You would think I was crazy, and rightly so. Why? Because when you believe you have truly good news, you want to spread the word.

A fierce battle for eternal souls is being waged between Christ and Satan. As Jesus approached His last week before the crucifixion, He said, "Now My soul is troubled, and what shall I say? Father, save Me from this hour? But for this purpose I came to this hour. Father, glorify your name" (John 12:27–28). Then Jesus said, "Now is the judgment of this world; now the ruler of this world will be cast out" (12:31). After the grueling test through the illegal trials and the horrible and humiliating pain of the cross, before He gave up His spirit, with a loud voice He gave the cry of victory, "It is finished!" The victory is won! Redemption is accomplished! Satan is defeated! The battle for people's souls has been won! No one will *have* to spend eternity in hell! In light of this glorious fact can we simply say, "I don't believe in talking about it. I just believe in living it?" Obviously that is not enough. When Christ rose from the dead, the disciples' sorrow was turned to rejoicing. They became indomitable and fearless in spreading the good news throughout the Roman Empire. They were eager to tell about it.

Of course, this is not to underestimate the great importance and value of a godly lifestyle. If we are not careful our actions may undo what we say. As the maxim puts it, "What you do speaks so loudly that I can't hear what you say." How we live should be consistent with our verbal sharing of the gospel. The Holy Spirit uses both in His convicting sinners of their need of the Savior.

102

PART FOUR
God's Act of Regeneration

CHAPTER 8

What Is Regeneration?

The preceding chapters have all been moving steadily toward the subject of regeneration. God's work in regeneration—giving a sinner life—is so great that Paul said each believer is a "new creation" (2 Cor. 5:17). This is more stupendous than even the creation of the universe!

As noted earlier, common grace, needful as it is, does not save. God's *saving* grace is necessary. When the gospel is received by faith, God brings about the miracle called regeneration.

THE EFFECTUAL CALL OF THE HOLY SPIRIT

In chapter 3 we briefly discussed three words that pertain to God's salvation: election, foreknowledge, and predestination (Rom. 8:28–30). God elected some to be saved, He foreknew (that is, loved) them, and He predestined their ultimate destiny. These three relate to God's work in eternity past. A fourth word is "called," and this transfers these three other acts into history. "Moreover whom He predestined, these He also called; whom He called, these He also justified; and whom He justified, these He also glorified" (8:30). Everyone whom God predestines, He calls, and each one who is justified is glorified. No one is lost in the process! ("Glorified" is yet future, but Paul spoke of it as past because it is as good as done.) Everyone whom God starts in this race finishes!

The starting gate in this race is labeled "called." Those who are called are those who have responded to the conviction of the Holy Spirit through the message of the gospel. The invitation to enter the race is offered to everyone, but not everyone accepts the offer. "Called," then, in Romans 8:30 means more than "invited." When we speak of the "call" of the gospel going out to the unsaved, we are referring to God's invitation to come to Christ. However, only those who respond with faith in Christ are the called (Matt. 22:14).

In Philippi, Paul, Silas, Timothy, and Luke preached the Word to women, including Lydia. That was the invitation, the general call. When Lydia responded, she was saved. That was what theologians call "the effectual call." The general call presents the message that "Christ died for our sins." But the hearer needs to believe (John 20:31).

In the general call in Philippi God led Lydia to listen to what the preachers said ("Lydia heard us," Acts 16:14). Then what happened? "The Lord opened her heart to heed the things spoken by Paul." She listened to all four speakers intently, but the Holy Spirit used Paul's message to open her heart. The word "opened" (*dianoigō*) stresses opening up wide, like double-folding doors. In Lydia's case all the elements are present: the message of the human witnesses; the convicting of the Holy Spirit; the response of the listener; the opening of Lydia's heart, the place of deepest reflection; and the effectual calling (salvation).

What is said about Lydia is presented in a doctrinal context by Paul about the neighboring church at Thessalonica: "God from the beginning chose you for salvation through sanctification by the Spirit and belief in the truth, to which He called you by our gospel for the obtaining of the glory of our Lord Jesus Christ" (2 Thess. 2:13–14). Paul referred to this effectual call when he said that the Christians in Rome and Corinth were "called to be saints" (Rom. 1:7; 1 Cor. 1:2). From the moment God opens our hearts to the truth of the gospel, we are His "called" ones.

Charles Spurgeon gave a beautiful illustration of the difference between the general call and the special call: "The general call of the gospel is like the sheet lightning we sometimes see on a summer's evening—beautiful, grand—but who ever heard of anything being struck by it? But the special call is the forked flash from heaven; it strikes somewhere. It is the arrow shot in between the joints of the harness."[1] Sheet lightning is impressive, but the forked flash is specific. Other verses that mention God's special call to salvation are 1 Corinthians 1:9; 1 Thessalonians 2:12; and 1 Peter 2:9.

THE MEANING OF REGENERATION

When God gives life to a spiritually dead person, we call it "regeneration." Now the new believer is a child of God, truly alive for the first time, and able to understand and feed on God's Word. The believer is born again, as Jesus said in John 3:3, 5, 7. The Greek word rendered "born" in these verses is *gennaō*, which speaks of God creating a new person. When unsaved individuals receive Jesus Christ by faith, they become "children of God" (1:12), born not by any human means but by God (1:13). They are born again to a living hope (1 Pet. 1:3) through the eternal Word of God (1:23). When Jesus spoke of being born "again" (John 3:3, 7), He used the Greek word *anōthen*, which can mean "from above" (see 19:11). That is, the new birth is a spiritual transformation that can be accomplished only by God.[2]

THE RESULT OF REGENERATION

Ronald Shea explains spiritual birth this way:

> Just as a man and a woman come together to produce a new person, a third person separate and distinct from the first two, so God "regenerates" a person. The seed or "sperma" of the Holy Spirit comes together with the lost sinner to produce a *new person!* This is why Paul is able to speak of the "old man" and the "new man" both present in us (Rom. 6:6; 7:15–20; Eph. 4:22–24; Col. 3:9). The old man is who we are before salvation. The Holy Spirit is God. . . . Some "genetic" component of man's spirit is joined by the "seed" of the Holy Spirit to create a *new man*. This new man is not "part" of God any more than a child is "part" of its parents. But as a father imparts certain genetic traits—a portion of his very *essence* to his child—so God passes certain "genetic" traits, part of His *essence* on to man in regeneration. . . .

For this reason, Scripture declares that those who experience this miracle actually become the *sons of God!* *"But as many as received Him, to them gave He power to become the sons of God, to those who believe in His name"* (John 1:12).[3]

This agrees with Peter's statement that believers are "partakers [*koinōnoi*, "'partners or sharers'"]) of the divine nature" (2 Pet. 1:4). This fact that believers take on God's very nature can help clarify some difficult passages. For example, how are we to understand 1 John 3:9: "Whoever has been born of God does not sin, for His seed remains in him; and he cannot sin because he has been born of God"? Does this verse contradict 1 John 1:8, 10, which say that every person, including Christians, sins? Some Bible translations of 3:9 seek to solve this dilemma by rendering the present tense of the verb for sin as a continual act. "No one who is born of God *practices sin* because His seed abides in him; and he cannot sin because he is born of God" (NASB, italics added). "No one who is born of God will *continue to sin* because God's seed remains in him; he cannot *go on sinning* because he has been born of God" (NIV, italics added). "Those who have been born into God's family do not sin, because God's life is in them. So they can't *keep on sinning*, because they have been born of God" (NLT, italics added).

Actually there are no words in the Greek New Testament to represent phrases such as "practices," "keeps on," or "continues." Those words are based on an understanding of the Greek tense that is now widely in dispute among Greek scholars. I. Howard Marshall says this "involves translators in stressing the present continuous form of the verb in a way which they do not do elsewhere in the New Testament."[4] C. H. Dodd noted that "it is legitimate to doubt whether the reader could be expected to grasp so subtle a doctrine simply upon the basis of a precise distinction of tenses without further guidance."[5] Other translations have not taken this interpretive liberty with the passage. For example, "Whosoever is born of God doth not commit sin; for his seed remaineth in him: and he cannot sin, because he is born of God" (KJV). "Whoever has been born of God does not sin, for His seed remains in him; and he cannot sin, because he has been born of God" (NKJV).

There is no need to add "practices," "keeps on," or "continues on" if one simply recognizes the meaning of "seed" in 1 John 3:9 (Greek, *sperma*) and its relation to *gennaō* ("born"). One of the traits God has passed on to those who are born of Him is that they cannot sin. That is, *no sin ever committed by a regenerate child of God has come from the new person inside who has been born of God. Instead every sin a regenerate person commits comes from his or her old sin nature.* Hodges puts it this way: "God's seed is His nature, given to every believer at salvation (John 1:13; 2 Pet. 1:4). The point here is that the child partakes of the nature of his Parent. . . . This 'new man' (or 'new self'; Eph. 4:24; Col 3:10) is an absolutely new creation. . . . Sin is not, nor ever can be, anything but satanic. It can never spring from what a Christian truly is at the level of his regenerate being."[6]

Understanding this verse in this way fits the context. The theme of 1 John is a believer's fellowship with God and with other believers. A key word in John is "abide" (*menō*).[7] The antithesis to abiding is sinning. The two cannot go together. When a believer sins, he is not abiding in Christ; he is out of fellowship with Him and is obeying Satan, the active agent energizing our old sin nature. That is out of character with who I am in Christ. On the other hand, when a Christian is abiding in Christ, enjoying fellowship with Him, he is living in the energy of the Holy Spirit through his new divine nature, which is born of God and he cannot sin.

The Concept of Life

In regeneration God gives us a new divine nature. But He also imparts life to children. This is *His* life, which is passed on to every believer.

Three Greek words are rendered by the English word "life." The least common (used only ten times) is *bios*, which refers to the things that accompany life, such as the "pride of life" (1 John 2:16), "this world's goods" (literally, "life of this world," 3:17), and the "cares, riches, and pleasures of life" (Luke 8:14). We might think of this as our terrestrial life. More significant is *psychē*, which occurs about one hundred times in the New Testament. Usually translated "soul," it refers to life received at birth. It speaks of one's personal existence as an individual.

The third word is *zōē*, which is the most frequently used of the three. (It is used more than 130 times in the New Testament.) It is often used of "eternal life," and the life implanted by the Holy Spirit in each one who believes in the Son (John 3:13–16). John 10:10–11 presents an interesting contrast between *zōē* and *psychē*: "I am come that they may have life [*zōē*]. . . . I am the good shepherd. The good shepherd gives His life [*psychē*] for the sheep." The Lord Jesus did not give up His *zōē*, for that would be impossible, but He did give His *psychē* in death.

We think of eternal life as endless blocks of time—and it is that. The favorite gospel song, "Amazing Grace," conveys this idea: "When we've been there ten thousand years, bright shining as the sun, we've no less days to sing God's praise than when we'd first begun." Life that extends forever in heaven is what we receive from God as a gift. Think of that magnificent truth! Jesus said, "And I give unto them eternal life, and they shall never perish; neither shall anyone snatch them out of My hand. My Father, who has given them to Me, is greater than all; and no one is able to snatch them out of My Father's hand" (10:28–29). However, the eternal life (*zōē*) the Lord gives is also intensive. Jesus said, "I am come that they may have life . . . more abundantly" (10:10). The believer's eternal life speaks of *quality* of life, as well as *length* of life. Jesus prayed on our behalf: "And this is eternal life, that they may know You the only true God, and Jesus Christ whom You have sent" (17:3). The more we know Christ, the more we love Him. And the more we love Him, the larger becomes our capacity to glorify Him.

The Birth Analogy

Childbirth illustrates several truths about regeneration. First, just as an unborn baby is totally helpless in the birthing process, so no one can contribute to his or her spiritual birth. Those who believe "were born, not of blood, nor of the will of the flesh, nor of the will of man, but of God" (John 1:13). Salvation is "not by works" (Eph. 2:9; Titus 3:5). Just as an infant cannot contribute to his birth, so no human can save himself.

Second, just as an unborn infant is in total physical darkness, so the unregenerate are in spiritual darkness (Eph. 5:8). But in regeneration God delivers us "from the power of darkness" (Col. 1:13), calling us "out of darkness into His marvelous light" (1 Pet. 2:9).

Third, just as a baby is a brand-new, unique creation of God breathing new air, so a new believer is a "new creation" (2 Cor. 5:17). This is not the "old man" or old self worked over. He is a "new man" (Col. 3:10) with "newness of life" (Rom. 6:4).

Fourth, just as a newborn infant is part of a family, so a new believer becomes part of God's family, the church. John expressed the wonder of this privileged place as children of God in 1 John 3:1: "Behold what manner of love the Father has bestowed on us, that we should be called the children of God!" Something of the awe of this truth is captured in The Living Bible paraphrase of this verse: 'See how very much our heavenly Father loves us, for he allows us to be called his children—think of it—and we really *are!*'"

The only way this intimate, family relationship with God can be experienced is through the new birth. You must have a divine implant of new life. The key to receiving that is faith, the subject of the next chapter.

CHAPTER 9
What Is Faith?

W e now come to what is perhaps the simplest—and yet the most difficult to accept— step in salvation, namely, faith. This is expressed by the word "believes" in the familiar verses of John 3:16–17. "For God so loved the world that He gave His only begotten Son, that whoever believes in Him should not perish but have everlasting life. For God did not send His Son into the world to condemn the world, but that the world through Him might be saved."

Charles H. Spurgeon expressed how sinners have difficulty receiving salvation simply by faith in Christ. "Oh, the many times that I have wished the preacher would tell me something to do that I might be saved! Gladly would I have done it, if it had been possible. If he had said, 'Take off your shoes and stockings, and run to John O'Groat's,' I would not even have gone home first, but would have started off that very night, that I might win salvation. How often have I thought that, if he had said, 'Bare your back to the scourge, and take fifty lashes,' I would have said, 'Here I am! Come along with your whip, and beat as hard as you please, so long as I can obtain peace and rest, and get rid of my sin.' Yet that simplest of all matters—believing in Christ crucified, accepting His finished salvation, being nothing, and letting Him be everything, doing nothing but trusting to what He has done—I could not get a hold of it."[1]

Everyone prefers the feeling of being able to do something to be saved. And once the door is open to this kind of thinking, the whole emphasis shifts away from salvation as a gift of God.

That kind of thinking accounts for the fact that none of the major religions of the world, with the singular exception of Christianity, offers salvation as a gift apart from any human effort at all. An example of this difficulty is seen in an encounter between Rambhau, a devoted Hindu, and David Morse, a Christian missionary in India.[2] Morse had befriended Rambhau and had explained that salvation is a gift. Then one day the Hindu told Morse he was going to crawl many miles on his knees to Delhi as a means of earning salvation. But before he planned to leave, he gave the missionary a small, heavy box.

"I have had this box for years," Rambhau said. "I keep only one thing in it. Now I will tell you about it. I once had a son."

"A son?" Morse responded. "Why, Rambhau, you never told me you had a son."

"My son was an excellent pearl diver. One day he found a most beautiful pearl, one of the largest ever found off the coast of India. But he had stayed under the water too long, and he died soon after he recovered the pearl. I have kept the pearl, and now I want to give it to you."

"Rambhau," Morse said, "this is an amazing pearl. Let me buy it. I'll give you ten thousand dollars for it, or if it takes more I will work for it."

"Sahib," said Rambhau, stiffening his whole body, "this pearl is beyond all price. No man in all the world has money enough to pay what this pearl is worth to me. I will not sell it to you. You may only have it as a gift."

"No, Rambhau, I cannot accept that. As much as I want the pearl, I cannot accept it that way. I must pay for it, or work for it." The old pearl diver was stunned. "You don't understand. Don't you see? My only son gave his life to get this pearl, and I wouldn't sell it for any money. Its worth is in the lifeblood of my son. I cannot sell this, but I can give it to you. Just accept it in token of the love I bear you."

The missionary was choked and for a moment could not speak. Then he gripped the hand of the old man. "Rambhau," he said in a low voice, "don't you see? That is just what you have been saying to God."

The diver looked long and searchingly at the missionary and slowly, slowly he began to understand.

"God is offering you heaven as a free gift. It is so great and priceless that no man on earth could buy it. No man on earth could earn it. His life would be millions of years too short. No man is good enough to deserve it. It cost God the lifeblood of His only Son to make the entrance for you into heaven. In a million years, in a hundred pilgrimages, you could not earn that entrance. All you can do is to accept it as a token of God's love for you, a sinner. Rambhau, of course, I will accept the pearl in deep humility, praying God I may be worthy of your love. Rambhau, won't you accept God's great gift of heaven, too, in deep humility, knowing it cost Him the death of His Son to offer it to you?"

"Sahib, I see it now. I have believed in the doctrine of Jesus for two years, but I could not believe that His salvation was free. Now I understand. Some things are too priceless to be bought or earned. Sahib, I will accept His salvation."

What right did Morse have to make such an offer to Rambhau? Is salvation a gift that is ours simply for the taking? Some Christian leaders say salvation requires more than simple faith. "*What must I pay to be a Christian?* . . . I say that the minimum amount a person must believe to be a Christian is *everything*, and that the minimum amount a person must give is *all*. . . . You cannot hold back even a fraction of a percentage of yourself. Every sin must be abandoned. Every false thought must be repudiated. You must be the Lord's entirely."[3] Another equally respected brother said, "Receiving Christ in the biblical sense is *more than* simply 'accepting' Him, or responding positively to Him."[4] He added that there are "five essential elements of genuine conversion, all so inextricably linked that it is impossible to eliminate any one of them from the biblical concept of saving faith."[5]

What Morse offered Rambhau—God's gift of salvation—can be received in a single moment of time. Yet some Bible teachers say that a lifetime of commitment is necessary in order for a person to know if he has eternal life.

WHAT IS THE GOSPEL?

The word "gospel" (*euangelion*) means "good news." It is sometimes used in a nonreligious sense, as in 1 Thessalonians 3:6: "But now that Timothy has come to us from you, and brought us good news [*euangelion*] of your faith and love, and that you always have good remembrance of us, greatly desiring to see us, as we also to see you." But the major use of *euangelion* is with a religious connotation. But when used in this way, what was the good news about?

The New Testament uses the word in two ways: "of the good tidings of the kingdom of God and of salvation through Christ."[6] In the Gospels *euangelion* is used by only Matthew and Mark and, in all but one instance, Matthew wrote of *euangelion* as "the gospel of the kingdom," which the prophets foretold and Jesus preached (Matt. 4:23; 9:35). This was also the message of John the Baptist (3:1) and of the twelve apostles when they were first sent out by our Lord (10:5–7). His covenant people, Israel, refused to repent and meet the spiritual conditions of the kingdom, and they rejected Christ as King at His first coming (Matt. 11–12; John 1:11). But at the end of the yet-future seven-year Tribulation (Dan. 12:1), Christ will again return to earth and present Himself to Israel as both Messiah and King. Even at the end of His ministry, therefore, when Jesus warned of the coming terrible destruction in the "great tribulation," He announced that "this gospel of the kingdom will be preached in all the world" (Matt. 24:14). What Christ instructed His disciples to pray for will come to pass: "Your kingdom come, Your will be done on earth as it is in heaven" (6:10). The only exception to this "gospel of the kingdom" in Matthew is "this gospel," in 26:13, which refers to Mary's anointing of Christ for His forthcoming death. This last usage introduces the theme that is predominant in the Epistles, and especially the Pauline writings.[7]

What was the *content* of the good news that especially Paul was commissioned to present? He stated this clearly in 1 Corinthians 15:1, 3–5: "Moreover, brethren, I declare to you the gospel [*euangelion*] . . . that Christ died for our sins according to the Scriptures, and that He was buried, and that He rose again the third day according to the Scriptures, and that He was seen by Cephas, then by the twelve." Paul wrote that when

God appointed him as an apostle, he was "separated to the gospel [*euangelion*] of God,...concerning His Son Jesus Christ our Lord" (Rom. 1:1, 3). At the end of his third missionary journey Paul told the elders of the church at Ephesus that his ministry was "to testify to the gospel [*euangelion*] of the grace of God" (Acts 20:24).

Some churches offer what they call the "full gospel," which supposedly includes tongues-speaking. Others plead for a "whole gospel," which envisions not just the redemption of individuals but the redemption of society. Others claim that a gospel that does not include discipleship is not good news. Surely, the church must take more seriously the need to disciple its members, but discipleship differs from the gospel that saves from eternal damnation. In the first century some Jewish believers taught that circumcision was necessary for Gentiles to receive salvation (Acts 15:1). But Peter, who had wrestled with this issue, presented the challenge: "Now therefore, why do you test God by putting a yoke on the neck of the disciples which neither our fathers nor we were able to bear? But we believe that through the grace of the Lord Jesus Christ we shall be saved in the same manner as they" (15:10–11).

Adding to the simple gospel of grace is not new. Human works or achievements are central to all non-Christian religions. And yet even some Christian leaders want to add requirements to the gospel, perhaps because they are disturbed by people who say they are believers but are not mature in Christ. Works have an allurement, but in the end they are disastrous to the gospel of grace.

How readily some fall into the trap of adding requirements to the gospel beyond simply believing that Christ died for our sins and rose from the dead. Even Peter, who had made such a clear statement to the Jerusalem Council, got trapped so that Paul "withstood him to his face, because he was to be blamed" (Gal. 2:11). In writing to the Galatians Paul spoke strongly against those who pervert the gospel: "I marvel that you are turning away so soon from Him who called you in the grace of Christ, to a different gospel, which is not another; but there are some who trouble you and want to pervert the gospel of Christ. But even if we, or an angel from heaven, preach any other gospel to you than what we have preached to you, let him be accursed [Greek, *anathema*; literally, 'under God's judgment']" (1:6–8).

SALVATION AS A GIFT

In Ephesians 2:8–9 Paul wrote of the precious truth of salvation: "For by grace you have been saved through faith, and that not of yourselves; it is the gift of God, not of works, lest anyone should boast." This word "gift" (*dōron*) is used nineteen times in the New Testament, but this is the only time God is referred to as the Giver. Salvation is a grace gift and it is received only by faith. Some say the gift is faith. However, the word "that," which "gift" refers back to, is a neuter pronoun in Greek, whereas the Greek word for "faith" is a feminine noun. The word "that" therefore more likely refers to the whole preceding clause, meaning that salvation is the gift of God.

A gift is "something that is bestowed voluntarily and without compensation."[9] Some people teach that the gift of salvation is a "costly gift" for the recipient, even going so far as to list what a person must pay in order to become a Christian. Of course, salvation was costly for the Giver. It cost our heavenly Father the sacrifice of His Son, and it cost the Son of God an ignominious death to pay the price for our sins. But Jesus paid it all—and so there is nothing left to pay. Obviously salvation is not cheap, but it *is* free! It is an insult to God to even think that we can add anything to God's marvelous plan of salvation.

Sometimes people give gifts as favors or bribes, with the anticipation of getting something in return. But such presents are not true gifts. A gift, by definition, is free, with no cost whatsoever. In salvation we are "justified freely [*dōrean*, 'as a gift'] by His grace" (Rom. 3:24)—without cost to the recipient. From His exalted throne, Christ, the Alpha and the Omega, said, "I will give of the fountain of the water of life freely [*dōrean*] to him who thirsts" (Rev. 21:6). In the last invitation in the Bible the Spirit of God said, "And let him who thirsts come. Whoever desires, let him take the water of life freely [*dōrean*]" (22:17).

THE MEANING OF FAITH

Many people are confused by the words *faith* and *believe*. Some suggest they mean two different things. Arthur Farstad pointed out that the words actually translate the same concept: "Oddly enough, the most important Gospel word-family in the Greek NT is obscured in English. This is because we translate the Greek verb *pisteuō* by the Anglo-Saxon word *believe*, and the related noun *pistis* by the totally unrelated word *faith* (from the Latin *fides*, by way of French). . . . Actually, *believe* and *faith*, as the Greek shows, are just the verb and the noun for a concept that is really no different in English than in Greek. That concept is *taking people at their word, trusting that what they say is true*."[10] *The American Heritage Dictionary* defines *faith* as "a confident belief in the truth, value, or trustworthiness of a person, idea, or thing." When the verb *believe* has an object (as a transitive verb) it means "to accept as true or real" or "to credit with veracity." When it does not have an object (as an intransitive verb), *believe* means "to have faith, esp. religious faith," "to have faith or confidence; trust," or "to have confidence in the truth, value, or existence of something."[11]

When these meanings are applied to some well-known verses, the point becomes clear that *to believe* and *to have faith* mean the same thing. "For God so loved the world that He gave His only begotten Son that whoever believes [or, has faith] in Him should not perish but have everlasting life" (John 3:16). "Believe [or, have faith in] on the Lord Jesus Christ, and you will be saved" (Acts 16:31). "For by grace you have been saved through faith [or, belief], and that not of yourselves; it is the gift of God" (Eph. 2:8). "But to him who does not work but believes [*pisteuō*] on Him who justifies the ungodly, his faith [or, belief] is accounted for righteousness" (Rom. 4:5).

We need to beware of the tendency to add meanings to these words that they were never intended to carry. For example, the Epistle of James uses *faith* sixteen times without ever needing a modifier, but one person writing on James added numerous adjectives before the word *faith*: "dead," "false," "shallow," "superficial," "nonsaving," "professed," "worthless," "unproductive," "deceptive," "true," "living," "saving," "genuine," "transforming," "complete," and "productive"[12]—an astonishing array of adjectives not even found in James. However, as I wrote elsewhere, *"It is not our job to encourage people to have faith in their faith but to enlarge the object of their faith.* The model of Christ in the upper room is most instructive. Knowing the lack of faith that Peter would exhibit on the night of his denial,

Christ does not question his faith. Rather, He proceeds to fill the object of his faith with revelation about God. He expands Peter's understanding of the resources he has in God the Father, God the Son, and God the Holy Spirit."[13] As Joseph Dillow rightly observes, "Faith is located in the mind and is persuasion or belief. It is something which 'happens' to us *as a result of reflection upon sufficient evidence*. . . . Saving faith is a reliance upon God for salvation. It does not include within its compass the determination of the will to obey, nor does it include a commitment to a life of works. To believe is to be persuaded and to be reliant and includes nothing else."[14]

Faith itself does not save. That is, we are saved only when we place our faith in the right object, namely, Jesus Christ.

Some people question the validity of faith *alone*. They believe that works are necessary along with faith. For support they refer to James 2:19, which says the demons believe and tremble. So, they argue, believing is not sufficient. But the question is, "What do the demons believe?" They believe that God is one (James 2:19), that is, they are monotheists. So are millions of others, and that is not sufficient to save. Demons do not believe that Jesus died for their sins and that they can be saved through placing their faith in Him. In other words, believing that God exists does not save. But believing that Jesus died for your sins and was raised again for your justification does save (Rom. 4:24–25).

WHAT MUST A SINNER DO TO BE SAVED?

We hear of many things that people do to seek to be saved, such as pray, confess, repent, and follow Christ, all of which are biblical, spiritual exercises. But we need to know from Scripture what a sinner *must* do to be saved.

The Gospel of John was written specifically to answer the question of what a sinner must do to be saved: "And truly Jesus did many other signs in the presence of His disciples, which are not written in this book; but these are written that you may believe that Jesus is the Christ, the Son of God, and that believing you may have life in His name" (John 20:30–31). When comparing John's Gospel with the Synoptic Gospels, we find that

92 percent of his material is unique, and he presents a more doctrinal reflection in contrast to the more historical approaches of the Synoptic Gospels.[15] Again, whereas John emphasized receiving the gift of eternal life by believing (John used *pisteuō* almost one hundred times), the Synoptic writers emphasized discipleship training for the kingdom (*pisteuō* occurs only thirty-four times in all three Synoptic Gospels together). Jesus' encounters with several individuals, as recorded in the Gospel of John, show what a sinner must do to be saved.

Nicodemus

Nicodemus was a "ruler of the Jews" (John 3:1), which meant he was a member of the Sanhedrin, the Jewish council of supreme authority in Jerusalem. As a Pharisee, he held Scripture in high regard. Most people thought the Pharisees were the ones who could identify the long-awaited Messiah when He came. Jesus referred to Nicodemus as "the" teacher of Israel, which may mean he was responsible for religious instruction in Israel. He may have come to faith in Christ the night he visited Jesus, or he may have done so later. Whenever it happened, he remained a secret believer like some others (12:42) until he and Joseph of Arimathea helped prepare Jesus' body for burial (19:39).

Jesus told Nicodemus, who should have known the Scriptures, that he needed spiritual birth (3:3, 5). This stood in glaring contrast to the teaching of the Pharisees, who emphasized their natural birth into the family of Abraham.

Jesus explained the need for spiritual rebirth by comparing Moses' lifting up the serpent in the wilderness to His own need to be lifted up, that is, on the cross (3:14; see Num. 21:4–9). The only thing the Israelites needed to do to be healed was to look at the brass serpent. To some people, however, simply looking on the serpent seems too simple. They call it "easy believism" or "cheap grace." Thus one writer of that persuasion states, "In order to look at the bronze snake on the pole, they had to drag themselves to where they could see it. They were in no position to glance flippantly at the pole and then proceed with their lives of rebellion."[16] However, this adds, unfortunately, to the simplicity of salvation. Dillow correctly observes, "Dragging themselves to see the serpent is, of course, not simply 'looking.' Neither is it found in the Old Testament text. Nowhere does [Numbers 21] say they had to drag themselves to where they could see the serpent. The serpent was lifted up so that they could see it!"[17] Look and live! That was what God required. It was not a matter of commitment or even being willing to commit.

Jesus followed up this simple illustration of a miraculous "look and live" with the words, "even so must the Son of Man be lifted up, that whoever believes in Him should not perish but have eternal life" (John 3:14–15). Jesus identified the "look" of faith with "believes." Strikingly in four verses Jesus repeated the words "believes in Him" (3:15–16, 18, 36) as the *only* condition for receiving "eternal life." These results are not conditioned on *how* one believes, but on *whom* one believes. In other words, salvation is not based on the *kind* of faith but the *object* of faith. Furthermore, on the negative side, Jesus holds people responsible for not believing: "He who believes in Him [the Son] is not condemned; but he who does not believe is condemned already, because he has not believed in the name of the only begotten Son of God" (3:18). The obvious implication is that sinners have the capacity to exercise faith (to believe) because God would not condemn sinners for not believing if, indeed, they have no capacity to believe. The issue, then, is simply to believe in Jesus Christ or not believe in Him.

Since Jesus made it so simple, why do so many people make it so difficult? Because in this decision sinners face the greatest battle of their lives with Satan, the enemy of their souls. Jesus spoke of this in His parable of the soils. "The seed is the word of God. Those by the wayside are the ones who hear; then the devil comes and takes away the word out of their hearts, lest they should believe and be saved" (Luke 8:11–12). The devil knows that sinners have the potential to believe and be released from his tyranny, so he and all the forces of hell fight furiously to keep sinners from believing. Paul explained this fact this way: "But even if our gospel is veiled, it is veiled to those who are perishing, whose minds the god of this age has blinded, who do not believe, lest the light of the gospel of the glory of Christ, who is the image of God, should shine on them" (2 Cor. 4:3–4).

The Woman at the Well

Jesus' encounter with the Samaritan woman (John 4) contrasts in several ways with His encounter with Nicodemus (John 3). John MacArthur portrays these contrasts well: "Nicodemus was a Jew; she was a Samaritan. He was a man; she was a woman. He was a religious leader; she was an adulteress. He was learned; she was ignorant [though she knew that 'Messiah is coming']. He was a member of the highest class; she of the lowest—lower even than an outcast of Israel, for she was a Samaritan outcast. He was wealthy; she was poor. He recognized Jesus as a teacher from God; she didn't have a clue who He was. The two of them could hardly have been more dissimilar."[18]

But the solution to their problems was the same, namely, God's gift of eternal life (3:16; 4:10). In order for them to "look" or "ask" (4:10), they needed to have a compelling object for their faith, that is, they needed to be persuaded that this One is who He claimed to be. Nicodemus was convinced that Jesus was "a teacher come from God" because of the miracles He performed (3:2). The woman at the well was persuaded by the fact that "He told me all things that I ever did" (4:29; see 4:19, 39).

The woman at the well wasn't concerned about her position in society because it wasn't that great anyway. But she was so excited about Jesus Christ that she left her waterpot, hurried back to Sychar, and said to her neighbors, "Come, see a Man who told me all things that I ever did. Could this be the Christ?" (4:28–29). Because of her testimony many believed. And when they heard Jesus for two days, many more believed because of His own words and said to the woman, "Now we believe, not because of what you said, for we ourselves have heard Him and we know that this is indeed the Christ, the Savior of the world" (4:42). They realized that He was not only a great prophet, like Moses, but He was indeed the Savior. In referring to their response, John used *pisteuō*, the verb "to believe" (4:39, 41–42), and in each case the persuasion that generated the believing was the word of the woman or of Christ Himself. Like Nicodemus they needed only to believe; salvation was by faith in Christ alone, plus nothing else.

The Nobleman and His Family

The account of a nobleman and his family in John 4:46–54 merits com-ment. Jesus had returned to Cana of Galilee where He had performed the sign-miracle of turning water to wine (4:46; see 2:1–12). Many had believed on Him then and the word had spread. When He appeared in town again, a nobleman, who had a son at the point of death, implored Jesus to come and heal him. A fact to note here is that twice the nobleman is said to have "believed" (4:50, 53). He first believed Jesus' promise that his son would not die. Is that a sufficient object for faith to receive eternal life? No! Believing that Jesus can and will heal is not enough to save and give eternal life. But it was a good thing to do, and undoubtedly it was part of God's common grace in preparing him for saving faith.

On the way to his home, the nobleman's servants met him and said, "Your son lives." When he asked them when the fever left him, he realized it was the precise time when Jesus had said, "Your son lives." Realizing that his son had been healed, the nobleman now knew that Jesus was more than a mere man. He placed his faith in Christ, not in the healing, and was born from above. And his whole household did the same. As F. F. Bruce noted, "On the previous day the nobleman had believed Jesus' reassurance; now, together with his household (wife, children, slaves, and other dependents), he believed in Jesus personally, acknowledging Him as the sent one of God."[19] A person may do many good and proper things, but saving faith must have as its object the understanding that Jesus is the Christ, the Son of God.

The Pharisees Who Sought to Kill Jesus

It may seem strange to include this account in discussing the point that faith in Jesus as the Christ, the Son of God, is the only condition for receiving eternal life. But let's look at the account. Jesus had healed a man on the Sabbath and so the Jews sought to kill Jesus (John 5:9, 16). Then in speaking to His enemies, He used the words "believe" and "receive" nine times (5:38–47). Jesus could have laid at their doorstep many other things that needed change, but there was one thing that kept them from eternal life and that was their failure to believe in Him. Jesus always stayed on the issue.

Many Disciples Who Did Not Believe

Jesus' feeding of the five thousand and His walking on the water were two other miracles He performed to encourage people to believe. However, many would-be disciples stumbled over the simplicity of faith in Him. Like many people today, His hearers asked, "What shall we do, that we may work the works of God?" (John 6:28). People have a difficult time recognizing that they can contribute *nothing* to their salvation. But Jesus kept to the issue by answering, "This is the work of God, that you believe in Him whom He sent" (6:29).

The Jews puzzled over His claim to be "the bread . . . from heaven" (6:41), but in His response He again affirmed, "He who believes in Me has everlasting life" (6:47). Yet many of His listeners did not believe and no longer followed Him (6:66). Listening to and learning about Jesus is not sufficient to gain eternal life. It is no substitute for belief in Him. Again, Christ focused on the issue. "But there are some of you who do not believe" (6:64). And John explained, "For Jesus knew from the beginning who they were who did not believe, and who would betray Him" (6:64). When Jesus asked the Twelve if they wanted to leave, Peter gave the gold-star answer: "Lord, to whom shall we go? You have the words of eternal life. Also we have come to believe and know that You are the Christ, the Son of the living God" (6:68–69).

The Man Born Blind

The Jews tried to kill Jesus (John 7:1), but "no one laid a hand on Him, because His hour had not yet come" (7:30). On the other hand, "Many of the people believed in Him, and said, 'When the Christ comes, will He do more signs than these which this Man has done?'" (7:31). As the momentum increased, Jesus continued to give knowledge of who He was, culminating in His claim to be God Himself: "Most assuredly, I say to you, before Abraham was, I AM" (8:58; see also Exod. 3:14).

Then Jesus performed another miracle: giving sight to a blind man. This sign-miracle highlights the contrasting responses of belief and unbelief. The man whose sight Jesus restored concluded that Jesus was a prophet (John 9:17), though he did not yet confess Him as Messiah. On the other hand, the spiritually blinded Pharisees refused to believe in Jesus, again because He healed on the Sabbath (9:14, 16). They attributed the man's congenital blindness to sin and threw him out. But Jesus asked him, "Do you believe in the Son of God?" Through what the man had seen and heard, he was ready to believe. But wanting to know more in order to inform his belief, he asked, "Who is He, Lord, that I may believe in Him?" Jesus graciously filled that need by responding, "You have both seen Him and it is He who is talking with you." The man's response was immediate: "Lord, I believe!" (9:35–38). And he worshiped Him. How beautiful and simple was the man's faith in Christ!

The Raising of Lazarus

Jesus' restoring Lazarus to life was the seventh great sign-miracle John singled out so "that you may believe that Jesus is the Christ, the Son of God, and that believing you may have life in His name" (John 20:31). Some who were mourning for Lazarus, remembering the previous miracle, asked, "Could not this Man, who opened the eyes of the blind, also have kept this man from dying?" (11:37). Jesus told them to roll back the stone from the entrance to the cave where Lazarus had lain dead for four days. Then he shouted, "Lazarus, come forth!" And Lazarus came out. Augustine said that if Jesus had not designated Lazarus by name, all the graves would have been emptied at His command (5:28)! Once again the response was twofold: "Then many of the Jews went away and believed in Jesus" (12:11).

What we must not miss in this encounter, however, is the discussion between Jesus and Martha before Lazarus was raised. Jesus' words to her show that saving faith in Christ involves believing certain facts about Him. "'I am the resurrection and the life. He who believes in Me, though he may die, he shall live. And whoever lives and believes in Me shall never die. Do you believe *this*?' She said to Him, 'Yes, Lord, I believe *that* You are the Christ, the Son of God, who is to come into the world'" (11:25–27, italics added). Zane Hodges has carefully explained this interchange.

Notice how Jesus here does more than simply identify Himself. Yes, He *is* the Resurrection and the Life. But He is more than that. He is the One who

126

guarantees that even if the believer dies, he will live again—that is, he will be resurrected. As the Life, He guarantees the believer will never die—that is, he or she will always have eternal life. Jesus' statement to Martha, therefore, is an identification of Himself in reference to everyone who believes in Him. Then comes the crucial question. Jesus asks Martha: "Do you believe this?" (John 11:26b). Notice the simplicity that is involved here. Jesus says: "I have just stated certain facts about Myself and the one who believes in Me. Do you hold these facts to be true? Is this what you believe about me?" And what is Martha's reply? Well, not surprisingly, it is a full-fledged articulation of the theme verse of 20:31. Martha replies: "*Yes, Lord, I believe that You are the Christ, the Son of God, who is to come into the world.*" Notice closely. Jesus says: "Do you believe *this?*" and Martha says: "I believe that You are the Christ." To believe what Jesus just stated about Himself is to believe that He is the Christ. Thus to believe that Jesus is the Christ is to believe He guarantees resurrection and eternal life to everyone who believes Him to be the Christ. . . . To deny or doubt this, is not to believe what John wants his readership to believe. If I believe it, I *know* that I have eternal life. There is no way I can believe what Jesus tells Martha, and yet not know whether I have eternal life or will be resurrected by Jesus.[20]

John has given us a definitive statement from the teachings of Jesus Himself as to what a person must do to be saved. Every occurrence of salvation recorded in John is in keeping with the purpose statement of his Gospel in 20:30–31. Certainly John's Gospel is a valid benchmark for testing every presentation and protecting us from "a different gospel, which is not another" (Gal. 1:6–7). When Peter preached on the death and resurrection of Jesus to Cornelius's household, the apostle concluded, "To Him all the prophets witness that, through His name, whoever believes in Him will receive remission of sins" (Acts 10:43). Peter said his message included "words by which you and all your household will be saved" (11:14). And at the Jerusalem Council he stated clearly that salvation is by faith alone in Christ. "But we believe that through the grace of the Lord Jesus Christ we shall be saved in the same manner as they" (15:11).

To the Jews in Antioch of Pisidia, Paul said, "To you the word of this salvation has been sent" (13:26). He then gave a clear statement about the death and resurrection of Christ (13:27–31). The Philippian jailer, fearing for his life because of the escape of his prisoners, drew his sword to kill himself. But out of the darkness came Paul's shout, "Do yourself no harm, for we are all here." The jailer called for a lamp, ran to them, and asked, "Sirs, what must I do to be saved?" Paul and Silas responded, "Believe on the Lord Jesus Christ, and you will be saved, you and your household" (16:27–31). With regard to saving faith, Jesus, John, Peter, Paul, and Silas were of one accord—salvation is by faith alone in Christ alone!

WILL INFANTS WHO DIE BE SAVED?

Since we do not know whether or how infants can exercise faith in Christ, this raises the question, will they go to heaven if they die? And what does this imply for the fact that salvation is obtainable only by faith in Jesus Christ? Roy B. Zuck has discussed this thoroughly in his book *Precious In His Sight: Childhood and Children in the Bible.* So rather than discuss it here, I am including his material on the subject as Appendix A.

CHAPTER 10

What Are Repentance and Justification?

W e turn now from what a sinner *must* do to be saved to what a sinner *may* do to be saved. In other words, a sinner *must* place his or her faith in Christ in order to be saved, but some sinners may also repent (and others may not) at the moment of regeneration. For centuries believers have differed on the meaning of the word *repentance*. Does it mean to "change one's mind," to "turn from sin," to "do penance," or is it simply a synonym for faith? And there is disagreement as to its object. Are we to repent of sin, idolatry, or dead works? Also Bible students disagree on who should repent. Is repentance for unbelievers, believers, or both?

A BRIEF HISTORICAL SURVEY

In the second century the church martyr, Justin, exhorted sinners to pray, fast, repent of past sins, and be baptized in order to be saved.[1] Repentance was one of the conditions for salvation. Later some church leaders equated repentance with penitence. They said weeping and wailing were necessary to win God's forgiveness. By the time of Augustine, many believed God's grace brought about regeneration, faith, and repentance in the sinner. However, at baptism only the prebaptismal sins were forgiven; therefore many early Christians waited until their deathbeds to be baptized. But what about the sins of people who had been baptized as infants? The answer was that they needed to practice penance. The church fathers were divided over how many times a person could repent after baptism; by the time of Augustine the number was unlimited. Penance for postbaptismal sins was the means by which a person could be reinstated in the church. Penance eventually came to include fasting, prayers, weeping, begging, abstinence for those married, shaving one's head, and similar acts. Penance could last a few days or many years. This view of repentance held sway right through the Dark Ages and the Renaissance until the Reformation.

The Reformers Martin Luther, John Calvin, and Ulrich Zwingli rejected the notion that postbaptismal sins could be atoned for by contrition, confession, and acts of penance. It was their belief that all sins (past, present, and future) are covered by the blood of Christ when a sinner repents and is baptized. Hence, acts of penance were unnecessary. For both Calvin and Luther, repentance was connected with faith and was a lifelong process in Christians. Calvin wrote, "Now it ought to be a fact beyond controversy that repentance not only constantly follows faith but is born of faith."[2] Reformed theologians, following Augustine and Calvin, held that regeneration precedes both faith and repentance, which are understood to be "conversion." In their view an unregenerate person cannot believe, and repentance is the fruit of faith. Charles H. Spurgeon and A. H. Strong[3] also saw the same order of events: regeneration, faith, and repentance.[4] Present-day theologians Millard Erickson and Bruce Demarest[5] reverse the order, pointing out that regeneration follows repentance and faith.

So some say repentance must precede regeneration, while others say repentance follows regeneration. And some say repentance is for the unregenerate and others say it is for the regenerate. What do the Scriptures say about this matter?

THE MEANING OF REPENTANCE

The verb "repent" (*metanoeō*) and the noun "repentance" (*metanoia*) are used several dozen times in the New Testament. Twenty-five occurrences are in the Gospel of Luke and the Book of Acts, and twelve are in the Book of Revelation. Significantly John never used these words in his Gospel, which has as its purpose bringing sinners to eternal life through belief in Christ. In Revelation, on the other hand, eight of the twelve uses of the verb are admonitions to churches. The word *metanoeō* is composed of *meta* ("after") and *noeō* ("to think or perceive"); thus its basic meaning is "to perceive afterward." This contrasts with *pronoeō* ("to perceive before-hand"). The common meaning of the noun *metanoia*, then, is a "change of mind."

THE OBJECTS OF REPENTANCE

In most instances in the New Testament the object of one's change of mind in repentance is not identified (God "commands all men every-where to repent," Acts 17:30; and "they should repent," 26:20). Other times repentance is be "toward God" (20:21). In other passages repentance is said to be in reference to sin (8:22; 2 Cor. 12:21; Rev. 9:20–21). Therefore Cook suggests that "repentance is that conscious change of attitude (mind), both spiritual and moral, regarding God, on the one hand, and sin, on the other."[6] Larry Moyer makes the following helpful observations about repentance.

> (1) Repentance clearly means to change the mind. (2) The object of repentance is not the same in every context, but is nonetheless in one way or another "Godward." (3) In salvation contexts, repentance either implies faith or is associated with faith. Therefore, when used in a soteriological context, repentance means to change one's mind about whatever is keeping one from trusting Christ and trust Him as the only means of salvation. Some may have to change their minds about their very concept of God. That is, they have to realize that He is indeed God and Christ is indeed His Son. Others may have to realize that their works cannot save them. Still others may have to change their minds about the seriousness of particular sins, admitting to God that they are indeed sins. But once an individual has changed his or her mind about whatever is keeping them from trusting Christ and trusts Him for salvation, both faith and repentance have taken place.[7]

WHAT IS REPENTANCE?

In the attempt to defend *sola fide* ("faith alone"), some Christians weaken the concept of repentance. For example, some have said that repentance is only a change of mind and not a change of one's life. However, if changing one's mind doesn't change one's life, what does it do? What did Solomon mean when he said, "For as he thinks in his heart, so is he" (Prov. 23:7)? Surely there is an inviolable principle that our actions are nothing more than the blossom of our deepest thoughts.[8] Jesus told Peter about the role of our thought processes: "Those things which proceed out of the mouth come from the heart, and they defile a man. For out of the heart proceed evil thoughts, murders, adulteries, fornications, thefts, false witness, blasphemies. These are the things which defile a man, but to eat with unwashed hands does not defile a man" (Matt. 15:18–20).

Peter got the point. He may have seemed dense at times and he may have stuck his foot in his mouth at other times, but when he got hold of a point, he used it deftly, as in his powerful message on the Day of Pentecost. In that sermon he spoke of the Jews' sin in crucifying Jesus (Acts 2:23), but he did not dwell on that. Instead his message was geared to changing their minds about who Jesus Christ really is (2:31–35). Then, after he had carefully stated his case, he hit them with the punch line that went straight to their hearts: "Therefore let all the house of Israel know assuredly that God has made this Jesus, whom you crucified, both Lord and Christ" (2:36).

"When they heard this, they were cut to the heart" (2:37). What is the heart? It is the seat of our deepest reflections and thus the source of all of our actions. So the Jews asked, "Men and brethren, what shall we do?" They had changed their minds about Jesus Christ. How do we know that? Because they urgently wanted to do something to rectify their previous actions. They now knew they had been wrong, but they did not know how to undo it. Their change of mind (or perspective) about Christ and their sins demanded a change of action.

How did Peter help them solve their pressing need to *do* something? He told them, "Repent, and let every one of you be baptized in the name of Jesus Christ for the remission of sins" (2:38). The Greek word rendered "for" is *eis*, which here may mean "on account of or because," not "in order to."[9] When were their sins remitted? Immediately when, having been convicted by the Holy Spirit, they were persuaded in their hearts of the truth of what Peter said about who Jesus really is. Baptism followed as an appropriate demonstration of repentance.

Perhaps some of what is called "easy believism" today is really not belief at all, because *belief is persuasion as a result of reflection on sufficient evidence* and, where that persuasion exists, *it will be reflected in one's perspective and lifestyle.* When Paul wrote, "Let this mind [from *phroneō*, 'to think'] be in you which was also in Christ Jesus" (Phil. 2:5), was he anticipating a change of mind *without* a change of action? Surely in using *phroneō* ten times in Philippians Paul anticipated more than simply a shifting of thoughts without a change in behavior. One writer expressed this principle this way: "Paul is suggesting that what we are in our thinking is what we are in reality. We are not necessarily what we think we are; rather, what we think, we are! Our words, our actions, and our attitudes are all expressions of our thoughts, our true selves."[10]

WHO NEEDS TO REPENT?

Can it be demonstrated that repentance is for unbelievers? Certainly Jesus said, "Thus it is written, and thus it was necessary for the Christ to suffer and to rise from the dead the third day, and that repentance and remission of sins should be preached in His name to all nations, beginning at Jerusalem" (Luke 24:46–47). The "all nations" here is literally "all the nations" (Greek, *panta ta ethnē*), the same as in Matthew 28:19. Anderson declared, "Surely these nations were not in covenant relationship with Yahweh. Of course, the individuals in these nations needed to *believe* in order to be saved (Mark 16:16), but it is very likely that the call to repentance preceded the invitation to believe."[11]

We see the universal command to repent in Paul's sermon on Mars Hill. As he looked around and saw rampant idolatry in Athens, he was roused to anger (Acts 17:16) when he thought of how the devil was deceiving the people in this demon worship (1 Cor. 10:20). Because the Athenians had little knowledge of the Hebrew Scriptures, Paul began with general revelation visible in creation itself (Acts 17:24–28), and he ended with a warning that a day of judgment is coming when the Man whom the true God has appointed and has raised from the dead will be the Judge. To these people, Paul said, "Truly, these times of ignorance God overlooked, but now commands all men everywhere to repent" (17:30). The words "all men everywhere" leave no doubt that the universal command to repent includes unbelievers. This parallels what we have seen previously about the common grace of God in revealing Himself in nature, which is not sufficient to save but can lead people, as in the case of Cornelius, to see the emptiness of paganism and to search for the true God. God responds to those who respond to the light they have. As Peter said, when reporting on his experience with Cornelius, "God has also granted to the Gentiles repentance to life" (11:18).

Repentance and faith are two separate things, though they may occur together, as seen in Acts 20:21, which refers to Paul's "testifying to Jews and to Greeks repentance toward God and faith toward our Lord Jesus Christ." As Calvin wrote, "For to include faith in repentance, is repugnant to what Paul says in Acts [20:21]—that he testified 'both to the Jews, and also to the Greeks, repentance toward God, and faith toward our Lord Jesus Christ'; where he mentions faith and repentance, as two things totally distinct."[12] Lewis Sperry Chafer wrote that "repentance toward God could not itself constitute, in this case, the equivalent of 'faith toward our Lord Jesus Christ,' though it may prepare for that faith."[13] In other words, genuine repentance *may* precede salvation by way of preparation, as in the case of Cornelius, but it is *not necessary* if the individual is ready for faith, as in the case of the Philippian jailer.

A final observation on repentance needs to be made with respect to its role with believers. Although John never used the word *repent* in his Gospel, he did use it in the Book of Revelation. Of the twelve times he used it there, eight of the occurrences are in relation to five of the seven churches of Revelation (2:5 [twice], 16, 21 [twice], 22; 3:3, 19). Surely the majority of people in those churches would have been believers. Although John did not use the word *repent* in his Epistles, it is certainly pictured in the confession and forgiveness/cleansing process stated in 1 John 1:9, which ought to be characteristic of believers throughout their lives. In confessing sin believers are changing their minds about sin (the Greek word for confess means "to think the same," that is, to hate sin, as God does).

In summary, repentance and faith are two distinct terms that should not be identified with each other. Repentance is for all people, unbelievers as well as believers. Repentance is not necessary (though it may often occur) for entering into an eternal saving relationship with Jesus Christ. But repentance on the part of believers is necessary for maintaining fellowship with the Savior. For unbelievers, repentance from sin and toward God (that is, changing one's mind or perspective about sin and God) prepares the individual for saving faith. (For more on repentance see Appendix B.)

GOD'S ACT OF JUSTIFICATION

Justification is a declaration by God, who is righteous, concerning a person who turns to Christ in faith. When I was a boy, I heard that "justified" means "just as if I'd never sinned." Well, that's a start, but it is much more.

The English words "justify" and "justification" are used differently today from their original meaning. Lorman Petersen illustrates this difference: "In present-day usage the justified man is an innocent man. Modern man uses the term to excuse his actions or to prove he was right in acting as he did, to vindicate himself either in principle or before the law. 'I was justified in disciplining my son because he lied to me'; 'The man was justified in killing the man because it was self-defense'; 'Further investigation will justify your action,' are typical statements."[14] When "justified" and "justify" are used this way, however, they have little in common with their usage in Scripture.

In the New Testament "propitiation" is mentioned four times in connection with the Atonement, "reconciliation" five times, but the "justification" word group occurs more than two hundred times.[15]

In the Old Testament the ideas of right, righteousness, justification, and similar concepts are associated with God's standards and His Law. Abraham pleaded for the righteous in Sodom: "Far be it from You to do such a thing as this, to slay the righteous with the wicked, so that the righteous should be as the wicked; far be it from You! Shall not the Judge of all the earth do right?" (Gen. 18:25). Here God is designated by the legal term "Judge" and Abraham's question expressed the certainty that God would act in accord with His moral law. Heathen gods, however, could not be depended on in this way; they reacted in capricious ways. Leon Morris addressed this contrast:

> Among the heathen the deity was thought of as above all law, with nothing but the dictates of his own desires to limit him. Accordingly his behavior was completely unpredictable, and while he had demands on his worshippers for obedience and service, there were few if any ethical implications of this service and none of a logically necessary kind. Far otherwise was it with the God of the Hebrews. The Old Testament does not conceive of anything outside Him which could direct His actions, and we must be on our guard against the thought of a law which was over Him. But Yahweh was thought of as essentially righteous in nature, as incorporating the law of righteousness within His essential Being. Accordingly He works by a method which may be called law—He inevitably punishes evil-doing and rewards righteousness. He himself acts righteously, and He demands that His people do the same.[16]

The Hebrew word *ṣedeq* refers to the standard God maintains in the world, the norm by which everyone must be judged. "Righteousness," then, is conformity to God's standard, and "justification" is God's declaring that a person is in right standing with God. The "righteous" person is the one who is accepted before God.

This action by God in declaring a person righteous is a legal pronouncement; "to justify" (*dikaioō*) means "to declare righteous" and not "to make righteous." This is not a process, as Roman Catholics teach. In their view justification is a lifelong process of cooperation between God and man.[17] Unfortunately some evangelicals and most liberal theologians view justification as inner moral change, rather than a declarative act by God. Morris makes the following helpful observations.

> When we turn to those passages where the verb "to justify" occurs, there can be no doubt that the meaning is to declare rather than to make righteous.

Thus we find . . . that judges "shall justify the righteous, and condemn the wicked" (Deut. 25:1). The forensic background is unmistakable and the verb can mean only "to declare righteous" or "to acquit." The same usage is seen in "I will not justify the wicked" (Ex. 23:7), and in the woe to them that "justify the wicked for reward" (Is. 5:23). The legal content of the term is brought out from another angle when we read, "let them bring forth their witnesses that they may be justified" (Is. 43:9), where legal proof based on the testimony of witnesses is the ground for justification. These are typical passages, and although there are places where the forensic note is not so strong they do not invalidate our conviction that the basic idea is one of acquittal.[18]

Morris adds, "Thus Jesus said 'every idle word that men shall speak, they shall give account thereof in the day of judgment. For by thy words thou shalt be justified, and by thy words thou shalt be condemned' (Matt. 12:36f.). The idea is clearly that of an assize such as the Jews conceived of at the day of judgment. . . . So it is in Acts 13:39 and Romans 3:4. This last passage refers to God as justified, which is enough to show that the meaning of the word must be something like 'declare righteous,' for it is impossible to think that the apostle (or, for that matter, the psalmist that Paul is quoting) meant that God was to be 'made righteous.'"[19]

Realizing that we are all sinners by birth and by choice and that we thus stand guilty before the holy and righteous God, the question arises: How can God declare righteous those who in fact are not so? Where is there any hope? Can sinful people ever obtain a favorable verdict from this Judge? Justification, Paul clearly stated, does not come by human effort. "By the deeds of the law no flesh will be justified in His sight" (Rom. 3:20).

If human effort cannot attain justification, the only other possibility is that God provides it. How was Abraham declared righteous? By his faith in God. "Abraham believed in the LORD, and He accounted it to him for righteousness" (Gen. 15:6; see also Rom. 4:1–5). "But now the righteousness of God apart from the law is revealed . . . even the righteousness of God, through faith in Jesus Christ, to all and on all who believe. For there is no difference; for all have sinned and fall short of the glory of

God, being justified freely by His grace through the redemption that is in Christ Jesus, whom God set forth as a propitiation by His blood, through faith, to demonstrate His righteousness, because in His forbearance God had passed over the sins that were previously committed, to demonstrate at the present time His righteousness that He might be just and the justifier of the one who has faith in Jesus" (3:21–26).

In this passage all the great concepts involved in justification—the righteousness of God, faith, grace, redemption, propitiation—are woven together in one majestic declaration. In these six verses "righteousness," "justified," "just," and "justifier"—all related words in Greek—occur seven times. Because Christ paid the full ransom price for sin forever and is the Propitiation that satisfied the holiness of our righteous God, God can be righteous while at the same time declaring believers righteous. And this justification is provided "freely [*dōrean*, 'as a gift'] by His grace [unmerited favor]" (3:24). As Paul wrote to Titus, we are "justified by His grace" (Titus 3:7). It is available to everyone through faith (Rom. 3:25–26; 5:1). When a person is persuaded of the genuineness of the offer of salvation and believes in Christ, at that moment he is clothed in the righteousness provided by Christ, so that His righteousness becomes his very own— God legally pronounces him justified. God subtracts the penalty of sin and adds the standing of righteousness. The believer then has an official standing as a member of the "royal family," clothed in the robe of Christ's righteousness.

As we are walking out of this majestic concert, Paul plays a postlude for us with these lingering notes: "Where is boasting then? It is excluded. By what law? Of works? No, but by the law of faith. Therefore we conclude that a man is justified by faith apart from the deeds of the law" (3:27–28). This is faith alone in Christ alone!

Then, after referring to Abraham being declared righteous (justified), Paul wrote, "But to him who does not work but believes on Him who justifies the ungodly, his faith is accounted for righteousness" (4:5). And to the Galatians Paul wrote that a person "is not justified by the works of the law but by faith in Jesus Christ" (Gal. 2:16), and that each believer is "justified by faith" (3:24; see also Rom. 5:1).

GOD'S WORK OF ADOPTION

"Adoption" is a beautiful word Paul used five times (Rom. 8:15, 23; 9:4; Gal. 4:5; Eph. 1:5) to portray the relational side of justification. The Greek word *huiothesia* stems from two Greek words that together mean "placing as a son." Whereas justification focuses on a believer's legal standing with his or her sins forgiven and being accepted as righteous in God's sight, adoption refers to the believer's intimate relationship with God our Father. When we were purchased out of the slave market of sin (redeemed) and declared righteous, God's Spirit took up residence in us. Thus Paul wrote, "For you did not receive the spirit of bondage again to fear, but you receive the Spirit of adoption [that is, the Holy Spirit who provides adoption] by whom we cry out, 'Abba, Father'" (Rom. 8:15). "Abba" is an Aramaic word that Jesus Himself used in praying to the Father (Mark 14:36). Adoption into God's family is part of his predestined plan for everyone who believes, for Paul wrote that God has "predestined us to adoption as sons [*huiothesia*] by Jesus Christ to Himself" (Eph. 1:5). Jesus Christ came to redeem sinners so that they "might receive the adoption as sons [*huiothesia*]" (Gal. 4:5).

Adoption means to take a person from another family and make him legally one's own child. The son's or daughter's former relationships are severed, and the individual is a member of the new family under the father's authority. In addition the adoptee enjoys the benefits of being an heir of his or her adoptive father's estate. In the spiritual realm a believer in Christ is not only *born* into the family of God as His child (John 1:12). He or she is also *adopted* with the full privileges and responsibilities of adulthood. Because of these two metaphors of birth and adoption, God addresses believers as both children and adults. As spiritually adopted children, believers enjoy the benefits of being in God's family, including being heirs of God (Rom. 8:17). Adoption, however, does not discount the need for growing in the Christian life. The spiritual resources available from the "Spirit of adoption" belong to the son or daughter of God from the moment of the new birth.

The fullest experience of our adoption will be ours when not only our soul is redeemed, but our body as well. "For we know that the whole creation groans and labors with birth pangs together until now. Not only that, but we also who have the firstfruits of the Spirit, even we ourselves groan within ourselves, eagerly waiting for the adoption, the redemption of our body" (Rom. 8:22–23). We may not look like sons of God now, but the full family likeness is sure to come. John declared, "Beloved, now we are children of God; and it has not yet been revealed what we shall be, but we know that when He is revealed, we shall be like Him, for we shall see Him as He is. And everyone who has this hope in Him purifies himself, just as He is pure" (1 John 3:2–3).

PART FIVE

God's Provision for Sanctification Salvation

CHAPTER 11

Why Is Sanctification Salvation Needed?

In Christ! Sins forgiven! Released from Satan's tyranny! Declared righteous! Accepted in the Beloved! Adopted into God's family! On the way to heaven! Possessing eternal life! All these spiritual riches became ours when by faith we received Jesus Christ as our Savior. With these truths surging through our hearts, every believer can identify with John Peterson's hymn "Heaven Came Down and Glory Filled My Soul."

> Heaven came down and glory filled my soul,
> When at the cross the Savior made me whole;
> My sins were washed away and my night was turned to day—
> Heaven came down and glory filled my soul!

THE NEGLECT OF SANCTIFICATION SALVATION

There is far more to salvation than most Christians have thought about. We become absorbed—and rightly so—with the marvelous *position* we have in Christ and the consequent safety and security it provides. But we tend to forget the present tense of salvation, the need to go on being saved from the *power* of sin.[1] That is why Christ our Advocate (1 John 2:1) intercedes for us in heaven. "Therefore He [Jesus] is also able to save to the uttermost [present tense] those who come [present tense] to God through Him, since He always lives to make intercession for them" (Heb. 7:25). Hebrews speaks of those who will inherit salvation (that is, future "glorification salvation," 6:12). If you were to ask me, then, "Are you saved?" and I were to give you a full biblical answer, I would have to say, "I *have been* saved from the penalty of sin (over fifty years ago), I *am being* saved from the power of sin (day by day), and I *shall* yet *be* saved (from the presence of sin, when I am in my heavenly home)."

Unfortunately we frequently use the word *salvation* exclusively to refer to justification or regeneration. Several years ago I spoke at the Annual Pastor's Conference of Moody Bible Institute. I had the good fortune of being preceded by two of my favorite speakers, Howard Hendricks and Warren Wiersbe. Having been edified by their messages, when it was my turn to speak, I said, "I want to praise God because I got saved this morning while Dr. Hendricks was speaking. And then I got saved again while Dr. Wiersbe was speaking." Not surprisingly, many in the audience looked confused. But then I explained what I meant. I said that one of the greatest problems of evangelicalism today is that many Christians who are saved are not *being* saved, that is, they are not growing in Christ and dealing with sin in their lives. Many American Christians are in the spiritual nursery feeding on milk. *We desperately need to get believers out of infancy and into the infantry.*

Think of how many more workers it takes to care for infants as compared to mature adults. When I hear preachers talking about hundreds of people coming to Christ, it makes me shudder to think of what happens to these spiritual babies who after birth are abandoned with no one to help them grow. Who, in obedience to Christ's commission (Matt. 28:19–20), will disciple these spiritual infants?

THE NATURE OF SANCTIFICATION SALVATION

In moving from "justification salvation" to "sanctification salvation," we are moving from what we received as a grace gift apart from any works (Rom. 3:24) to what we are to "work out" (Phil. 2:12–13) with a view to reward (2 Cor. 5:10). The former is "not of works" (Eph. 2:8–9) and the latter is through "good works" (2:10). Sanctification salvation pertains to those who have been "made alive" in Christ, not those who are "dead in trespasses and sins" (2:1). Sanctification salvation relates to the outworking of the truth that we have been declared righteous by faith in Jesus Christ. In justification sinners can bring nothing to God, but in sanctification believers are invited by God, as partakers or sharers with Him of the divine nature, to do good deeds. We are "created . . . for good works" (Eph. 2:10), and God has ordained that our works will determine the position of service we receive when Christ reigns in the future Millennium (Matt. 5:12; 16:27; 19:27; Rev. 3:21; 22:12). This period of sanctification, between our being begotten by God (born again) and our being raptured or resurrected into His presence, is a training period for the coming kingdom. Whereas justification took place in a moment as a legal, positional transaction, sanctification is progressive throughout our lives.

Progressively becoming more like Christ (2 Cor. 3:18) is the essence of sanctification. However, we live in a world that opposes Christ (John 15:18–25; James 4:4), so we face constant pressure to lose our focus on Christ. Believers live in a tension between two biblical doctrinal polarities—separation and fellowship. On the one hand, the Bible warns believers to separate from sin and unbelief (the word *sanctify* means "to set apart"). On the other hand, the Bible often encourages believers to maintain fellowship with fellow believers as well as to reach out to those who are without Christ. A believer who emphasizes separation but neglects fellowship and outreach tends toward being *isolated*. But a Christian who seeks fellowship without separation from sin is in danger of being *saturated* by the world.

Our Lord's prayer to the Father for His disciples provides the proper balance for these two issues: "They are not of the world, just as I am not of the world. I do not pray that You should take them out of the world, but that You should keep them from the evil one" (John 17:14–15). What does Satan, the "evil one," want? He would like for God's people either to be isolated from the world so that unbelievers never see their "light" or experience their "salt" (see Matt. 5:13–16) or to be so saturated with the ways of the world that they fail to be effective Christian witnesses. Satan doesn't care which of these avenues we take—isolation from the world or saturation with the world—just so long as we miss Christ's method, which is *penetration* of the world.

The Lord presented to His disciples a commission: "Behold, I send you out as sheep in the midst of wolves. Therefore be wise as serpents and harmless as doves" (10:16). Have you ever heard a more impossible situation than that? Have you ever known of sheep existing in the midst of wolves? Never! Sheep *in* wolves, perhaps, but not *in the midst* of wolves. The only thing that can make that possible is the presence of the Shepherd. It is impossible to maintain a proper biblical balance without consistently focusing on Christ. As Jesus prayed, He doesn't want God the Father to take us out of the world. He wants us to be *in* the world but not *of* the world. Paul wrote along a similar line in Philippians 2:14–16: "Do all things without complaining and disputing, that you may become *blameless and harmless,* children of God without fault *in the midst of* a crooked and perverse generation, among whom you shine as lights in the world, holding fast the word of life" (italics added).

Another verse that addresses the subject of separation is 2 Corinthians 6:14, "Do not be unequally yoked together with unbelievers." This verse has often been used to prove that evangelical churches should not be a part of liberal denominations (which may be right), but there was no such thing in the Corinthian experience. Also the verse is often used to teach that believers should not marry unbelievers (which certainly grows out of biblical principles), but this verse cannot be talking about mixed marriages because only three verses later he wrote, "Therefore, come out from among them and be separate, says the Lord. Do not touch what is unclean, and I will receive you" (v. 17). If the "unclean" thing is the unbelieving partner in a mixed marriage, then Paul was telling the believing spouse to divorce the unbeliever. But that cannot be what Paul meant, because it would contradict what he wrote earlier in 1 Corinthians 7:12–13. Obviously Paul was not referring to marriage in 2 Corinthians 6:14.

To understand the relevance of this verse to the doctrine of separation, we must see it in light of the culture of Corinth. As I wrote elsewhere, Corinth was

> a place of vulgar pleasure and gross immorality. But the factor which is too often overlooked is that this was immorality with a religious sanction of the state. In fact, to fail to partake in the worship of the gods would be

treason to the state. Thus, it was common for Christians of first-century Corinth to hold on to their pagan ritual which was an integral part of their life, and still try to be faithful to that faith which they really believed, namely, Christianity. Another reason for carrying on their pagan practices was their strong gregarious spirit. Their innumerable societies which played a large part in their lives all had their chapels, priests, and rituals. Apparently there were some Corinthians who did withdraw from the official temple rites, but not from the social-religious associations. If one were to refrain from participation, it would mean almost complete ostracism from the community. Furthermore, the Corinthians had a very defective sense of Christian liberty which was evidenced by their insistence, to give one example, that Christian liberty involved the right to gratify sexual impulse in promiscuous intercourse with prostitutes. Thus, the obligation of loyalty to the state, the pressures of society, and the carnal, immature, latitudinarian spirit of the Corinthian Christians were all contributing factors in the prevalent unbiblical fellowship of Christian and pagan.[2]

Clearly, then the unbelievers in 2 Corinthians 6:14 were pagan idolaters in whose festivals believers were constantly being urged to participate.[3] This verse emphatically calls for Corinthian believers to discontinue their practice of being wrongly associated with paganism. Why? Because the Christian life is incompatible with the conduct of the heathen, who are pulling an entirely different kind of "yoke." Such associations were inappropriate because believers, Paul said, are "the temple of the living God" (6:16). This temple metaphor is gripping when we realize that the Greek word Paul used is not *hieron* (the temple including its courts and auxiliary buildings) but the *naos* (the inner sanctuary), where God made His presence known above the mercy seat.

When an idol or an idolatrous practice is introduced into the temple of God, that becomes, as Calvin called it, a "sacrilegious profanation."[4] Yet, ironically, relationships with the world resulted in their cutting off fellowship with Paul, the very one who had led them to Christ and discipled them. Paul wanted to have full fellowship with them (6:11–12), but that fellowship was broken by the Corinthians' failure to separate from pagan practices.

Believers are to be separate from pagans because they have nothing in common. In 2 Corinthians 6:14–16 Paul spelled out this contrast in five ways:

Righteousness	*No Fellowship*	Lawlessness
Light	*No Communion*	Darkness
Christ	*No Accord*	Belial (Satan)
Believer	*No Part*	Unbeliever
Temple of God	*No Agreement*	Idols

Literally, 2 Corinthians 6:17 can be read this way: "Therefore, come out at once from the midst of them and be immediately separated, says the Lord, and the unclean thing do not continue touching." The key word is "separate," and several Greek words are translated by that word. *Chorizō* speaks of physical separation, as in the case of couples being divorced (Mark 10:9). *Apochorizō* describes a more decisive physical separation, as when Paul and Barnabas parted and went different ways (Acts 15:39). The word used in 2 Corinthians 6:17 is *aphorizō*, which can be used both in a physical sense and also in a figurative way meaning "to mark off from others by boundaries" or "to render distinct," as when Paul spoke of himself as "separated to the gospel of God" (Rom. 1:1) or "separated me from my mother's womb" (Gal. 1:15). The latter instance is not the physical separation of the child from the mother's womb but Paul's recognition of the purpose of God, "who set me apart, devoted me to a special purpose from before my birth, and before I had any impulses or principles of my own."[5] He was not physically removed from other people; he was marked out as distinct and different. Suppose you have a garden with rows of carrots, beets, lettuce, marigolds, beans, and roses. The marigolds and roses could be said to be separate (*aphorizō*), not by physical removal from the others but by distinction in their midst.

As Roy Laurin wrote, "This separation does not mean segregation. To live a separated life does not mean that we have to segregate ourselves from the world. . . . One can live *in* one sphere and still be living *by* the other sphere."[6] This is consistent with what Jesus said to the disciples,

"Behold, I send you out as sheep in the midst of wolves" (Matt. 10:16). And this was the kind of separation the Lord practiced, for He was "separate from sinners" (Heb. 7:26) and yet the Pharisees said of Him, "How is it that He eats and drinks with tax collectors and sinners?" (Mark 2:16). While Jesus was in fact "a friend of tax collectors and sinners" (Matt. 11:19), He was separate from them in His character. "Though He lived amongst sinners, He was infinitely apart from them, in nature and character, motive and conduct."[7]

Christians are to go out *among* the wolves, but while they are among them, they are to be looking to the Shepherd (Heb. 12:2–3). It is dangerous for a sheep to be in the midst of a pack of wolves, but they are safe if they stay close to the Shepherd, together with the rest of the flock of God. This is why the Scriptures repeatedly portray our Christian life as a race that demands discipline (1 Cor. 9:24–27) and as a fight and a warfare (Eph. 6:10–20). This is also why our Lord and the apostles repeatedly (almost a hundred times) spoke of future reward at the judgment seat of Christ as a motive to encourage us to "hang in there" when the "going gets tough."[8]

THE MEANS OF SANCTIFICATION SALVATION

The Word of God

The primary means of spiritual life and growth is the Scriptures. The Word of God is so basic that Jesus likened it to our daily food. Refusing Satan's suggestion to live by miracles, Jesus said, "Man shall not live by bread alone, but by every word that proceeds from the mouth of God" (Matt. 4:4; see Deut. 8:3). To new believers, Jesus advised, "If you abide in My word, you are My disciples indeed. And you shall know the truth, and the truth shall make you free" (John 8:31–32). And Jesus assured His apostles, "You are already clean because of the word which I have spoken to you. Abide in Me, and I in you. As the branch cannot bear fruit of itself, unless it abides in the vine, neither can you, unless you abide in Me" (15:3–4). And knowing that His time for discipling the apostles was quickly coming to a conclusion, He left them to the Father's keeping, but He prayed, "I have given them Your word. . . . Sanctify them by Your truth. Your word is truth" (17:14, 17).

The apostle Peter stressed that God's Word is needed as food to nourish believers: "As newborn babes, desire the pure milk of the word, that you may grow thereby, if indeed you have tasted that the Lord is gracious" (1 Pet. 2:2–3).

The Spirit of God

For the Word of God to help us grow spiritually, its ministry must be accompanied by the Spirit of truth (John 14:16–17). The Word of God apart from the Spirit of God is lifeless. On the other hand, the Spirit of God without the Word of God is mute. To put it another way, focusing on the Word of God apart from the Spirit of God leads to formalism, whereas focusing on the Spirit of God apart from the Word of God leads to fanaticism. But focusing on both—the Word of God and the Spirit of God—will lead to growth into the image of Christ.[9]

In Ephesians 5:18 Paul wrote, "Be filled with the Spirit," and in Colossians 3:16 he said, "Let the word of Christ dwell in you richly." Though these commands differ, the results are the same, thus suggesting their close relationship. These verses therefore suggest that it is not possible for God's Word to dwell in believers unless they are filled with the Spirit; and conversely, Christians can't be filled with the Spirit without the Word of Christ dwelling in them.

Second Corinthians 3:18 summarizes sanctification beautifully: "But we all, with unveiled face, beholding as in a mirror the glory of the Lord, are being transformed into the same image from glory to glory, just as by the Spirit of the Lord." Paul was addressing people who have turned to the Lord and therefore have had the veil of unbelief taken away (3:15–17). The word "beholding" suggests a continuous looking, as in a mirror, so that we take on the reflection of what we are looking at.

When Paul wrote that we behold "the glory of the Lord," what did he mean? He was referring, I believe, to Jesus Christ, because He "has declared" God the Father (John 1:18). And we see Christ through the written word of God. What a privileged people we are to behold the incarnate God in the person of Jesus Christ revealed in the Word of God. To behold Jesus is to behold "the glory of the Lord." And to keep on looking to Jesus results in our being "transformed." The Greek verb for "transformed" is *metamorpheō*, from which we get our word "metamorphosis." A butterfly begins as a microscopic egg, which becomes a larva, which after about five days becomes a caterpillar. Then after about twenty days the caterpillar becomes a beautiful butterfly. What was once a crawling caterpillar is now a butterfly, able to fly up to a thousand miles in its lifetime. No longer is it bound to the earth; it can fly from flower to flower, enjoying the sweet nectar of God's great and wonderful creation. So it is with those who have been "unveiled" by believing in Christ. A new world is opened to explore, a new life in which to enjoy the glory of the Lord. As we behold His glory, we are changed or transformed, being made more like Christ by the Spirit of the Lord. Thus the Holy Spirit is an essential means to our sanctification, or spiritual development. Years ago this beautiful process got me so excited that I took this verse (2 Cor. 3:18) as my life verse and I keep it before me regularly. In fact, my oldest son wrote it on parchment in beautiful calligraphy and framed it for me.

The Church of God

God created us not to live in isolation from each other but in relationship to each other. Thus when a person is saved by faith in Christ, God places that new Christian into the family of fellow believers called the church, the body of Christ.[10] Just before His ascension the Lord Jesus spoke of the coming formation of this body, which began on the Day of Pentecost by the baptizing work of the Holy Spirit (see 1 Cor. 12:13). After Jesus ascended and was installed as Head (Col. 1:17) of the body which He created and placed in the Holy Spirit, He gave gifts to each member (Eph. 4:7–8) and designated appropriate leaders "for the equipping of the saints for the work of ministry, for the edifying of the body of Christ" (4:12). Therefore as Christ views His church, He sees its members—all believers in this church age[11]—united together under leadership in local churches where the members minister their gifts, serving each other so "that there should be no schism in the body, but that the members should have the same care for one another" (1 Cor. 12:25).

Jesus Christ does not intend for the members of His body to live independently of each other. Yet we live in a society in which the greatest disease, according to social scientist Robert Bellah, is individualism. In his bestseller *Habits of the Heart*, Bellah quoted Alexis de Tocqueville, who offered a comprehensive and penetrating analysis of the relationship between character and society in America. Tocqueville warned that "some aspects of our character might eventually isolate Americans from one another and thereby undermine the conditions of freedom."[12] Responding to this danger, Bellah's landmark book portrays the conflict between our fierce individualism and our urgent need for community and commitment to one another.

This disease of individualism has penetrated many churches as well. Ted Peters, of Pacific Lutheran Seminary, noted that Western culture has thrown off "the authority of the king to tell us what to do, and we rejected the authority of the church to tell us how to think."[13] As a result of Freudian influence, "the internal constraints of inhibiting moral codes are now seen as illicit restrictions upon the freedom of the self."[14] Peters said we are therefore moving into the future "with loyalty to a concept of the human being as an autonomous and independent self, responsible for creating its own values and priorities, subject to no external authority, and charged only with fulfilling its own self-defined potential for living."[15] Peters then related this problem to religion. "Members of the viewing public will soon be able to sit at home and watch the religion of their choice; and in addition, by pushing buttons on a hand-held console, they will be able to order a book being recommended or make a financial pledge. It will be religion without geographical proximity, without eye-to-eye contact, without personal commitment, without fellowship. It will be religion totally at the consumer's disposal."[16] And that was written two decades ago!

Yet the "go-it-alone" phenomenon is apparently not entirely new, for the writer of Hebrews wrote that some in the first-century church were in the habit of "forsaking the assembling" [of themselves] (Heb. 10:25). The word "forsake" (*kataleipō*) was a strong word for abandon and was used in the military to convey what we mean by AWOL. God said that absenting ourselves from meeting with other believers is a "willful sin" (10:26). As we hear and respond to the preached Word, we should relate to each other by considering one another (10:24) and "exhorting one another" (10:25). By following this directive of our Lord, we are able to stimulate others to acts of "love and good works" (10:24). But refusing to do so leads to God's discipline and chastisement (10:27).

Several years ago God corrected my faulty thinking about being faithful in church attendance and ministering to others. As president of Western Seminary, for many years every weekend I was speaking in a different church or conference someplace in the country. So the only time I could get together with my family in our church was for the midweek Bible study and prayer meeting. One Wednesday evening, as all six of us got into the car, my oldest child, Rebecca, said, "Daddy, let's sing!" So I let her choose the song and then Tim had a song for us to sing. As we drove along, each one of us chose a song.

When we arrived at the church I felt spiritually stimulated, and I was eager to get in and hear a good message from our pastor. I bounded up the stairs and into the auditorium. To my disappointment, the pastor wasn't there. The visiting speaker chose a difficult passage of Scripture to speak on, and he did not expound it well at all. I could hardly wait for him to get through, and I thought to myself, "Why didn't I stay home? I could have read the Bible and prayed and gotten more out of the Word than listening to this poor message." While he was speaking, I had a nice smile, but on the inside I was asking myself, "When is he ever going to get through?" Finally, he concluded, and I said, under my breath, "Thank you, Lord," and turned to walk out.

I reached my hand back to grab Ruth's hand, and it wasn't there. So I turned around to see where she was, and I noticed she had turned to talk to the lady next to her—Mrs. Findley, an elderly lady of eighty-six at the time. I still had enough presence of mind not to interrupt their conversation, so I waited. As I was waiting, I heard Ruth saying this: "Mrs. Findley, my husband and I have often wanted to thank you for your faithfulness to Jesus and His people here in this church." She cited several examples and then said, "Do you remember that six weeks ago we had an ice storm here in Portland and most of us did not come to the midweek service. And the people who normally picked you up didn't come for you that night. They felt it wouldn't be safe to go out on the ice. But you believed it was important to be here, so you walked six blocks on the ice to be present with God's people. We just want to thank you for your faithfulness."

Mrs. Findley grabbed Ruth's hand and squeezed it as the tears began to come down the wrinkles in Mrs. Findley's cheeks, and she said, "Ruthie, I want to thank you for that. Do you know I have been complaining to God all week long. I have felt I am just a useless, worthless old woman who doesn't do anyone any good. Oh, I have done good in the past. I have played the piano and the organ. I have sung in the choir and directed the choir. I have taught Sunday school, and I've been a department superintendent. I have led the women's missionary society. There is hardly anything in this church that I haven't done except preach from the pulpit. But I am not doing anything now. I just get in everybody's way and I have to be driven here and there. So I said to the Lord, 'Lord, why don't you take me home to heaven. You've taken my mother and my father home. You've taken my husband home. You've taken my only sister home. And now, Lord, you've even taken some of my own children to heaven, but you haven't taken me home yet.' But tonight, Ruthie, you have helped me see why He wants me to stay here. He wants me here so I can pray for you."

I was so chagrined! Ruth had not received from the preacher's message any more than I had. But she had the presence of mind to recognize that she could minister to a woman next to her.

Some time later Mrs. Findley moved into the Baptist Retirement Home in Portland. The retirement-home workers retrieved an old pump organ from a back room and dusted it off. She got her spindly, arthritic fingers going again, and she played that organ every morning for a group of older people who got together to sing for no one else's good but theirs and God's. They bought her a big Bible with large print, which she read every morning to a blind lady who couldn't read. And every day for eight years she prayed for my ministry until she died at age ninety-four. To the end of her life she was thinking more of what she could do for others than what she could do for herself. We need more people like her!

In our disease of self-love, which we call narcissism, we often ask, "What can I get out of church?" rather than "What can I give?" And we feel that if there is nothing to get we needn't be there.

Quoting a Syrian poet, John F. Kennedy said, "Fellow Americans, ask not what your country can do for you, but what you can do for your country." I would like to lift that to a much higher level by saying, "Fellow members of the body of Christ, ask not what your church can do for you, but what you, because of the grace of Christ, can do for your church." When you do that, God will bless you, for He delights to pour out His blessings on those who obey Him.

The Chastening of God

Another means by which God sanctifies us, saving us from the power of sin, is His chastening. The writer to the Hebrews addressed this subject in Hebrews 12:5–11. Writing to believers, he said, "My son, do not despise the chastening of the LORD, nor be discouraged when you are rebuked by Him; for whom the LORD loves He chastens, and scourges every son whom He receives" (12:5–6; compare Rev. 3:19). The "chastening" and "scourges" mentioned here have nothing to do with payment for the penalty of sin. The atonement of Christ on the cross was a righteous and infinite payment that satisfied the demands of God's holiness forever for all who receive that payment in faith (Rom. 3:23–26). However, God doesn't want any believer simply to coast into heaven.

When God disciplines believers because of sin in their lives, it is because of His love for them. It is like the love of a father for a son, who needs correcting. Every believer experiences the Lord's discipline; we are all "partakers" of it (Heb. 12:8). The word "partakers" translates *metachoi* ("companions, sharers"), a word used five times in Hebrews (1:9; 3:1, 14; 6:4; 12:8).[17] The Lord's chastening is designed to lead us to confess our sins, and it is "for our profit, that we may be partakers of His holiness" (12:10, NIV). Paul urged Timothy to accept discipline from the Lord, much as a soldier endures hardship. "You therefore must endure hardship as a good soldier of Jesus Christ. No one engaged in warfare entangles himself with the affairs of this life, that he may please him who enlisted him as a soldier" (2 Tim. 2:3–4).

Christ has enlisted us as soldiers, not as spectators or tourists. Recently I read with intense interest an article in *USA Today* entitled "Rangers' 'Elite' Tag Is Hard-Won." The article began with these words: "To become a Ranger, a soldier is supposed to suffer." It continued, "He is supposed to do without food, sleep, and shelter—all the while making smart decisions about complex, technical problems he might encounter in wartime as the best of the best of the U. S. Army... 'I want them rigorously trained so that they can be successful on the battlefield,' says Army Secretary Togo West Jr. . . . The Rangers are the Army's super-infantry, ready to go and fight anywhere on 11 hours notice. They conduct raids, infiltrate hostile turf and take part in secret commando units like the one that got caught in the firefight in Somalia. To prepare them—and sift out those who can't make it—the Army gives aspiring Rangers a hard dose of what they'd experience in war. Suffering is an important ingredient. . . . It's an experience as close to real combat as absolutely possible."[18]

The Christian life parallels those soldiers' experiences in suffering, hardship, deprivation, and more. Also the Rangers received special positions of leadership in the U.S. Army. Similarly Jesus Christ will assign special positions of service in His millennial kingdom in keeping with how well His soldiers trained (Rev. 2:26–27). Just as some soldiers in training don't make it, so some soldiers of Christ fail to persist (for example, Demas, 2 Tim. 4:10; see also 2:12), and they will lack positions of honor in the Millennium.

However, the Rangers' training simulates warfare, whereas God's soldiers are in real warfare with the most fierce enemy, Satan himself (Eph. 6:12; 1 Pet. 5:8). Also as a result of our disciplined training we will be privileged to serve in Jesus' reign of peace and righteousness in the Millennium.

Another contrast is that those who conduct the training of army personnel sometimes make mistakes in deciding which dangers and hardships they allow their trainees to endure. But our all-wise and all-powerful God never leads us into a battle for which He has not prepared us. Here is His promise concerning battle strategy: "No temptation has overtaken you except such as is common to man; but God is faithful, who will not allow you to be tempted beyond what you are able, but with the temptation will also make a way of escape, that you may be able to bear it" (1 Cor. 10:13).

God administers discipline and training in a variety of ways. Sometimes it is simply a strong rebuke, as when Jesus rebuked Peter (Matt. 16:23). Other times the discipline may be sudden death, as in the case of

Ananias and Sapphira (Acts 5:1–11). Or some other punishment may be needed. For example, when Moses struck the rock rather than speaking to it (Num. 20:7–12), God did not allow him to lead Israel over the Jordan River into the Promised Land (Deut. 31:2). Other times God disciplined the nation Israel for sins of its leader, so that godly men like Daniel went into captivity along with the nation.

Whether severe or not, God's chastening is directed by His sovereign purposes. He loves us infinitely and has infinite power to accomplish His good purposes in us (Rom. 8:28). At the same time He holds us responsible for our actions. Paul said cautiously, "For I know of nothing against myself, yet I am not justified by this; but He who judges me is the Lord. Therefore judge nothing before the time, until the Lord comes, who will both bring to light the hidden things of darkness and reveal the counsels of the hearts. Then each one's praise will come from God" (1 Cor. 4:4–5). In the light of this Paul kept on training, knowing that he had not reached the finish line yet: "Therefore I run thus: not with uncertainty. Thus I fight: not as one who beats the air. But I discipline my body and bring it into subjection, lest, when I have preached to others, I myself should become disqualified" (9:26–27).

About twelve years later, when Paul was facing execution at the finish line, he did not hesitate to claim confidently, "For I am already being poured out as a drink offering, and the time of my departure is at hand. I have fought the good fight, I have finished the race, I have kept the faith. Finally, there is laid up for me the crown of righteousness, which the Lord, the righteous Judge, will give to me on that Day, and not to me only but also to all who have loved His appearing" (2 Tim. 4:6–8).

These, then, are four ways God seeks to deepen our walk with Him, to encourage us to be more Christlike, to have victory over the power of sin in sanctification: the Word of God, the Spirit of God, the church of God, and the chastening of God.

CHAPTER 12
What Are Some Evidences of
Sanctification Salvation?

S anctification salvation is a process over the lifetime of the believer. What, then, are the experiences we should expect to see in the child of God? Or to put it in the words of John 15:1–16, what "fruit" may we expect to experience?

The Believer Repents and Submits

Merrill Tenney entitled his commentary on the Gospel of John *The Gospel of Belief*. This is a worthy title because, as noted earlier, John used various forms of the verb "to believe" (*pisteuō*) almost one hundred times in his Gospel, and he is the only one of the four Gospel writers to include a statement of purpose (John 20:30–31). He did not use the verb "repent" (*metanoeō*, "to change one's mind") even once in the Gospel of John. Yet when he addressed the churches of Asia Minor in Revelation 2 and 3, he used *metanoeō* eight times in his letters to five of the seven churches. It is apparent that in these two books John used "believe" for the unregenerate and "repent" for the regenerate. Believers need to develop a moment-by-moment practice of allowing the means of sanctification (the Word of God, the Spirit of God, the church of God, and the chastening of God) to bring them to repentance and consequent growth into maturity in Christ. As believers use these means of sanctification, they will gain insights that require a change of mind, which in turn will enable them to change their actions. To change our actions, we need to change our thinking (to repent) and to submit to the Holy Spirit for power to put the change into action.

The church at Corinth failed to respond to the means of sanctification, resulting in a number of believers becoming weak, sick, and dying (1 Cor. 11:28–32). Their thinking had resulted in carnal behavior (3:1–3). The problem was not a lack of good teaching, for Paul had personally taught them for eighteen months (3:2). The truth had not taken root, that is, they had not repented, and the problem had worsened; so Paul repeatedly asked, "Do you not know?"[1] The first instance of this is in 3:16–17: "Do you not know that you are the temple of God and that the Spirit of God dwells in you? If anyone defiles the temple of God, God will destroy him. For the temple of God is holy, which temple you are." Three times in this one verse Paul used the word "temple" (*naos*, inner sanctuary). Even with all its imperfections, the congregation at Corinth was still seen as God's sanctuary. God so longed for the local church at Corinth to be pure that Paul said, literally, "If anyone corrupts [*phtheirō*] the temple of God, God will corrupt [*phtheirō*] him." The word *phtheirō* means "to destroy by means of corrupting, and so bringing into a worse state. . . . It is used of marring a local church by leading it away from the condition of holiness of life and purity of doctrine in which it should abide."[2]

Years ago I was invited to speak at a large downtown Baptist church. As I approached the opening into the auditorium, I saw a sign that read, "You are now entering the sanctuary. Please be quiet." I walked up to the platform and, taking my seat next to the pastor, I said, "When I came through the door, I saw the sign, 'You are now entering the sanctuary.' I would like to suggest a correction. When I came through that door, the sanctuary entered the auditorium." My point was that God dwells in people, not in buildings.

Some prefer to call a church auditorium the worship center. But whatever you call it, it is not a sanctuary. A sanctuary (*naos*) is the dwelling place of God, and God does not dwell in buildings today. God condescends to making believing human beings His sanctuary, the place where

He manifests His glory. As Paul wrote, "Do you not know that your body is the temple of the Holy Spirit who is in you, whom you have from God, and you are not your own? For you were bought at a price; therefore glorify God in your body and in your spirit, which are God's" (6:19–20).

When my wife, Ruth, and I were in college, we belonged to a church that had more formality than I was used to. One Sunday morning my landlord (an elder in the church and a building contractor in town) and I together with other men were standing in front of the church building. Checking my watch, I found we were almost late, so I said to my friend, "Come on! Let's go in." He responded, "You go on in. I want to finish this," referring to his cigarette. I said, "Come on, and bring it in with you." He looked at me quizzically and said, "What? Bring this in there?" "Sure, why not?" I replied. He then asked, "Don't you know that the church is the temple of God?" I simply responded, "No, that is not the temple. I thought you had that thing sticking in the temple right now." And, believe it or not, he threw that cigarette away, and it was the last one he ever smoked. What happened? He repented and submitted—just that quickly. God the Holy Spirit used a single word of His Word that suddenly came alive through the vehicle of a fellow church member. Of course, it doesn't often happen that quickly. Sometimes God has to let disciplinary measures such as lung cancer take place before a person changes.

Let me ask, Was that man more righteous and more acceptable to God because he stopped smoking? No! How can a person be more acceptable to God than when He wrapped us in the righteousness of Christ and we were declared righteous (justified) and were "accepted in the Beloved" (Eph. 1:6)? You can't get any better positionally in Christ than you were the moment you believed. What happened to my friend was that suddenly he got a vivid picture of who he was in Christ. It becomes significant, then, where we take our "temple" and what our temple looks at, listens to, says, and does. We are God's temple and He bought us at a great price. Thus, as we move on to maturity in Christ, we enlarge our capacity to let our light shine better (Phil. 2:14–16). That's why the writer of Hebrews said, "Let us lay aside every weight, and sin which so easily ensnares us, and let us run with endurance the race that is set before us, looking unto Jesus, the author and finisher of our faith" (Heb. 12:1–2).

The Believer Exercises Priesthood

The main idea in priesthood is access to God. Under the Mosaic Law the high priest was limited to one appearance in the tabernacle's Most Holy Place in an entire year. He had access to the mercy seat, where the very presence of God was revealed. But when the Law was abolished at the cross, the Lord did away with the Old Testament priesthood. So in the early days of the church the apostles served as pastors and teachers but they never claimed to be priests. Hence in striking contrast to the rest of the world, the church has leaders but not priests. William Arndt wrote, "In the Gentile world outside of Palestine ... the absence of priests must have attracted attention. The heathen saw that the Christian churches had elders, likewise called bishops (overseers), but if one looked for priests, there was disappointment. The pagan religions had priests. ... Priests played an important role in the religions of the Hellenic world. Similarly the Romans had their priests; the emperors had the title of *pontifex maximus*. The Egyptians, as we know from ancient history, had priests who superintended and conducted the religious worship. How strange it must have seemed to an interested observer that the new religion, that of Christ, was not provided with religious functionaries of this nature."[3]

This observation leads to a remarkable fact: While the Christians had none who were set apart from the others as priests, the truth is that in the New Testament *every* Christian is called a priest. In the former dispensation Israel *had* a priesthood, but in the present dispensation the church *is* a priesthood. This privilege of access to God on the part of every Christian must have been overwhelming to the writer of Hebrews. After he stated the "unthinkable," namely, "Let us therefore come boldly to the throne of grace" (Heb. 4:16), he went into a five-chapter defense of the privilege (Heb. 5–9) before he resumed the argument in chapter 10 with these words: "Therefore, brethren, having boldness to enter the Holiest by the blood of Jesus, by a new and living way which He conse-crated for us ... and having a High Priest ... let us draw near with a true heart in full assurance of faith" (10:19–22). Having boldness and hav-ing Christ as our own High Priest, we are to draw near to the Lord in prayer. Privilege begets responsibility. The greatest privilege any human being can have is to talk with God. God talks to us through the Scriptures, and we talk to Him in prayer. We need to be sure we do not treat precious privileges tritely.

While the *privilege* of a priest is access to God, the purpose is *service* for God. First Peter 2:9 refers to believers as a "royal priesthood." Alexander Findlay paraphrased these words as "a priesthood in the service of a king."[4] Chafer's discussion on the believer's ministry as priests focuses on service: the service of sacrifice, the service of worship, the service of intercession.[5]

Where should Christians start, then, in exercising their role as God's royal priests? One sacrifice Israel made is still valid today and will be forever. It is the sacrifice of thanksgiving. This was a public proclamation of who God is and what He does. Many of the psalms highlight the sacrifice of thanksgiving (see, for example, Pss. 95:2; 100:4; 105:1; 147:7).

When the disciples asked Jesus to teach them to pray (Matt. 6:9–13; Luke 11:1–4), He gave them a pattern for prayer,[6] beginning with an ascription of praise to God for who He is ("Our Father in heaven," whose name is "hallowed"). And the final directions of Hebrews include the following exhortation: "Therefore by Him let us continually offer the sacrifice of praise to God, that is, the fruit of our lips, giving thanks to His name. But do not forget to do good and to share, for with such sacrifices God is well pleased" (Heb. 13:15–16).

Why is praise called a "sacrifice"? Because praise, like a sacrifice, is costly. In the very first church, prayer was one of its four main corporate activities. The new believers were to be trained in the discipline of prayer (Acts 2:41–42). Furthermore, the apostles adjusted their priorities of ministry to make prayer their number-one commitment, even ahead of the ministry of the Word: "We will give ourselves continually to prayer and to the ministry of the word" (6:4). As a result, Peter, James, John, Stephen, and others experienced great boldness for God.

What might God do if the leaders of churches in America today would set the same priorities for themselves as the leaders did in Acts 6? What would happen if as much time and effort were spent on concerted prayer as is spent on lobbying Congress today to try to "Christianize" our nation? Obviously the first-century Christians did not lobby the Roman senate or emperors. Yet they turned the world upside down for Christ (17:6). Have we lost the priorities of the early church? A ray of hope in this regard is seen in the recent book *Blinded by Might: Can the Religious Right Save America?* (Grand Rapids: Zondervan, 1999), in which columnist Cal Thomas and pastor Ed Dobson, two former leaders in the Moral Majority, reevaluate their priorities for the local church.

What would happen if our churches took seriously Paul's exhortation in 1 Timothy 2:1–4: "Therefore I exhort first of all that supplications, prayers, intercessions, and giving of thanks be made for all men, for kings and all who are in authority, that we may lead a quiet and peaceable life in all godliness and reverence. For this is good and acceptable in the sight of God our Savior, who desires all men to be saved and to come to the knowledge of the truth"? Our power with respect to our governmental leaders is not in our pocketbooks, our prestige, or our political correctness; it is our royal priesthood. Responding to this power, however, calls for spiritual maturity.[7]

The Believer Moves on to Maturity

Another evidence that sanctification is taking place in a believer's life is that he is maturing spiritually. Of course, not all believers move ahead spiritually at the same pace, and some seem not to grow at all (1 Cor. 3:15; 2 John 8). As a result at the judgment seat of Christ they will lose out on rewards and on positions of service in Christ's coming millennial reign (2 Tim. 2:12). While discussing the fascinating work of Christ, who is a High Priest after the order of Melchizedek, the writer of Hebrews said some of them were spiritually dull (Heb. 5:12–14). Apparently they had made progress, but something tripped them up in the race, and they had retrogressed. In their case it may have been the Roman oppression against the Jews, which culminated in the destruction of Jerusalem in A.D. 70. Sometimes the cause of spiritual retrogression is persecution (John 12:42–43), while other times it may be doctrinal deviation (1 Tim. 1:18–20) or worldly allurement (2 Tim. 4:10)—but Satan always has several fiery darts in his weaponry to fit the occasion. Paul's question to the Galatians is appropriate: "You ran well. Who hindered you from obeying the truth?" (Gal. 5:7).

The writer to the Hebrews backed up his charge about his readers' spiritual dullness with evidence. Apparently he knew how long they had been saved, for he said, "By this time you ought to be teachers" (Heb. 5:12). Obviously God does not want every believer to become a "teacher" in the formal sense of that term. But everyone is to be progressing in communicating what God has given them. Apparently God has a time line for each of us, an individual time line that takes into account all the variables in one's life. Yet God anticipates progress.

All of us who are parents have had the privilege of enjoying our children at each stage of growth. I recall being invited to dinner by one of my students whose lovely wife prepared an elaborate meal, which in itself was a task. The difficulty was increased dramatically by her six-month-old baby who was crying to be fed. Wanting to be helpful, my wife offered to feed the baby. It had been awhile since she had done that, but she felt she could rise to the occasion. The food was soft and should have gone down nicely. But when Ruth put the spoon to the baby's mouth, the baby spit it out. The food went down the baby's chin and onto her pretty Sunday dress, and then she gave a great big grin. We all smiled and said, "Isn't she cute?" Nobody said, "That little rebel. We ought to whip her good!" Why? We all know the answer. "She's just a little baby." Understanding that fact, we made allowances for the baby. However, we would not respond the same way if the person were a teenager spitting food out of his mouth. We would call the doctor or dial 911.

While God recognizes the fact of spiritual infancy, He does not desire that believers stay in that condition. Paul chided the Corinthians for being spiritual babies (1 Cor. 3:1–3).

They were believers—he called them "brethren"—but they were not "spiritual" brethren. Rather they were "carnal," or "babies" in Christ, that is, spiritually immature Christians. Not holding them culpable, he gave them a diet appropriate for babies; he said they were not yet capable of handling "solid food" (3:2). Although the Corinthians were taught by the premier teacher of that day, they were not judged culpable for their carnality after Paul had been there in Corinth for eighteen months. But when they received this letter, they were at least four years old in Christ and some, if not most, or all of them were *still* carnal.

John Calvin observed, "But he [Paul] does not mean that they were completely carnal, without even a spark of the Spirit of God, but that they were still much too full of the mind of the flesh, so that the flesh prevailed over the Spirit, and, as it were, extinguished His light. Although they were not entirely without grace, yet they had more of the flesh than of the Spirit in their lives, and that is why he calls them carnal. That is plain enough from his adding immediately, that they were 'babes in Christ,' for they would not have been babes, if they had not been begotten, and this begetting is the work of the Spirit of God."[8]

Unfortunately some Christians remain in a carnal state an inordinate length of time, so they become culpably carnal, having failed to move on to spiritual maturity in Christ. In the case of these Corinthians many of them experienced divine chastisement in the form of weakness, sickness, and even untimely death (11:30–31). This was in spite of the fact that they had been washed, sanctified, and justified in the name of the Lord Jesus by the Spirit of God (6:11). Just as we expect progress physically and mentally in our children, so God expects His children to progress spiritually. When progress is not forthcoming through the diet of "the pure milk of the word" (1 Pet. 2:2), God uses increasingly stricter measures.

The Hebrews were told they needed to be taught again the "first principles" (*stoicheia*, Heb. 5:12). This Greek word is also used later in 6:1, where it is rendered "elementary principles." It refers to learning spiritual "basics." In music, learning the basics means learning the notes; in chemistry, it is learning the elements; in mathematics, it is learning the numbers. When I was in grade school, we memorized the addition, subtraction, multiplication, and division tables. We had to do it perfectly. When I went to high school, because I liked math, I took every course they offered in mathematics: beginning algebra, advanced algebra, plain geometry, solid geometry, calculus, trigonometry. They never let me take a high school course on the tables I learned in grade school. Why not? Because in high school we were to put into practice the *stoicheia* we memorized years before. We never had to recite the tables again because we used them and so we never lost them. But if we hadn't used them, we would have forgotten them and would have had to learn them all over again.

In Hebrews 5:12 two statements stood in parallel form: "you need someone to teach you again the first principles," and "you have come to need milk." The first is a plain literal statement and the second is a figurative statement; thus the "milk" is a figurative description of the *stoicheia*, the Word of God.

What is the difference between spiritual "milk" and "solid food"? From my earliest days as a Christian, I remember being taught that "milk" is the gospel and "meat" (KJV) is doctrine. As I began to think of that later, it troubled me because the gospel is certainly doctrine, and where in Scripture are some doctrines designated "milk" and others "meat"? I've heard some prophecy buffs refer to prophecy as "meaty" in contrast to other less "meaty" subjects. Actually, I believe Hebrews gives us the meaning. The one "who partakes only of milk" is said to be "unskilled," a word that in Greek means "without experience."[9] His problem is not ignorance; he may have much great information. But he is destined to lose it and to have to be taught all over again unless he experiences it.

A person may memorize a driving manual word for word, but the first time he gets into a car and has to start up a hill, you don't want to be behind him. His problem will not be ignorance; it will be lack of experience. A spiritual infant, then, is one who is on "milk," who may have little or much information from the Word of God, but he or she lacks experience.

What, then, is "solid food"? We are helped by Jesus' words when He said, "My food is to do the will of Him who sent Me, and to finish His work" (John 4:34). He did not say, "My food is to *know* the will of Him who sent Me" but "My food is to *do* the will of Him who sent Me" (italics added). And this is the very definition that is given to "solid food" in Hebrews 5:14: "But solid food belongs to those who are of full age, that is, those who by reason of use have their senses exercised to discern both good and evil." The spiritually mature person is one who not only knows the "word of righteousness" (5:13), but also one who uses it in distinguishing good from evil. Moving on to maturity (6:1) requires gaining a firm grasp of God's revelation in His Word, and it calls for retaining it by applying it in life. Experience without the Word, and the Word without experience, are both inadequate. To grow in Christ, we need to know God's Word and we need to experience it.

CHAPTER 13

What Are Other Evidences of Sanctification Salvation?

As seen in the previous chapter, sanctification salvation, or spiritual growth, is evidenced by believers dealing with sin, exercising priesthood, and moving on to maturity through living out God's Word. Now we want to consider two other evidences.

The Believer Develops Stewardship

Many people think "stewardship" means "giving" or "tithing." But it's far more than that. Paul wrote, "Let a man so consider us, as servants of Christ and stewards of the mysteries of God. Moreover it is required in stewards that one be found faithful" (1 Cor. 4:1–2). The word "steward" (*oikonomos*) combines the two words "house" (*oikos*) and "law" (*nomos*); thus a steward is the administrator or manager of a house or an estate.[1] "A steward is a person who has been given the right of independent action, in his own name, but to the advantage of another. In other words a steward is one to whom another has entrusted his property for administration, in the expectation that he will deal responsibly with it, that he will nurture and multiply it."[2] In the first-century Roman world a steward was a slave who administered all the affairs of his master's household, although he himself owned none of it. He was a manager, not an owner. He was entrusted by the owner to manage an estate on his behalf.

In Jesus' parable of the minas (Luke 19:11–27) a master (symbolizing Jesus Himself) gave each of ten of his servants a mina (about four months' wages) and told them he was going on a long journey. They were to do business with the minas, and when he returned he would evaluate what they had gained by trading and would give them positions in his kingdom commensurate with their faithfulness. This is what we are to do in administering what God has entrusted to us.

In 1 Corinthians 4:1 Paul said he was a manager entrusted with "the mysteries of God." What are these mysteries? To the Greeks "the mysteries" were religious rites and ceremonies practiced by secret societies. Those who were initiated into these "mysteries" became possessors of certain knowledge, which was not imparted to the uninitiated.[3] The "mysteries of God," however, are just the opposite. They are not things God has hidden; they are things that reveal the person and will of God. Moses wrote, "The secret things belong to the LORD our God, but those things which are revealed belong to us and to our children forever, that we may do all the words of this law" (Deut. 29:29). The New Testament word "mystery" does not mean something mysterious (as in the English word). Instead it refers to what can be made known only by divine revelation, and is made known in a manner and at a time appointed by God.[4]

What has God revealed to us, which we are responsible to "manage" or oversee as His stewards? They include, but are not limited to, the following:
- the Scriptures (2 Tim. 2:15; Jude 3)
- your church (1 Cor. 12:25–26; Heb. 10:24–26)
- your spouse (Eph. 5:22–33)
- your children (Eph. 6:1–2)
- your spiritual gifts (Rom. 12:3–8; 1 Pet. 4:10–11)
- your physical body (1 Cor. 6:19–20)
- your neighbor (Matt. 22:39)
- your mind (Rom. 12:2)
- your time (Eph. 5:15)
- your money (2 Cor. 9:6–7, 12–13).

As stewards of these items, we are not expected to be perfect; instead we are to be faithful. "It is required in stewards that one be found faithful" (1 Cor. 4:2).

The Believer Achieves Good Works

The Bible repeatedly emphasizes the need for believers to do good, not in order to be saved from the *penalty* of sin, but because we need to go on being saved from the *power* of sin. The following verses (with italics added) show the Bible's strong emphasis on "good works.".

Let your light so shine before men, that they may see your *good works* and glorify your Father in heaven. (Matt. 5:16)

And God is able to make all grace abound toward you, that you, always having all sufficiency in all things, may have an abundance for *every good work*. (2 Cor. 9:8)

For we are His workmanship, created in Christ Jesus for *good works*, which God prepared beforehand that we should walk in them. (Eph. 2:10)

Being confident of this very thing, that He who has begun a *good work* in you will complete it until the day of Jesus Christ. (Phil. 1:6)

That you may walk worthy of the Lord, fully pleasing Him, being fruitful in every *good work* and increasing in the knowledge of God. (Col. 1:10)

That the women adorn themselves . . . with *good works*. (1 Tim. 2:9–10)

Be . . . the wife of one man, well reported for *good works*: if she has brought up children, if she has lodged strangers, if she has washed the saints' feet, if she has relieved the afflicted, if she has diligently followed every *good work*. (5:9–10)

The *good works* of some are clearly evident, and those that are otherwise cannot be hidden. (5:25)

Those who are rich in this present age. . . . Let them do good, that they be rich in *good works*, ready to give, willing to share, storing up for themselves a good foundation for the time to come, that they may lay hold on eternal life. (6:17–19)

He will be a vessel for honor, sanctified and useful for the Master, prepared for every *good work*. (2 Tim. 2:21)

All Scripture is given . . . that the man of God may be complete, thoroughly equipped for every *good work*. (3:16–17)

In all things showing yourself to be a pattern of *good works*. (Titus 2:7)

Jesus Christ, who gave Himself for us, that He might redeem us from every lawless deed and purify for Himself His own special people, zealous for *good works*. (2:13–14)

Remind them to be subject to rulers and authorities, to obey, to be ready for every *good work*. (3:1)

This is a faithful saying, and these things I want you to affirm constantly, that those who have believed in God should be careful to maintain *good works*. (3:8)

And let our people also learn to maintain *good works*, to meet urgent needs, that they may not be unfruitful. (3:14)

And let us consider one another in order to stir up love and *good works*. (Heb. 10:24)

Now may the God of peace . . . make you complete in every *good work* to do His will. (13:20–21)

These references to good works leave no doubt about the premium God places on good works. In addition, it is striking that Jesus Christ, in His first statement to *each* of the seven churches of Revelation, said, "I know your works" (Rev. 2:2, 9, 13, 19; 3:1, 8, 15). Since that was Jesus' first order of business for each of those churches, we, too, should be buying up every opportunity to do what is important to God. Yet many Christians either overemphasize works by saying they are essential for a person to be saved from sin's penalty, or they deemphasize works, failing to see that works give evidence of faith and of ongoing salvation from sin's power.[5]

In the Middle Ages masses of people were obligated by the church to carry out works, including various forms of penance, as a way to appease God. But in the Reformation the truth of justification by faith alone apart from works was rediscovered. With their newfound freedom in Christ, some believers reacted against works, saying they were totally unnecessary. Joseph Ton of Romania told me of a denominational group in Eastern Europe that has taken the position that works are detrimental to faith and thus are to be altogether banned. A different situation has developed in America. Lacking a sense of responsibility for Christian duty and good works, many Christians practice a kind of spiritual license, indifferent to good works.

Ultimately, everyone, unregenerate and regenerate, will be judged by their works. At the Great White Throne judgment the unregenerate dead, "small and great," will be resurrected to stand before God and to be "judged according to their works" (Rev. 20:12–13). Their works will demonstrate that they deserve eternal condemnation (20:15). Somehow in the infinite mind of God every work ever performed by every unsaved person is a matter of record. People who have taken their chances on their works as a means of gaining entrance to heaven will find that their works fall short of God's righteous demands for eternal fellowship with Him. When the "books" in heaven reveal that unbelievers fall short of what is required, another book, the Book of Life, will be opened to show that their names are not written there.

Regenerate people, those who have been clothed in the righteousness of Jesus Christ, will also be judged by their works. But they will not appear at the Great White Throne judgment. Instead, they will appear at the judgment seat of Christ in heaven (2 Cor. 5:10). There they will be judged by their works—not to determine punishment, for that has been cared for eternally by Jesus' sacrifice on the cross—but to determine whether they will receive or lose rewards (1 Cor. 3:12–15).

The following illustrates the difference between these two judgments.

SALVATION

Christians		Non-Christians
Judgment Seat of Christ		Great White Throne Judgment
(2 Cor. 5:10)		(Rev. 20:11–12)

┌───┐
│ "To each person according to what he has done" (Rom. 2:6). │
└───┘

⇩   ⇩   ⇩

Loss of reward	Reward	Lake of fire
Fire	Rest	
Disqualification	Inheritance	

Saved   ***Condemned***

The only time Jesus Christ mentioned "good works" was in His Sermon on the Mount: "You are the light of the world. . . . Let your light so shine before men, that they may see your good works and glorify your Father in heaven" (Matt. 5:14, 16). Yet Jesus said that *He* is "the light of the world" (John 8:12). Is this a contradiction? No. Think of it this way. On a bright, sunny day we may say, "The sun is the light of the world." But when nighttime comes we might say, "The moon is the light of the world." Both statements are true. The light of the moon, however, is not inherent light; it reflects the light of the sun. Similarly Christ, as the Light of the world, has inherent light, and Christians reflect His light.

This is the essence of our fellowship with Christ, as John noted: "God is light and in Him is no darkness at all. If we say that we have fellowship with Him, and walk in darkness, we lie and do not practice the truth. But if we walk in the light as He is in the light, we have fellowship with one another, and the blood of Jesus Christ His Son cleanses us from all sin" (1 John 1:5–7). Zane Hodges explained that "two things are true of believers who walk in the light: (a) they are in fellowship with God and (b) they are being cleansed from every sin. So long as there is true openness to the light of divine truth, a Christian's failures are under the cleansing power of the blood of Christ."[6]

The key to good works is unbroken fellowship with Jesus Christ. As we walk in the light, we reflect His light, much as the moon reflects the light of the sun. First John encourages believers to deal with the defilement of sin, and to express the love of God in practical ways. When we do, then people around us can see Christ in us and glorify our Father in heaven. This is the key point that Jesus made to the disciples in His Upper Room Discourse. He said, "All men will know that you are My disciples, if you have love for one another" (John 13:35).

Our love calls not only for words but also for good works. "Let us not love with words or tongue, but with actions and in truth" (1 John 3:18 NIV). When Christ said "that they may see your good works" (Matt. 5:16), He used the Greek word *kalos* for "good," which stresses primarily the outward form, in contrast to *agathos*, which stresses inner goodness.

James 2:24 ("You see then that a man is justified by works, and not by faith only") is often misunderstood. Hodges gives this helpful explanation: "There are *two kinds* of justification, not one kind conditioned on faith *plus* works. James' words do *not* mean a man is justified by works, and not [justified] by faith only [or, alone]."[7] Instead, James was saying that a "by-faith justification is not the *only* kind of justification there is. There is also a by-works justification. The former type is *before God*; the latter type is *before men*."[8] When James asked the question, "Was not Abraham our father justified by works when he offered Isaac his son on the altar?" (2:21), he was stating that we demonstrate to others our genuine faith in Christ through our works.

We need to encourage our people to be stimulated to "love and good works" (Heb. 10:24). We ought to be as zealous for doing good works as we are for seeing people come to Christ. In fact, this might be one of the most effective means of bringing people to the Savior.

Are we carrying out good works in our churches? What can we do, for example, to help the poor and needy in our communities? How can we enlist our young people to help minister to others in need? Can we encourage them, for example, to help an older couple whose house needs painting? Could they have a car wash to raise money for paint, and then paint the house? Could some adults be encouraged to visit elderly people in nursing homes once a week? Could some men in your church be-friend some fatherless boys in an inner-city environment? Scores of similar opportunities are available. We simply need to be aware of them and to channel our people to carry out "good works" on behalf of people, both saved and unsaved, in need. These kinds of ministries could revi-talize our churches, and cause the world to take note of our love and glorify God. As we maintain good works, we let our light shine, and we give evidence of our sanctification salvation by God for His glory.[9]

CHAPTER 14

How Do Spiritual Gifts Relate to
Sanctification Salvation?

THE IMPORTANCE OF SPIRITUAL GIFTS

One of the areas mentioned in the last chapter for which believers are responsible as stewards is that of spiritual gifts. While the subject of spiritual gifts is not normally included in books on salvation, I am including a brief discussion of spiritual gifting here because using their spiritual gifts is one of the ways believers can exercise their stewardship and can help build up each other in the sanctification salvation process.

Four New Testament passages address the subject of believers' spiritual gifts: Romans 12:3–8; 1 Corinthians 12–14; Ephesians 4:11–16; and 1 Peter 4:10–14.

In the Romans passage Paul urged his readers to present their bodies to God for His use and to be transformed by the renewing of their minds so that they could exercise their spiritual gifts effectively. If a Christian is not dedicated to the Lord and is conformed to the world's sinful ways, he cannot use his or her spiritual gifts most effectively for God's glory. And how did Paul introduce the subject of spiritual gifts in Romans 12? By drawing an analogy to the physical body: "For as we have many members in one body, but all the members do not have the same function, so we, being many, are one body in Christ, and individually members of one another" (12:4–5). The apostle extended this metaphor more graphically in 1 Corinthians 12:12–27. Just as the human body has many parts (diversity) but they all function together (unity), so in Christ's one body, the church, believers have differing spiritual gifts (12:4, 12, 14, 20, 27).

The biblical teaching on spiritual gifts is not a subject simply to banter about in seminars. Spiritual gifts are the *means* by which believers are to serve one another in and through the local church. Spiritual gifts are "for the profit of all" (1 Cor. 12:7) by which we teach, encourage, and build up one another. The gifts given by the Holy Spirit are basic to the development of the body of Christ, the church. They are tools in our hands to be used for the benefit of others.

The idea of Christians serving each other by means of their spiritual gifts, however, has not always been recognized. For a thousand years before the Reformation the Roman Catholic clergy viewed themselves as God's priests, intermediaries between God and humans. One of the doctrines the Reformers championed was the priesthood of all believers. Yet they did not give much attention to the tools God gives believers for ministering for Him. The Roman Catholic priest did almost everything for the people. He read the Bible for them. He prayed for them. He did everything in the church for the people instead of getting them involved. However, the Scriptures do not suggest that only the clergy are to engage in ministry. Instead, the Bible indicates that all the "saints" (believers) are to be engaged in "the work of the ministry" (Eph. 4:12). Just as every part of the human body contributes to its growth, so all believers are to be equipped by spiritually gifted leaders (4:11–16). Then as the Lord's followers are engaged in the work of ministry, the body of Christ is edified and believers become spiritually mature. This helps us see how spiritual gifting is related to sanctification salvation.

Unfortunately many pastors still see themselves as responsible for doing all the "church work," and many congregations are content to let their pastors do it. These pastors are caught in the "Jack-of-all-trades" syndrome. Some of my students caught me in this attitude some years ago when I was serving as president of Western Seminary. Arriving early on campus one bright, sunny morning, I was captivated by the beauty of the rose garden at the entrance to my office. They were in gorgeous bloom, and the rays of the morning sun were shining over the top of them and catching the little beads of dew, making them glisten. As I looked at them, I magnified the Lord for His handiwork. But then I looked and saw large blades of grass spoiling the beauty of the rose bed. My first thought was, "Why hasn't the gardener taken care of that? What a mess." And so I began to pull out the grass. The ground was soft so that I could fairly easily pull those long roots out. A few blades led to a few more blades, until I had completed the job of weeding the rose garden—while I was dressed in my suit and tie! After I finished the job, I backed up and looked at what I had done and thought, "Now that is the way it ought to look. That is really beautiful."

Then I turned around and to my surprise several students had quietly gathered behind me. One of the more daring ones said, "Oh, Dr. Radmacher, is that what God has called you to do?" He had the strange idea that someone else was hired to do that! But more important, he knew there was something on my desk he hadn't received back from me yet, that I alone could do—and that was his ungraded test paper. The gardener could weed the garden when he had time, and he was being paid to do that. But by my doing what God had *not* given me to do, I was leaving undone what God *had* given me to do. At the same time I rationalized that I didn't have time to get to that paper-grading because there was just too much else to do. Spiritual gifts are like that. We ought not neglect what God has given us in order to do something for which He has gifted someone else.

A number of years ago, when I wrote an article on this problem for *Moody Monthly*,[1] the artwork with the article portrayed a pastor as a taxi-cab driver, delivery boy, local plumber, office boy, baby-sitter, recreation director, and custodian. Some pastors feel they are doing God a great service by doing everything in the church. They face the danger of thinking they are "omnicompetent."

But not even God does everything. He gives us tools to work with, assigns us jobs to do, and evaluates our success for future positions in the kingdom. Actually, thinking we can do everything is arrogance, which heads God's list of sins that He hates (Prov. 6:17). Of course, it is often easier for a pastor to do something himself than to take the time to train an appropriately gifted person.

The apostles in the first church were on the verge of getting trapped by the needs of widows who were neglected in the daily distribution of food: "Now in those days, when the number of the disciples was multiplying, there arose a complaint against the Hebrews by the Hellenists, because their widows were neglected in the daily distribution" (Acts 6:1). Apparently the apostles had set the trap themselves earlier when they took on the task of handling the money (4:37). But God alerted them to the fact that it was not pleasing to Him for them to leave prayer and the Word of God to serve tables. Serving (*diakoneō*) was not the problem, because that was their assignment in the "ministry [*diakonia*] of the word" (6:4). However, the "tables" and the "word" were two different ways of serving, tasks that required different people with different gifts. Wisely, therefore, they restructured their priorities: "We will give ourselves continually to prayer and to the ministry of the word." They didn't leave the tables unattended, however, for they searched out gifted people to care for those tasks (6:3).

Ephesians 4 begins by stating that all believers, not just some, have a "calling," that is, a vocation in the body of Christ. Furthermore, when Jesus ascended, He gave "gifts," that is, tools, for carrying out that vocation (4:7–10). In addition, He appointed people in five special ministry functions for equipping the church (4:11). Two of these, "apostles and prophets," are designated as the "foundation" of the church (2:20), thus leaving three others, "evangelists, pastors, and teachers,"[2] to develop the superstructure. Most importantly, Jesus Christ is the Chief Cornerstone from whom the living stones take their lines as they are placed in the superstructure (2:20–22).

COMMONLY ASKED QUESTIONS ABOUT SPIRITUAL GIFTS

What Is a Spiritual Gift?

The Greek word for a spiritual gift is *charisma*, which builds on the word *charis*, "grace." Thus a spiritual gift is a gift of grace. And this grace is "measured" out to each believer by the ascended Christ (Eph. 4:7–8). Furthermore, a spiritual gift is "a manifestation of the Spirit . . . for the profit of all" (1 Cor. 12:7) and is distributed to each believer by the Holy Spirit "as He wills" (12:11). Thus a spiritual gift may be defined as a supernatural capacity of grace designated by Christ and distributed to each believer at the moment of regeneration for the edification of the church to the glory of God. A spiritual gift is not a natural talent, although natural talents may often be a channel for spiritual gifts. For example, the gift of encouragement may be a means of exercising the talent of singing or writing. Also a spiritual gift does not refer to a place of service such as that of a youth minister or a nursery attendant. Just as there are various gifts, so there are various ministries and activities in which those gifts can be exercised (12:4–6). For example, two believers may have the gift of teaching, but one may function more effectively with adults whereas another teacher delights in ministry to children.

Who Decides Which Gifts Are for Us?

Several Bible verses indicate that God alone determines which spiritual gifts believers receive.

- "As God has dealt to each one" (Rom. 12:3).
- "Distributing to each one individually as He wills" (1 Cor. 12:11).
- "But now God has set the members, each one of them, in the body just as He pleased" (12:18).
- "And God has appointed these in the church" (12:28).
- "But to each one of us grace was given according to the measure of Christ's gift" (Eph. 4:7).

Paul wrote to Timothy about the "gift of God" (2 Tim. 1:6), that is, his gift which was given him by God. Receiving a spiritual gift does not come after much prayer or by becoming spiritually mature, or by working hard for them. Only God decides who receives which gifts.

Some Christians, however, point to 1 Corinthians 12:31, which some versions translate as a command: "But earnestly desire the best gifts." However, I think that a more likely rendering is an indicative statement: "You are striving after the greater [more demonstrative] gifts." This seems to be suggested by the contrast in the following words in verse 31: "And yet I show you a more excellent way," the way of exercising whatever gift you have in a spirit of love not self-centeredness (13:1–8). As Michael Griffiths observes, "The force of this verse is to tell us that we should *not* seek gifts which we do not possess."[3]

Does Every Believer Have a Spiritual Gift?

Each passage on spiritual gifts uses the word "each one" (Rom. 12:3; 1 Cor. 12:7, 11; Eph. 4:7; 1 Pet. 4:10), thereby affirming that each believer has at least one spiritual gift.

No one of the spiritual gifts is limited to either men or women. However, it is important to distinguish, on the one hand, between the gifts of the Spirit given to all the members of the body of Christ, and the office of elder which is to be held only by men. In the New Testament the leadership of the nuclear family as well as the extended family, the church, is the responsibility of men. All members of the body, both male and female, are to use their gifts in submission to those in authority over them (Heb. 13:17).

When Does a Believer Receive His or Her Spiritual Gift(s)?

Peter wrote that "each one has received a gift" (1 Pet. 4:10). And Paul said that "to each of us grace was given according to the measure of Christ's gift" (Eph. 4:7). The past tense "received" and "was given" suggests that every believer receives a spiritual gift at the moment he or she is justified by God's grace. This is part of each believer's "salvation package" to be worked out (Phil. 2:12–13). Obviously the only time common to all believers in the past is the moment when they placed their faith in Christ.

Must Spiritual Gifts Be Developed?

Yes, our gifts must be developed.[4] As Paul admonished Timothy, "Do not neglect the gift that is in you" (1 Tim. 4:14), and "stir up the gift of God which is in you" (2 Tim. 1:6). As stewards of these gifts from God, we are to discover them and then develop and deploy them. Just as natural talents do not come fully developed at birth, so spiritual gifts do not come fully developed at the new birth. Just as singers, writers, or musicians need to develop and use their talents, so preachers, teachers, evangelists, and encouragers need to develop and use their spiritual capacities.

Of course if a believer does not develop his spiritual gift(s), that does not mean he is less spiritual than someone who does. Failure to develop them does not mean that person will lose his or her gifts, but it will result in loss of reward at the judgment seat of Christ. Even the most worldly church in the New Testament, the church at Corinth did not lack spiritual gifts (1 Cor. 1:7), but they failed to exercise them properly.

How Many Spiritual Gifts Are There?

As noted earlier, four New Testament passages address the subject, but no one of them lists all the gifts. So we need to bring together the gifts mentioned in all four passages in order to have a composite picture.

First Peter 4:10–11 groups the gifts in two categories: speaking and serving: "As each one has received a gift, minister it to one another, as good stewards of the manifold grace of God. If anyone speaks, let him speak as the oracles of God. If anyone ministers, let him do it as with the ability which God supplies, that in all things God may be glorified through Jesus Christ." Though Peter did not cite specific examples of gifts, he did state that those who have "speaking" gifts are to communicate God's "oracles," that is, the Scriptures. And those who have "serving" gifts are to serve not in their own strength but with God's enabling.

In Romans 12:3–8 the apostle introduced a selective list by first mentioning in verse 6 the two categories of speaking (prophecy) and serving (ministry).[5] Then he gave five specific examples. Two are speaking gifts—teaching and encouraging—and three are serving gifts—giving, leading, showing mercy. In 1 Corinthians 12:28–31 Paul mentioned some speaking gifts and then added a "sign gift" category with four gifts in that group. These four were miraculous "signs"[6] that authenticated the supernatural ministry of the gospel message to hearers in the beginning years of the church (see the diagram on the next page).

Putting the lists in these passages together gives a total of sixteen gifts:
- speaking gifts: prophecy (preaching), teaching, exhortation, word of wisdom, work of knowledge;
- serving gifts: faith, discernment of spirits, helps, mercy, administration, leadership, giving;
- sign gifts: miracles, healings, tongues, interpretation of tongues.[7]

Biblical Categories of Spiritual Gifts

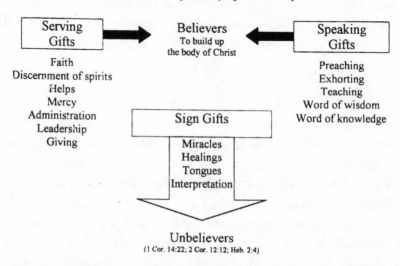

Believers, as "good stewards" of God's grace (1 Pet. 4:10), are to be faithful in discovering, developing, and exercising their spiritual gifts for the good of others and for God's glory (4:11). As they do this, they give evidence of their sanctification.[8]

PART SIX
God's Certainty of Salvation

CHAPTER 15

Is the Believer's Salvation Secure?

When I was a college sophomore on a summer missions trip in Europe, our ship docked for a short time in Cobh, Ireland. Among the people who came aboard to sell their wares was a quaint little Irish lady with some handmade lace. Talking with a distinguished-looking customer, she shared the reality of her salvation through Jesus Christ and her eagerness for heaven. The man chided her a bit about her assurance of heaven. He said it was presumptuous and perhaps even egotistical to think that she was good enough to be sure of heaven. I'll never forget her radiant response: "Oh, sir, you mistake me. You see, it is not my reputation that is at stake. It is Jesus Christ who made the promise." The man did not have a clue about the gift of eternal life through Christ. But the Irish lady correctly understood that God, on whom she had focused her faith, would keep her secure in Christ. How could she have such confidence?

DEFINING THE DOCTRINE

Charles Ryrie gives this concise definition of the believer's security in Christ: "Eternal security is that work of God which guarantees that the gift of salvation, once received, is possessed forever and cannot be lost."[1]

A number of theologians have used the term "perseverance of the saints" to refer to the security of the believer. For example, the Westminster Confession reads, "They whom God hath accepted in his Beloved, effectually called and sanctified by his Spirit can neither totally nor finally fall away from the state of grace, but shall certainly persevere therein to the end and be eternally saved." The terms *persevere* and *perseverance*, however, can be misleading. As Louis Berkhof said, "The doctrine of perseverance requires careful statement, especially in view of the fact that the term 'perseverance of the saints' is liable to misunderstanding. . . . We should guard against the possible misunderstanding that this perseverance is regarded as an inherent property of the believer or as a continuous activity of man, by means of which he perseveres in the way of salvation."[2] That misunderstanding came to fruition in A. W. Pink's summary statement: "God preserves His people in this world through their perseverance."[3]

This is the viewpoint of what is today called "lordship salvation." A leading proponent of this view, who believes in eternal security, has said he believes that "the Puritan's terminology is more appropriate; they spoke of the perseverance of the saints. The point is not that God guarantees security to everyone who will *say* he accepts Christ, but rather that those whose faith is genuine will prove their salvation is secure by persevering to the end in the way of righteousness."[4] Of course, no one believes that "God guarantees security to everyone who will *say* he accepts Christ."

The problem is that the word *perseverance* on the other hand, as many use it today, has switched its focus from God to man. Again Ryrie noted, "Perseverance seems to focus on the believer as the one who perseveres through the power of God. Security and preservation, on the other hand, seem to focus on God as the One who secures our salvation."[5] Also the so-called perseverance of the saints fails to account for Christians who do *not* persevere to the end in faithfulness to God (1 Cor. 11:27–32). More importantly, it does not give the attention that the Bible gives to the believers' gain or loss of reward at the judgment seat of Christ. Unfortunately many interpreters say those passages on reward or the lack of it speak of an absence of salvation rather than a failure of believers to persevere.

For the first twenty years of my life I was taught that eternal security is a doctrine of the devil. We were taught that a person could lose his or her salvation and thus be in and out of the family of God. My wife, too, grew up under that teaching. She was sensitive spiritually, so if she missed a midweek prayer meeting, she was not sure she was still saved.

When I went to church on Sunday and came under deep conviction of sin, someone would put his arm around me and say, "Wouldn't you like to go forward?" So I did. When I got to the altar, I got different instructions. Sometimes a person would tell me I needed to "hang on to God," and I tried to do it. Other times I was told to "let go and let God." On still other occasions I was told to "pray through." So I would stay there awhile, hoping that I had prayed long enough. But then Monday came, and I had lost it all again. My confusion was increased by seeing dynamic leaders fall into sin and turn away from the Lord.

I knew nothing about justification then. The term I regularly heard was "surrender." I thought of God as a general who was all-powerful and who would win in the end. I felt that if I surrendered to Christ, it would kill my joy in this life, but yet it would make things a whole lot better for me in eternity. As I weighed that through, I concluded that it would be better to be miserable for a short period of time and happy for eternity, than happy for a short period of time and miserable for eternity. I accepted Christ as my Savior at age fourteen, but my life didn't change appreciably because I was basically untaught; so for six years I was on a spiritual roller coaster.

In my early twenties I began to be taught what God is really like, particularly His sovereignty. Both my wife and I found that as we began to feast on what God is truly like, His peace overwhelmed us. We learned that God's love is unconditional, that He is for us, not against us. I realized that He loved me so much, that though I was His enemy, He gave His precious Son to die for my sins.

So for my wife and me, the grandest experience in our lives has been to understand the doctrine of the security of the believer because of the character of God who stands behind that doctrine.

This idea of the keeping work of the triune God, then, ought not be a storm center for debates between Calvinists and Arminians. Frankly, I don't think either John Calvin or Jacob Arminius would be on the side of most contemporary Calvinists or Arminians. Furthermore we need to remember who the real enemy is. Satan delights in getting our focus off the greatness and goodness of our God and on to each other. What really matters is who God is and what He did with respect to us at the moment of saving faith in His Son and our Savior. Jesus prayed to the Father, "And this is eternal life, that they may know You, the only true God, and Jesus Christ whom you have sent" (John 17:3). It was this knowledge that caused Paul, bound with chains and waiting for his execution, to write, "I am not ashamed, for I know whom I have believed and am persuaded that He is able to keep what I have committed to Him until that Day" (2 Tim. 1:12).

DEFENDING THE DOCTRINE

Eleven marvelous works of God demonstrate that a person who truly believes in Jesus Christ is eternally safe and will never lose his or her salvation. Four of these works relate to God the Father, three to God the Son, and four to God the Holy Spirit.

Actions of God the Father

The sovereign purpose of God. All of us have had days when nothing works out the way we had planned. We make plans, and sometimes they come to pass and sometimes they don't. But this has never been true of God. He accomplishes what He sets out to do. We are controlled by circumstances, but He isn't. He controls and creates circumstances. And the greatest demonstration of that is fulfilled prophecy. In Jesus' first coming He fulfilled more than three hundred prophecies. One example is the timing of His Triumphal Entry. On Palm Sunday I love to preach about *the day* God picked for Christ to enter Jerusalem. The classic work, *The Coming Prince*, by former Scotland Yard detective, Sir Robert Anderson, documents it.[6]

For God to fulfill the triumphal entry of Christ into Jerusalem to the exact day, as prophesied by Daniel 173,880 days before (Dan. 9:25–26),[7] God had to control every event, big and small, in between. Obviously, to prophesy, you have to be in control of history. So if God can fulfill His purpose with respect to His Son, He can also fulfill His purpose with respect to His children. "And we know that all things work together for good to those who love God, to those who are the called according to His purpose. For whom He foreknew, He also predestined [100 percent of them] to be conformed to the image of His Son, that He might be the firstborn among many brethren. Moreover whom He predestined, these [100 percent of them] He also called; whom He called, these [100 percent of them] He also justified; and whom He justified, these [100 percent of them] He also glorified" (Rom. 8:28–30).

Ryrie observed, "This daring statement could not be made if any one of the group could lose his salvation. If so, then the ones whom He justified would not be the same number as the ones He glorified. But the text says they will be the same."[8] Chafer added, "The failure of one soul to be saved and to reach glory whom God has ordained to that end means the disruption of the whole actuality of divine sovereignty. If God could fail in one feature, be it ever so small, He could fail in all. If He could fail in anything, He ceases to be God and the universe is drifting to a destiny about which God Himself could know nothing."[9]

Everything our sovereign God sets out to do, He most certainly will accomplish. So we need to ask ourselves, What is God's purpose in saving a person? What has He set out to do? Paul answers these questions: "In Him [Christ] also we have obtained an inheritance, being predestined according to the purpose of Him, . . . that we who first trusted in Christ should be to the praise of His glory" (Eph. 1:11–12). That is His sovereign purpose—that believers ultimately, with all their present imperfections, will one day be in heaven and will be to the praise of God's glory. Each believer, a trophy of God's grace, will bring glory to Him for all eternity. This phenomenal thought—that at the end of this process called salvation we will actually bring glory to Christ eternally—is beyond our comprehension. Yet that is why He saved us.

The infinite power of God. Some Christians believe a saved person can be lost. When you ask them, "What can 'unsave' a Christian?" they usually answer, "Sin." But they would have to admit that everyone sins and that no one reaches heaven on the basis of a sinless life. So they say it's important not to commit "big sins." Yet James wrote that "whoever shall keep the whole law, and yet stumble in one point, he is guilty of all" (James 2:10). He didn't distinguish between big and little sins.

Because of God's omnipotence every believer is kept secure. This is why Jesus said, "And I give them [My sheep] eternal life, and they shall never perish; neither shall anyone snatch them out of My hand. My Father, who has given them to Me, is greater than all; and no one is able to snatch them out of My Father's hand" (John 10:28–29). Along with God's sovereign *purpose* to present every believer to the praise of His glory, He has the *power* to carry out that purpose. "Therefore He is also able to save to the uttermost [completion] those who come to God through Him, since He always lives to make intercession for them" (Heb. 7:25). Peter rejoiced that we have been begotten "to an inheritance incorruptible and undefiled and that does not fade away, reserved in heaven for you, who are *kept by the power of God* through faith for salvation ready to be revealed in the last time" (1 Pet. 1:4–5, italics added). Paul stated with confidence, "I know whom I have believed and am persuaded that He is able to keep what I have committed to Him until that Day" (2 Tim. 1:12).

The immeasurable love of God. The well-known verse, John 3:16, begins with the words "For God so loved the world." In Greek the word "so" is at the beginning of the sentence, so that the idea in the verse is, "In this way, God loved us." As Paul wrote, "God demonstrates His own love toward us, in that while we were yet sinners, Christ died for us" (Rom. 5:8). This holy God found a way to extend His love to us while we were yet lost in sin. Whoever heard of a love like that? Since He did this while we were enemies, will He not then love us enough to keep us now that we are His children? This leads to the two "much more's" of Romans 5:9–10: "Much more then, having now been justified by His blood, we shall be saved from wrath through Him. . . . much more, having been reconciled, we shall be saved by His life."

Paul concluded one of the greatest chapters in the Bible with this strong statement: "For I am persuaded that neither death nor life, nor angels nor principalities nor powers, nor things present nor things to come, nor height nor depth, nor any other created thing, shall be able to separate us from the love of God which is in Christ Jesus our Lord" (8:38–39). Little wonder that Paul prayed that the Ephesians would "be able to comprehend with all the saints what is the width and length and depth and height—to know the love of Christ which passes knowledge" (Eph. 3:17–18).

The work of the Father. What about Jesus' words in John 15:2, "Every

branch in Me that does not bear fruit He takes away"? Does this statement mean God removes salvation for some Christians and sends them
to hell? Not at all! The answer lies in understanding that the Greek verb
airō rendered "takes away" also means "lifts up."

One time in Israel, as our tour group was going by bus from Bethlehem
to Hebron, we were driving past many miles of vineyards. Unlike our
vineyards in the United States, which are kept up all year on wires or
trellises, the grapevines in Israel, especially in the southern part, lay on
the ground during the cold winter months. But when the spring comes,
the vinedressers begin to lift up the stocks. They put a rock under the top
of each stock to hold it up off the ground. As we were driving, we came to
a section of ground where all of the vines were "lifted," and I saw for the
first time what Jesus was talking about.

We pulled the bus to the side of the road, and the workers in the vine-
yard gave us a lesson in Israeli viticulture. They explained that in the spring
they carefully lift the branches to allow the heat of the sun to envelop them
and thus control the ripening of the fruit. They said that if they allowed the
branches to lay on the ground, hundreds of little tiny roots would sink into
the surface of the soil where there would not be sufficient moisture to produce anything but little sour grapes. But if the workers lifted the branches
up off the ground, then they would get their moisture from the main roots
that went deep into the soil. What a picture of our divine Vinedresser. God
lifts the branches (believers) so they will produce spiritual fruit.[10] John
Mitchell, late founder and beloved teacher of Multnomah School of the
Bible, expressed this truth of John 15:2 this way:

> Many expositors believe verse 2 means the Lord takes the branch away in
> judgment. I do not accept this.... The primary meaning of the Greek here
> is "to raise up," not "to take away." Verse two should read this way, "Every
> branch in Me that does not bear fruit He raises up." What is the purpose of
> the husbandman? He goes through the vineyard looking for fruit. But here
> is a branch on the ground, not bearing any fruit. What does he do? Cut if
> off? No. He raises it up, so the sun can shine upon it, and the air can get to
> it. Then it will bear fruit. Some Christians don't bear fruit. What's the mat-
> ter with them? They need to have the Son shining on them. When a believer

is out of fellowship with God and is occupied with the things of the world, he is not bearing fruit. The husbandman must come along and lift the branch, raising it up and bringing the individual believer back into fellowship in order that he or she might bear fruit. God's purpose is to gather fruit, not render judgment.[11]

John 15:2 adds that God purges or cleanses the branches that bear fruit so that they will bear *more* fruit. Here the verb is *kathairō*, which in this passage does not mean "to prune," as some Bible versions render it. Pruning of vines takes place in the fall after the grapes have been harvested (referred to in 15:6),[12]"but here in verse 2 Jesus was speaking of the vinedresser's action in the spring. The cleansing by the divine Vinedresser refers to removing bugs and disease from the branches and to removing small unwanted suckers, that is, "cleaning up" the branches. As believers obey God's Word (15:3), they are cleansed of sin; they can bear even more spiritual fruit.

Rather than suggesting that some believers can lose their salvation, Jesus was showing us the special care God the Father has for all believers, the "branches." With His eternal purpose, infinite power, and fathomless love, God keeps every believer secure in Him. Also He is at work in believers to help them stay in fellowship with Him and to keep them clean through the Word.

Actions of God the Son

Jesus Christ is also active in sustaining every believer, as seen in His promise, His prayer, and His work.

The promise of the Son of God. Jesus Christ said of everyone who believes in Him, "And I give them eternal life" (John 10:28). Here is a simple unconditional promise. He didn't say, "I give them life until they sin." Nor did He say, "I give them temporal life." The Son of God, who brought the universe into existence and maintains it (Col. 1:16–17), simply affirmed, "I give them eternal life." Then He added, "They shall never perish."[13] "Never" in Greek is a strong negative. "When Jesus says, 'never,' He means exactly what He says. . . . 'and I give unto them eternal life; and they shall never, in no wise, under any consideration, perish.' Why? Because 'no man is able to plunder them out of My hand.'"[14]

Then Jesus said, "My Father, who has given them to Me, is greater than all; and no one is able to snatch them out of My Father's hand" (John 10:29). How marvelous to contemplate, that Jesus Christ views each believer as a personal gift from the Father! Would God the Father take back a gift He gave to His own Son? Certainly not. Our salvation is secure because we belong to Christ. Also no one can remove a believer from the Father's hand. W. B. Hinson, a great pastor in Portland, Oregon, during the early decades of this century, used to say, "The Lord takes you and puts you into the Father's hand, and then He covers you with His other hand. How are you going to get out?" When we are tempted to doubt our salvation, we should dwell on this wonderful fact. "And this is the promise that He has promised us—eternal life" (1 John 2:25).

The prayer of the Son of God. When Jesus promised that believers will never perish, He backed up that promise with His prayer in John 17. And as Jesus said, His prayers are always heard by the Father (11:41–42). Many people think of the prayer given by the Lord in Matthew 6:9–13 as "the Lord's Prayer." But Jesus' prayer in John 17 is actually the *Lord's* prayer, and the one in Matthew should be seen as the *disciples'* prayer. John 17 is a foreview of the intimate and effective ministry our Lord now continues to have on behalf of His own. Marcus Rainsford noted, "What the Savior had spoken from God to them He now speaks to God of them, and for them; so faithful is Christ that He will never say anything to us that He will not say for us."[15]

Near the beginning of this prayer, Jesus Christ noted that He has *authority* to give eternal life (17:2) to everyone whom the Father has given to Him. Nine times in this prayer Jesus referred to believers as those whom God the Father gave Him (17:2, 6 [twice], 7, 9, 11, 12, 24 [twice]). In other words, they were first God the Father's, and then were the Father's gift to the Son. Believers are God's gift to Christ, and Christ is God's gift to us. Thus people who come to Jesus demonstrate that they belong to the Father.

It is interesting to note what Jesus did *not* say to the Father about His followers. He did not talk about their failures or frailties. Instead he mentioned their faith: "They have kept Your word" (17:6). He pointed to their faith, not their works. They believed His Word.

For whom was Jesus praying? "I do not pray for the world but for those whom You have given Me" (17:9). Were these only the eleven disciples? No, for in verse 20, He said, "I do not pray for these alone, but also for those who will believe in Me through their word." So God the Son, who promises eternal life, buttresses that promise with His own prayer—and His prayer never goes unanswered because He always prays in the Father's will.

What did Jesus pray for His own? First, He prayed that God the Father would preserve and protect each believer. "Holy Father, keep through Your name those whom You have given Me" (17:11). In this request Jesus was asking the Father to exercise His sovereign power, not according to our merit, but in accord with His character and commitment to them. Other requests Jesus made in this prayer are that believers would experience His joy (17:13), that they would be protected from the influence of the world, the present evil system that opposes God (17:15), that they would be united (17:21), that they would "behold My glory which You have given Me" (17:24). To be with Him and to behold His glory refers to their being in heaven.

Would a prayer by God the Son to God the Father go unanswered? Hardly! To deny the safekeeping of the believer is to imply that this prayer of the Son of God will not be answered. Chafer concluded, "It is reasonable to believe that each individual ever to be saved by the grace of God through the Savior, Jesus Christ, was in the ages past individually presented as a particular love gift from the Father to the Son [and] if one of these jewels should be missing from the whole company, the Lord would be deprived as only infinity could be injured by imperfections."[16]

The work of the Son of God. Another factor that guarantees each believer's security is Jesus' work on their behalf, a subject Paul addressed in Romans 8:33–34. He asked rhetorically, "Who shall bring a charge against God's elect?" And then he answered his own question: "It is God who justifies" (8:33). Inasmuch as everyone who has believed on Jesus has already been justified (3:26; 6:7; 8:30), how could God or anyone else lay a charge against them? As Chafer wrote, "A justification which is not subject to human merit could hardly be subject to human demerit. . . . God, having justified the ungodly (Rom. 4:5), will not and cannot contradict Himself by charging them with evil, which charge amounts to the reversing of their justification."[17]

Reinforcing his argument, Paul said, "Who is he who condemns? It is Christ who died, and furthermore is also risen, who is even at the right hand of God, who also makes intercession for us" (8:34). This verse, Robert Cook writes, makes it clear that "if someone is to be condemned it must be Christ for it is on Him, not man, that salvation rests in the first place. Anything that affects the believer affects Him because we are united to him. Since this is true, any blame for defection from faith, the loss of eternal life by any child of God, would rest in Christ Jesus."[18] Think of the accomplishments of Christ in this verse on behalf of believers: Christ died, He is risen, He is at God's right hand, and He intercedes.

The substitutionary death of the sinless Son of God was a full and sufficient payment for the sins of all mankind (1 John 2:2). There is no sin that can be charged against the one who has been "freed from sin" (Rom. 6:7) without denying the efficacy of the death of Christ. There is no difference in the solution of the problem of sin for the regenerate than for the unregenerate. Both are dependent on the validity of the sacrifice of Christ.

The fact of Christ's resurrection guarantees the believer's resurrection. Paul wrote of this in Romans 6:5: "For if we have been united together in the likeness of His death, certainly we also shall be in the likeness of His resurrection." If a Christian can lose his or her resurrection life, then so can Christ. "Now if we died with Christ, we believe that we shall also live with Him, knowing that Christ, having been raised from the dead, dies no more" (6:8–9). The life a believer receives in regeneration is the resurrection life of Christ, which cannot perish.

Seated at God's right hand, Christ is the believer's Advocate. Believers still live with the problem of a sin nature (1 John 1:8, 10), but God has provided Christ as our Advocate to deal with that problem (2:1). When Satan accuses us of sin (Rev. 12:10), our righteous Advocate points to His work on Calvary, which covers our sin. Whenever a Christian sins, Christ the Advocate rises to their defense and forgives them, even without their asking for it. However, a believer's fellowship with the Lord is restored as he or she confesses that sin (1 John 1:9).

Jesus also intercedes for us on a continuing basis to promote our ongoing sanctification and maturity in Christ. Because He continues forever,

Christ "has an unchangeable priesthood. Therefore He is also able to save to the uttermost those who come to God through Him, since He always lives to make intercession for them" (Heb. 7:24–25). Priests on earth keep changing, but our High Priest before God never changes. The One who brought us into God's family is the same One who now intercedes for us. A preview of this ministry is seen in John 17, as discussed earlier. Will Christ's priestly intercessory work on behalf of believers go unheeded? Certainly not! This too is part of His work that keeps every believer safe in Him for all eternity.

Actions of the Holy Spirit

Several ministries of the Holy Spirit also show that God keeps His own secure forever.

The Holy Spirit regenerates us. In the act of generating physical life two things come together—a sperm cell from the father and an ovum or egg from the mother. When God grants conception, a miracle of life takes place and a new person is conceived and born. That person will continue to exist forever. In a similar way, the Holy Spirit miraculously implants the divine seed (Greek, *sperma*, 1 John 3:9) so that a believer is born from above (John 3:3), without any human contribution (1:14)[19] and immediately becomes a partaker of the "divine nature" (2 Pet. 1:4). It is plain to see that the resulting life is eternal. "In the instance of human generation, a being originates who did not exist before and will go on forever. Likewise, in spiritual regeneration a being originates which was not identified as such before and this being will go on forever."[20] One who is born by the Holy Spirit and placed in God's family cannot be unborn.

The Holy Spirit protects believers. Anticipating the fact that He would not be bodily present with His disciples at the birth of the church (John 14:25; 16:4–7), Jesus assured them that He would give them another "Helper" (*paraklētos*, "one called alongside to help"). As "the Spirit of truth" (14:15–17), the Holy Spirit would teach and guide them (14:26; 15:26–27; 16:13–15). Entrusted by God the Father with the priceless gift of these believers, Jesus Christ in turn entrusted them to the Holy Spirit, who has the ability to protect them and keep them.

As recorded in each of the four Gospels, Jesus had predicted that He would baptize believers in the Holy Spirit (Matt. 3:11; Mark 1:8; Luke 3:16; John 1:33). These verses picture Christ placing believers *in* the care and safekeeping of the Holy Spirit.[21] As noted earlier, Jesus' prayer in John 17 included the request that God the Father would keep believers safe (17:11). And this prayer is answered by the Holy Spirit. Thus the protecting ministry of the Holy Spirit, in answer to Jesus' prayer, is another means by which God assures believers that they are eternally secure.

The Holy Spirit indwells His church. What did Jesus mean when He told His disciples in the Upper Room, "I will not leave you orphans" (John 14:18)? He meant that God the Father would send "another Helper, that He may abide with you forever—the Spirit of truth, whom the world cannot receive, because it neither sees Him nor knows Him; but you know Him, for He dwells with you and will be in you" (14:16–17). Jesus was looking forward to that unparalleled event, the birth of the church, that took place on the Day of Pentecost. On that day the number of the disciples was miraculously expanded and they were formed into one body of Christ and placed in the care of the Holy Spirit. The Spirit of God would make the members of the church, both individually and corporately, the temple of God (1 Cor. 3:16; 6:19; 12:27). In whole and in part, believers are God's sanctuary, the place where His glory is seen. The Holy Spirit *indwells* (lives in) every believer, a marvelous fact that cannot be undone even when believers sin.

Believers at Corinth were "sanctified," "saints," and "enriched in everything" by Christ (1 Cor. 1:2, 5). Yet in much of 1 Corinthians, Paul pleaded with them to change their ways and turn from their sinful practices. If Christians could lose their position in Christ because of sinful behavior, this church in Corinth would surely be an example. However, rather than saying they would lose their salvation, Paul said they would lose rewards. Their works would be burned because of their carnality, strife, and division, but they "will be saved, yet so as through fire" (3:15). Here is a clear example of the contrast between the surety of salvation based on the free gift of eternal life and the uncertainty of eternal reward based on works.

The Corinthian church was condoning sexual immorality in its membership. But Paul called on them to "deliver such a one to Satan for the destruction of the flesh, that his spirit may be saved in the day of the Lord Jesus" (5:5). Here, too, we see a distinction between the gift of eternal life ("saved in the day of the Lord Jesus") and loss of reward ("the destruction of the flesh," that is, physical death and being disqualified for reigning with Christ [9:29, 2 Tim. 2:12]). Even though these Corinthian Christians were guilty of defrauding each other (1 Cor. 6:6–8), they, like all believers, were indwelt by the Holy Spirit. "Or do you not know that your body is the temple of the Holy Spirit *who is in you*, whom you have from God, and you are not your own? For you were bought at a price; therefore glorify God in your body and in your spirit, which are God's" (6:19–20, italics added). Imagine how they grieved the Spirit (Eph. 4:30) by joining His temple to a harlot. This would result in serious loss for them in the future millennial kingdom of God. But through all of this the Holy Spirit remains in His temple. Though grieved by the sins of believers, the Holy Spirit still indwells them. He is "in our hearts" (2 Cor. 1:22).

The Holy Spirit seals believers. In ancient times a seal was a sign of ownership and security.[22] To make a seal, cylinders or signet rings were pressed into wet clay or soft wax. Some were in simple design and others were ornate, but they all had the same purposes. To those who belong to God, the Holy Spirit is like a seal, guaranteeing that we are owned by God and are secure in Him. Three times Paul wrote that the Holy Spirit seals us. "Now He who establishes us with you in Christ and has anointed us is God, who also has sealed us and given us the Spirit in our hearts as a guarantee" (2 Cor. 1:21–22). "In Him you also trusted, after you heard the word of truth, the gospel of your salvation; in whom also, having believed, you were sealed with the Holy Spirit of promise, who is the guarantee of our inheritance until the redemption of the purchased possession, to the praise of His glory" (Eph. 1:13–14). "And do not grieve the Holy Spirit of God, by whom you were sealed for the day of redemption" (4:30).

Each of these references indicates that the time of the sealing is when a person believes in Christ. And the sealing will last until the day of redemption, that is, until Christ returns (see Rom. 8:23). Since the Holy Spirit guarantees our inheritance (Eph. 1:14), we obviously are secure for eternity.

Here, then, are eleven wonderful actions of God that guarantee our salvation: the sovereign purpose, immeasurable power, infinite love, and careful vine-tending of God the Father; the promise, prayer, and work of God the Son in His atoning death, resurrection life, unending advocacy, and intercession; and the regenerating, protecting, indwelling, and sealing work of God the Holy Spirit. Any one of those actions by itself is sufficient to end all doubt about the certainty of salvation. How wonderfully reassuring to know that God guarantees that our salvation is an eternal possession and cannot be lost!

CHAPTER 16

How Can a Believer Have Assurance of Salvation?

I n the previous chapter we discussed the doctrine of eternal security, the fact that a believer's source of security is in God alone. But not everyone who is secure in Christ has the assurance of that security. What can give believers assurance of their salvation? Is it possible for any believer to know for sure that he or she is saved?[1]

During a ministry in Europe several years ago I presented the gospel to a man in Amsterdam. When I asked if he would like to receive eternal life through faith in Jesus Christ, he responded, "I do not know if I am among the elect." "When do you plan to find out?" I asked. "Well, I won't know that until I die." "Won't that be too late?" I asked. He responded, "If I die and find out that I am not among the elect, I will do the best I can to glorify God in hell." He was right on one count, for the Scriptures say a day is coming when even "those under the earth" will "confess that Jesus Christ is Lord, to the glory of God the Father" (Phil. 2:10–11). But what terrible confusion. Unfortunately confusion is not limited to the man on the street because Bible teachers are sometimes confusing on the subject of salvation and the assurance of it.

A Bible teacher whom I highly respect has stated that Christians, to be sure of their salvation, must pay a price.

What must I pay to be a Christian? I must pay the price of my self-righteousness. . . . I must pay the price of those sins I now cherish. I must give them up. Every one. . . . I must pay the price of my own understanding of life of what it is all about. . . . I must pay the price of this world's friendship. I will be in the world but not of it. . . . I must pay the price of my plans for my life. I have many ideas for what I want to do and be, but I must give them all up. . . . I must pay the price of my own will. That sinful selfish will must go entirely. . . . The minimum amount a person must believe to be a Christian is *everything,* and . . . the minimum amount a person must give is *all.* I say, "You must give it all. You cannot hold back even a fraction of a percentage of yourself. Every sin must be abandoned. Every false thought must be repudiated. You must be the Lord's entirely."[2]

Those holding this view believe in what is called "lordship salvation." But how does one know if he has ever paid enough? Can such a person have any genuine sense of being sure he or she is saved? Other Bible teachers, on the other hand, do not place any such conditions on having assurance of salvation. They teach that assurance is based solely on a person having trusted in Christ as Savior.

How do we know which view is correct? The answer is found in noting two important distinctions the Bible makes.

TWO SIGNIFICANT DISTINCTIONS

The Gift versus the Prize

A passage lordship-salvation adherents often refer to in support of their view is Luke 9:23–26: "Then He said to them all, 'If anyone desires to come after Me, let him deny himself, and take up his cross daily, and follow Me. For whoever desires to save his life will lose it, but whoever loses his life for My sake will save it. For what profit is it to a man if he gains the whole world, and is himself destroyed or lost? For whoever is ashamed of Me and My words, of him the Son of Man will be ashamed when He comes in His own glory, and in His Father's, and of the holy angels." One writer says that based on these verses, "It is impossible to be a Christian without self-denial."[3] In the parallel passage in Matthew, the statement is added that when the Son of Man comes again, "He will reward each according to His works" (16:27).

To whom was Jesus addressing those remarks? To all the disciples, not just some of them. What is the subject matter? Following Him and receiving a good return on the investment of their lives rather than being ashamed of Him and enduring shame when Christ returns. And what is the result of all of this? Luke mentioned shame as a negative result (see also Mark 8:38), and Matthew mentioned reward, a positive result.

Was Jesus, then, discussing how to be justified forever? No. He was speaking of sanctification salvation, not eternal salvation. Salvation is without cost (Rom. 3:24), apart from works (4:5; 11:6; Eph. 2:9), conditioned only on believing in Jesus Christ (John 1:12; 3:16; Eph. 2:8). Salvation is a *gift*. However, no mention is made in Luke 9:23–27 or its parallel passages[4] about eternal life or salvation as a gift from God. Instead, He was discussing the matter of reward for believers who serve Him faithfully and loss of reward for those who don't. Jesus' words are similar to what Paul wrote in 2 Corinthians 5:10, "For we must all appear before the judgment seat of Christ, that each one may receive the things done in the body, according to what he has done, whether good or bad."

When Christ comes in glory (Matt. 16:27), He will measure out reward in relation to whether we have invested our lives for Him or not (16:25). When Peter asked what the disciples would receive for leaving everything behind for Jesus' sake, the Lord responded, "Assuredly I say to you, that in the regeneration, when the Son of Man sits on the throne of His glory, you who have followed Me will also sit on twelve thrones, judging the twelve tribes of Israel. And everyone who has left houses or brothers or sisters or father or mother or wife or children or lands, for My name's sake, shall receive a hundredfold, and inherit eternal life" (19:28–29).

Faithful stewardship by believers will determine their position of service with Christ in His coming millennial kingdom. However, simple trust in Christ as one's Savior is the basis for receiving eternal life. If the requirement for receiving rewards is mistaken for the requirement for receiving eternal life, the result is endless confusion.

Both concepts—eternal life as a gift, and reward in return for faithful service—are included in 2 Timothy 2:11–13: "This is a faithful saying:

For if we died with Him, we shall also live with Him. If we endure, we shall also reign with Him. If we deny Him, He also will deny us. If we are faithless, He remains faithful; He cannot deny Himself."

The introductory heading, "This is a faithful saying," is unique to the Pastoral Epistles and introduces a poem that may have been put to music and sung by the early church.[5] When we desire to make a truth more vivid, we put it in poetic form, and to make it even more memorable, we put it to music. This is an unusual approach for Paul, but the four conditional stanzas, each introduced by "If," call attention to two important but distinct truths, namely, the gift and the reward. If the conditions are true—"If we died," "If we endure," "If we deny," "If we are faithless,"—then the consequences are certainly true.

The first stanza—"For if we died with Him, we shall also live with Him" (2:11)—would have been vivid to Timothy, for he had been with Paul in the home of Gaius when Paul received this revelation (Rom 16:21, 23). At the very moment a person believes in Christ, he is identified with Jesus' death and resurrection. Paul asked, "Do you not know that as many of us as were baptized into Christ Jesus were baptized into His death?" (Rom. 6:3). Then he added, "Now if we died with Christ, we believe that we shall also live with Him, knowing that Christ, having been raised from the dead, dies no more" (6:8–9). As many as died, live! There is no slippage at all. Not even one! And to reinforce that truth, the parallel stanza in 2 Timothy 2:13 declares, "If we are faithless, He remains faithful; He cannot deny Himself."

This kind of faithful commitment is so foreign to what we see every day among fellow human beings that Paul reinforced this with the explanatory statement, "He cannot deny Himself." God keeps His word; He does not lie. "He who promised is faithful" (Heb. 10:23).

An Irish saint was correct when she said, "It is not *my* reputation that is at stake. He is the one who promised." Bob Wilkin put it well: "*Our faithfulness is not part of the equation. It is His faithfulness that determines whether we stay saved or not.*"[6] Though Peter boasted, "I will lay down my life for Your sake" (John 13:37), Jesus, knowing what Peter would really do, nevertheless encouraged him with words of comfort (14:1–4). This is unconditional love! In essence, Jesus affirmed, "You are Mine. And

I am yours forever." Because eternal life is a gift from God (Eph. 2:8), He does not give it and later charge for it. "Let him who thirsts come. Whoever desires, let him take the water of life *freely*" (Rev. 22:17, italics added).

"Between the two pillars of certainty 'we shall live with Him' and 'He remains faithful' lay two alternatives that were fully conditional"[7]—"if we endure," and "if we deny Him." As believers, our home with Christ in heaven is secure, but our position of service with Christ in the Millennium depends on whether we endure hardships patiently and faithfully or whether we "deny" Him by failing to undergo difficulties with patience and loyalty to Him.

This was not a new concept to Timothy, for during Paul's first imprisonment, Paul had written to believers in Philippi: "For to you it has been granted on behalf of Christ, not only to believe in Him, but also to suffer for His sake" (Phil. 1:29). Paul was assured that he would have a part, along with all other believers, in the first resurrection (1 Cor. 15:51–52; 1 Thess. 4:16–17), but yet he knew the need to "press toward the goal for the prize of the upward call of God in Christ Jesus" (Phil. 3:14).

In 2 Timothy Paul had been urging Timothy to endure suffering. He urged him to resist the temptation to be ashamed of the testimony of the Lord and of Paul, His prisoner (1:8). As a good soldier Timothy was not to become entangled with the world (2:3–4). And like an athlete and a hardworking farmer, he was to be diligent and faithful. Paul also reminded Timothy that the apostle had endured suffering even to the point of chains (2:9). All this was preparatory to the sentence in 2:12: "If we endure, we shall also reign with Him." The verb "to endure" literally means "to remain under." The related noun is usually rendered "endurance." These words are often used in exhortations to believers.

The Epistle of James is a book on how to respond to trials and temptations in the Christian life: "My brethren, count it all joy when you fall into various trials, knowing that the testing of your faith produces patience. But let patience have its perfect work, that you may be perfect and complete, lacking nothing" (James 1:2–4). A reward is promised: "Blessed is the man who endures temptation; for when he has been approved he will receive the crown of life [a special dimension of eternal life, John 10:10] which the Lord has promised to those who love Him" (1:12). After two admonitions to "be patient" (5:7–8), James reminded his readers that "the Lord is at hand" and "the Judge is standing at the door" (5:8–9). Then he added, "we count them blessed who endure" (5:11).

James must have listened well to the words of Jesus: "Blessed are those who are persecuted for righteousness' sake, for theirs is the kingdom of heaven. Blessed are you when they revile and persecute you, and say all kinds of evil against you falsely for My sake. Rejoice and be exceedingly glad, for great is your reward in heaven" (Matt. 5:10–12). Why did Jesus say believers who are persecuted are blessed and are to rejoice about such persecution? Did He mean we should simply "take it on the chin" without complaining? He meant more than that, for He said, "great is your reward in heaven." Those who endure hardship for the name of Christ will be revealed; they will reign with Christ when he returns. "Behold, I am coming quickly and My reward is with Me" (Rev. 22:12). This points to the judgment seat of Christ, when believers will be judged for the way they served the Lord, and many of them will receive rewards (1 Cor. 3:12–15; 2 Cor. 5:10).

Cal Thomas wrote a news release about Samuel Lamb, pastor of one of China's best-known "house churches." Many of the believers who worship in house churches are persecuted by the government. "Pastor Lamb, who is 72, has served more than 21 years in prison for his faith. In 1990, the government closed his house church and confiscated his property. Yet he perseveres. He averages 400 worshipers per service, and he leads four per week. . . . 'Each time they arrested me and sent me off to prison, the church grew,' he tells me with a smile as attractive as his faith. 'Persecution was good for us. The more they persecuted, the more the church grew. That's been the history of the church. . . . You must have a mind to suffer,' he tells me. 'If you have a mind to suffer, you can stand it. But if you don't have a mind to suffer, you can be broken.'"[8] For those who have this kind of endurance Jesus said, "Great is your reward in heaven." Those who lose their lives for Jesus' sake (Matt. 16:25), putting Him first, above possessions and family, will receive a "hundredfold" (19:29). As Paul told Timothy, believers who endure suffering for Christ will reign[9] with Him (2 Tim. 2:12).

What happens if we grow weary in the time of testing? We are to look to Jesus, who set an example for us by enduring the cross and hostility from sinners (Heb. 12:2–3), and we are to remember our past victories over struggles (10:32–39). If we disobey the Lord, then He chastens us as sons (12:5–11) and warns us of the severity of the coming judgment (10:26–31).

But what if a believer denies the Lord? To "deny" means to say "no,"[10] which is the opposite of the word that John used for maintaining fellowship or abiding with Christ: "If we confess our sins [that is, 'if we say yes or agree with God about our sins'], He is faithful and just to forgive us our sins and to cleanse us from all unrighteousness" (1 John 1:9).

If we say no to the opportunity to endure for Christ, He in turn will deny us (2 Tim. 2:12), that is, He will say no to what would have been an opportunity to reign with Him in His coming millennial kingdom (Rev. 3:21). Jesus told His disciples, "Therefore whoever confesses Me before men, him I will also confess before my Father who is in heaven. But whoever denies Me before men, him I will also deny before My Father who is in heaven" (Matt. 10:32–33).

Paul's four-stanza hymn in 2 Timothy 2:11–13 clearly sets forth what is certain for believers and what is contingent on what we do in our lives. If we keep this distinction clear, we can avoid the uncertainty that confuses many Christians about the security of their eternal salvation. At the same time the challenge to "endure" rather than "deny" is a strong motivation to live for Christ in light of future rewards. Paul wrote, "But I discipline my body and bring it into subjection, lest, when I have preached to others, I myself should become disqualified" (1 Cor 9:27). Thankfully, more than a decade later, as Paul faced execution, he could triumphantly claim, "I have fought the good fight, I have finished the race, I have kept the faith. Finally, there is laid up for me the crown of righteousness, which the Lord, the righteous Judge, will give to me on that Day, and not to me only but also to all who have loved His appearing" (2 Tim. 4:7–8). Let's keep pressing on to the prize!

Believing versus Abiding

Another way to avoid confusion about one's assurance of salvation is to keep in mind the distinction between believing and abiding. In his first epistle the apostle John kept these distinct. He wrote that eternal life comes through believing in Christ (1 John 5:13), whereas fellowship with Him (1:3) comes through abiding in Him. With respect to "our fellowship with the Father and with His Son Jesus Christ," it is appropriate to evaluate our stewardship of the resources God has entrusted to us so that our "joy may be full" (1:4) and we may receive reward in the future.

With respect to the gift of eternal life (Eph. 2:8–9), however, it is totally inappropriate to consider our faithfulness in works as a basis for assurance of the gift. Paul was adamant on this point: "But to him *who does not work* but believes on Him who justifies the ungodly, his faith is accounted for righteousness" (Rom. 4:5, italics added). Hodges's comment's are most cogent: "In the face of this assertion, how can anyone suppose that 'works' must nevertheless be the real grounds on which I am assured of my salvation? That is, how can good works be indispensable to my certainty that I am justified *without works?* . . . It is as though God had said, 'My justification is for the person who does *not* work, but *assurance* of my justification is only for someone who *does!*' Any form of theology that reduces to that stands self-condemned."[11]

Louis Berkhof, late president and professor of dogmatic theology at Calvin Theological Seminary, commented on the agreement of Calvin and Luther on this single basis of assurance:

> In their common opposition to Rome they both describe it [the doctrine of justification by faith] as an act of free grace, and as a forensic act which does not change the inner life of man but only the judicial relationship in which he stands to God. They do not find the ground for it in the inherent righteousness of the believer, but only in the imputed righteousness of Jesus Christ, which the sinner appropriates by faith. Moreover, they deny that it is a progressive work of God, asserting that it is instantaneous and at once complete, and hold that *the believer can be absolutely sure that he is forever translated from a state of wrath and condemnation to one of favor and acceptance.*[12]

How different this is from contemporary advocates of lordship salvation, who deny that a person can have assurance of heaven before death.

Placing one's trust in Christ for salvation is the basis of assurance. Works are not the *means* to salvation, nor are they the *measure* of whether we have salvation.

Assurance of eternal salvation by believing. The Gospel of John emphasizes assurance of eternal life that comes from believing in Christ. First John, on the other hand, stresses assurance of fellowship with Christ that comes from abiding in Him. John's Gospel was addressed to the unregenerate: "And truly Jesus did many other signs in the presence of His disciples, which are not written in this book; but these are written that you may believe that Jesus is the Christ, the Son of God, and that believing you may have life in His name" (John 20:30–31). Interestingly this written statement comes right after John recorded Thomas's demand to "see" (20:25) and Jesus' response, "Blessed are those who have not seen and yet have believed" (20:29).

Special blessing, in other words, is available to those who simply believe God's written record (without actually seeing Jesus). F. F. Bruce addressed this difficulty of believing without seeing: "This last beatitude had a special message for the readers of this Gospel when it was first published; it has the same message for readers of the Gospel today. They had not seen, and neither have we; yet they might believe, and so may we. Thomas was no different from the other disciples in this respect; they did not believe until they saw: if they believed a week earlier than Thomas, that was because they saw a week earlier than he. . . . But since the apostolic generation passed from the earth, all believers in the crucified and risen Lord have believed without seeing, and to them is assured the special blessing here pronounced by Him."[12]

How then does God give assurance to those who believe? First John 5:9–13 answers this question: "If we receive the witness of men, the witness of God is greater, for this is the witness of God which He has testified of His Son. He who believes in the Son of God has the witness in himself; he who does not believe God has made Him a liar, because he has not believed the testimony that God has given of His Son. And this is the testimony: that God has given us eternal life, and this life is in His Son. He who has the Son has life; he who does not have the Son of God does not have life. These things I have written to you who believe in the name of the Son of God, that you may know that you have eternal life, and that you may continue to believe in the name of the Son of God."[14]

This passage, along with others, makes it clear that *assurance* of eternal salvation comes from exactly the same source as the *reception* of eternal salvation, namely, by trusting in Christ. In other words, "assurance is of the essence of saving faith."[15] The words "witness" and "testimony" translate the same word *martyria*, which is used six times in verses 9 and 10. The thrust of the paragraph is the testimony of God Himself concerning His Son (5:9), and the one who believes this testimony has an inner persuasion or testimony in his heart.[16] On the other hand, the one who does not believe it says, in effect, that God lies (5:10).

What is the "content" of God's testimony? That is answered in 5:11–12: "God has given us eternal life, and this life is in His Son. He who has the Son has life; he who does not have the Son of God does not have life." The essence of God's testimony to us is that He gives eternal life to those who trust in His Son. As John wrote in his Gospel, "For God so loved the world that He gave His only begotten Son, that whoever believes in Him should not perish but have everlasting life" (John 3:16). Why did John write "these things" about believing His Son? So that "you may *know* that you have eternal life" (1 John 5:13, italics added). This is a strong word of assurance of eternal life to those who believe in the Son of God. This, too, parallels what Jesus said in John 5:24: "Most assuredly, I say to you, he who hears My word and believes in Him who sent Me has everlasting life, and shall not come into judgment, but has passed from death unto life." Jesus did not say that if we believe in Him we *may* have eternal life or *shall* have it. He said we have it the moment we believe in Him. He did not say He gives eternal life after a person is baptized or after a person denies himself or after a person carries out a number of good works. No. Jesus gives eternal life as a gift to those who simply trust in Him.

Assurance of continuing fellowship by abiding. Whereas the believer's works have no part in giving assurance of eternal salvation (1 John 5:11–13), works are central to assurance of *fellowship* with God. Because of this, John said, "If we say that we have fellowship with Him, and walk in darkness, we lie and do not practice the truth" (1:6). In 1 John, to love other believers is the epitome of righteousness and experiencing fellowship with the Lord.

In John's writings the key word for fellowship is "abide" (*menō*), which he used thirty-four times in his Gospel (eleven in John 15) and twenty times (all in a figurative sense)[17] in 1 John. The English word "abide" means to wait for, to endure without yielding, to bear patiently, to remain stable or in a fixed state, or to continue in a place.[18] And *menō*, the Greek word for "abide," has the same meanings.[19] Jesus never spoke to the unregenerate about abiding. Dillow is correct in saying that "'remain' never signifies the initiatory event of saving faith but [rather] the enduring relationship of walking in fellowship. The very meaning of the word 'remain' implies staying in a position already obtained or entered into and not entering a position or state for the first time. If a nonbeliever should ask, 'What must I do to be saved?' only another gospel would answer, 'Remain in Christ.' We remain in Christ (i.e., remain in fellowship) by keeping His commandments *after* we have been saved."[20]

This truth is seen in John 8:30–32: "As He spoke these words, many believed in Him. Then Jesus said to those Jews who believed in Him, 'If you abide in My word, you are my disciples indeed. And you shall know the truth, and the truth shall make you free.'" In discussing abiding, Jesus was addressing those *who had already believed in Him*. But then the basis for becoming a disciple, He said, was abiding in His Word. Two things are readily apparent. First, eternal life is received by believing in His name (John 3:16), but that did not make these believers disciples. Second, discipleship comes by abiding in God's Word.

The Gospel of John, as mentioned, is addressed primarily to the unsaved. But in the Upper Room Discourse, Jesus was speaking of fellowship, not justification, because He was addressing His disciples. In John 15:1–8 Jesus spoke of Himself as a Vine, believers as the branches, and God the Father as the Vinedresser. We noted in the previous chapter that 15:2 refers to the work of the Father performing the two steps of vine-tending (lifting and cleansing) in the spring to prepare the vines to bear fruit. Then in verse 3 Jesus said, "You are already clean because of the word which I have spoken to you." In other words, Jesus was saying that everything was now in readiness. The fruiting season was upon them. And they could bear "fruit," "more fruit" (15:2), and "much fruit" (15:5) as they were abiding in Him ("abide" and "abides" are mentioned seven times in 15:4–8).

In 15:4–5 Jesus turned from what the Father does (15:2) and He (Jesus) does (15:3) to what the disciples must do in order to bear fruit: "Abide in Me, and I in you. As the branch cannot bear fruit of itself, unless it abides in the vine, neither can you unless you abide in Me. I am the vine, you are the branches. He who abides in Me, and I in him, bears much fruit; for without Me you can do nothing." A child of God can *experience* the benefits of God's work only to the extent that he or she believes and acts on it. God will not do for us what He has given us to do. The Father will bring us into a place of potential productivity (15:2) and Jesus will provide nourishment from His Word (15:3), but God will not bear the fruit for us. As Jesus said, He appointed us to "go and bear fruit" (15:16). Thus in verses 4–5 Jesus enunciated for believers the working principle of abiding: No fruit is possible without abiding, but abundant productivity comes with abiding.

When believers abide in fellowship with Christ, they bear much fruit (15:5), their prayers are answered (15:7), and they have joy (15:11). But what happens when believers don't abide in Him? Verse 6 gives the answer. "If anyone does not abide in Me, he is cast out as a branch and is withered; and *they* gather them and throw them into the fire, and they are burned" (italics added). Reflect again on the situation of those disciples. They belonged to Christ, but they were weak. And they would soon abandon the Lord at His trial and crucifixion.

Who would be watching the apostles during that time? Unbelievers. And those onlookers may well be referred to by the word "they" in 15:6. "They" cannot refer to the disciples because they are referred to by the word "you" in verses 4 and 7. Bearing fruit may well mean having love for each other, because twice Jesus said believers are to "abide in My love" (15:9–10). And this gives evidence to the unsaved that we are His disciples: "By this *all* will know that you are My disciples, if you have love for one another" (13:35, italics added).

Jesus then said, "By this My Father is glorified, that you bear much fruit; so you will be My disciples" (15:8). The word "be" conveys the idea of "prove to be" (NASB). As Robertson states, it means "'become' my disciples (learners) in the fullest sense of rich fruit-bearing according to the text in 8:31."[21] The unbelieving world ("they") needs to see the love of

Christ's disciples for one another. If they don't, they toss us on the trash heap along with many others they consider phonies. Thus Jesus was illustrating in 15:6 that branches that don't bear fruit are useless. They have no practical value because the very people they are seeking to reach discount them and even demean them.

Abiding in Christ results in abundance of fruit and in answered prayer: "If you abide in Me, and My words abide in you, you will ask what you desire, and it shall be done for you" (15:7; see also 15:16; 16:26–27). Answered prayer is conditioned on the disciple's abiding in Jesus and on Jesus' words abiding in the disciple. But the greatest result of our abiding in Christ is that God the Father "is glorified" (15:8). This reminds us of Jesus' command, "Let your light so shine before men, that they may see your good works and glorify your Father in heaven" (Matt. 5:16).

After giving this teaching about abiding in Christ by using the allegory of the vine and the branches, Jesus said, "These things I have spoken to you, that My joy may remain [menō] in you, and that your joy may be full" (John 15:11). This recalls the purpose statement of 1 John: "And these things we write to you that your joy may be full" (1 John 1:4). Apparently, then, this section in the Upper Room Discourse is expanded in 1 John.

The first critical concern John warned about in this epistle was sin.[22] He wrote, "My little children, these things I write to you [in 1:5–10], so that you may not sin" (1 John 2:1). Our slavery to sin was broken by our Lord Jesus Christ at the cross (Rom. 6:7), but sin destroys fellowship with Christ. How, then, can we take advantage of what Christ accomplished for us on the cross? We need to recognize that the standard for fellowship is God Himself. "God is light and in Him is no darkness at all" (1 John 1:5). If we[23] are walking in any darkness (that is, sin; 1:6) at all, we have closed ourselves off to fellowship with the Lord.

One night this truth hit me very strongly. In discussing a thorny doctrinal issue with a student, my wife, Ruth, came out of the kitchen and suggested an answer that I felt revealed that she didn't understand the issue. I cut her off quite abruptly, and she went back to the kitchen. A short time later, she mentioned her idea again, and I was as ungracious as before. After the student left, my relationship with Ruth was strained, but I managed to ignore it for I go to sleep easily. But it was not easy for Ruth to get to sleep.

I tend to be an early riser, so I was up much before Ruth and on my knees in the other room in prayer. I had hardly begun when God brought to my mind 1 Peter 3:7: "Husbands, likewise, dwell with them with understanding, giving honor to the wife, as to the weaker vessel, and as being heirs together of the grace of life, that your prayers may not be hindered [*enkoptō*, 'to cut into, interrupt']." It was as though God was saying to me, "Your trying to talk with Me is of no use. You have something to take care of with Ruth." I went into the bedroom, and rather than being asleep, she was sitting up in bed reading her Bible. I said, "Honey, I am really sorry for the unkind way I treated you last evening. Will you forgive me?" Her response was beautiful. We hugged and kissed, and then I went back to my place of prayer and had a wonderful time with the Lord. This was a vivid lesson to me about how our fellowship with God is affected when we sin. I couldn't pray effectively until I dealt with this problem. David knew this too. He wrote, "If I regard iniquity in my heart, the Lord will not hear" (Ps. 66:18). Sin hinders our fellowship with God.

In view of the devastating effect of sin, how may a regenerate person have assurance of *fellowship* with God? God has provided two things to enable us to deal with sin, which disrupts fellowship. First, the most basic provision is "walk[ing] in the light" (1 John 1:7). The truth ("light") exposes our sin nature, or capacity from which sin arises, and helps control it. When this is true, we have fellowship with Christ and we are cleansed from potential defilement by the blood of Jesus Christ. If, however, this potential defilement becomes actual and we commit sin, God has given us a second provision: "If we confess our sins, He is faithful and just to forgive us our sins and to cleanse us from all unrighteousness" (1:9). The word "our" is not in the Greek; instead, "sins" is preceded by the word "the." So the verse literally reads "He is faithful and just to forgive us *the sins.*" What sins? The ones we confess. If we confess the sins we know, God forgives us of those sins. But He does more than that. He is also faithful to cleanse us from *all* unrighteousness. Hodges commented, "When I am honest with God and confess the sins I am aware of, His forgiveness and cleansing extend to *everything* that is wrong with me. 'All unrighteousness' is dealt with by His grace so that, after my confession to Him, I can walk with Him, knowing that my harmony with Him is fully repaired. What a perfect provision! Let's not torment ourselves with our unknown failures. When God is ready to reveal them to us, he will (see Phil 3:15). Meanwhile, honest confession of known sin will bring complete restoration to fellowship with our gracious heavenly Father."[24]

These two provisions mean that no believer in Jesus Christ need ever be overcome by his or her sin. There is provision at the cross and at the Father's throne.

Here we have an objective basis for knowing we are in fellowship with God, just as we have an objective basis for assurance of our eternal salvation. So there is no need to continue in doubt.

A second important subject Jesus mentioned in the Upper Room Discourse, which is expanded in 1 John, is the devil, the active agent of darkness and evil. Jesus spoke of him at least four times in that discourse (John 13:2, 27; 14:30; 16:11). When Christians traffic in sin, even seemingly "small" sins, they are walking out of the light into the darkness, out of fellowship with Christ into Satan's trap.

Expounding on Jesus' words about Satan, John referred to him six times as "the wicked one" (1 John 2:13–14; 3:12 [twice]; 5:18–19) and three times as the "devil" (3:8 [twice], 10). "The devil," John wrote, "has sinned from the beginning" (3:8), but of Christ, John said, "In Him there is no sin" (3:5). Now what should we expect to see in the one who *abides* in Him, the sinless One? John answered, "Whoever abides in Him does not sin" (3:6), and "He who says he abides in Him ought himself also to walk just as He walked" (3:6). As noted earlier, several Bible versions say 3:6 should be rendered "does not sin habitually." However, "it cannot be shown anywhere in the New Testament that the present tense can bear this kind of meaning *without the assistance of other words.*"[25] Nor was John saying that sinless perfection can be achieved in this life, for in 1:8, 10 he called such an idea a lie. But he was saying that when a Christian sins, this means he or she is not abiding but is walking in the darkness (1:6). Sin and fellowship with Christ are incompatible. When a believer sins, therefore, that person needs to recognize that he or she has followed the devil. At any given moment in our lives we are saluting one or the other of two masters—either Jesus or Satan, either sin or righteousness.

A believer has a new divine nature, which can never be the source of sin (3:9). When sin takes place in a believer's life, it can only be because he or she is walking in the energy of Satan (like Ananias and Sapphira who were Christians but who were "filled" with Satan, Acts 5:3, not the Holy Spirit). Satan uses the world system to appeal to believers through their old sin nature or capacity to get us to do his will—and when we do, the result is sin. On the other hand, the Holy Spirit uses the Word of God, which is the truth, to appeal to us through our divine nature to do His will—and when we do, the result is always righteousness.

The two parallel statements in 1 John 3:7–8 literally read, "the one who does righteousness is righteous" and "the one who does sin is of the devil." Here John was not talking about the believer's position in Christ; instead he spoke of the practical outworking of the believer's life. The central thrust in 1 John is precisely the same as the Upper Room Discourse: "If we love one another, God abides in us, and His love has been perfected in us" (1 John 4:12; see John 15:9).

CONCLUSION

Sin in a believer's life does not affect his or her regeneration, but it does impair the believer's fellowship with Christ. Assurance of salvation is based solely on belief in Christ. If a person has received the gift of eternal life through faith in Christ, he can rest assured that nothing will alter that. His or her salvation is secure forever and is not dependent on works. However, following regeneration, believers are to do good works, to be faithful to the Lord. They are to abide in Christ, to fellowship with Him. No Christian need doubt his regeneration, because God's Word is true. Jesus said that everyone who believes in Him "has everlasting life, [and] . . . has passed from death into life" (John 5:24)—and God does not lie!

CHAPTER 17
What Is Glorification?

In this study we have seen that salvation has past, present, and future tenses. We have been saved from the penalty of sin forever—"justification salvation"; we are being saved moment by moment from the power of sin—"sanctification salvation"; and with eager anticipation we look forward to being saved from the presence of sin altogether—"glorification salvation." The glorification of the redeemed is so certain that in Romans 8:30 Paul looked on it as an accomplished fact: "And whom He justified, these He also glorified." Looking ahead to our glorification in God's presence Paul wrote, "Knowing the time, that now it is high time to awake out of sleep; for now our salvation [that is, glorification salvation] is nearer than when we first believed. The night is far spent, the day is at hand. Therefore let us cast off the works of darkness, and let us put on the armor of light" (Rom. 13:11–12).

THE REDEMPTION OF OUR BODIES

Our mortal bodies, along with the whole creation, still experience the curse of sin, sickness, and death. "For we know that the whole creation groans and labors with birth pangs together until now. Not only that, but we also who have the firstfruits of the Spirit, even we ourselves groan within ourselves, eagerly waiting for the adoption, the redemption of our body" (Rom. 8:22–23).

Believers are children of God because we have received "the Spirit of adoption" (8:15), that is, the Holy Spirit has adopted us into God's family. But the results of the adoption will not be complete until we receive our resurrection bodies.

As we get older, we can identify with Paul's statement that "our outward man is perishing" (2 Cor. 4:16). But when Christ returns at the Rapture, all church-age believers will be given resurrected bodies. "We shall all be changed—in a moment, in the twinkling of an eye. . . . The dead will be raised incorruptible, and we shall be changed. For this corruptible must put on incorruption, and this mortal must put on immortality" (1 Cor. 15:51–53). Believers already in heaven will receive bodies that will not decompose; the corruptible will become incorruptible. And believers who are still alive at the Rapture will be given bodies like that of Christ; the mortal will put on immortality.

Paul likened death and the resurrection to sowing a seed and the growth of a plant from that seed. "What you sow is not made alive unless it dies. . . . The body is sown in corruption, it is raised in incorruption. . . . It is sown a natural body, it is raised a spiritual body" (15:36, 42, 44). Believers are waiting for this transaction, when our lowly bodies will be made like Christ's resurrection body. As Paul said, "Our citizenship is in heaven, from which we also eagerly wait for the Savior, the Lord Jesus Christ, who will transform our lowly body that it may be conformed to His glorious body, according to the working by which He is able even to subdue all things to Himself" (Phil. 3:20–21). And John put it this way: "Beloved, now we are children of God; and it has not yet been revealed what we shall be, but we know that when He is revealed, we shall be like Him, for we shall see Him as He is" (1 John 3:2).

Looking forward to this glorification salvation, Peter gave praise to God. "Blessed be the God and Father of our Lord Jesus Christ, who according to His abundant mercy has begotten us again to a living hope through the resurrection of Jesus Christ from the dead, to an inheritance incorruptible and undefiled and that does not fade away, reserved in heaven for you, who are kept by the power of God through faith for salvation ready to be revealed in the last time" (1 Pet. 1:3–5). Peter also wrote that "the God of all grace" has "called us to His eternal glory by Christ Jesus" (5:10). Every believer can join with Peter in thanking God that someday their bodies—weak, in pain, frail, dysfunctional—will be changed and made perfect, fit for occupying heaven forever. Because Christ indwells us, He is our "hope of glory" (Col. 1:27).

THE ENTRANCE TO OUR HEAVENLY HOME

What a thrill it is for Ruth and me to listen to Diane Susek sing "Finally Home."

> When engulfed by the terror of tempestuous sea
> Unknown waves before you roll,
> At the end of doubt and peril is eternity,
> Tho fear and conflict seize your soul.
>
> When surrounded by the blackness of the darkest night,
> Oh, how lonely death can be.
> But at the end of this long tunnel is a shining light,
> For death is swallowed up in victory.
>
> But just think of stepping on shore and finding it heaven;
> Of touching a hand, and finding it God;
> Of breathing new air and finding it celestial;
> Of waking up in glory and finding it home.

Everybody longs for a permanent, secure place, and God has set aside such a home for every one of His children. Jesus said, "I am going to prepare a place for you" (John 14:2). Will we be with Jesus? Yes, Jesus said we will be with Him forever. He promised, "I will come again and receive you to Myself; that where I am, there you may be also" (14:3). And He prayed to God, "Father, I desire that they also whom You gave Me may be with Me where I am, that they may behold My glory which You have given me" (17:24).

Our ultimate home will be in the holy city, the New Jerusalem, which God will bring down on the new earth *after* the victorious millennial reign of our Lord Jesus Christ on the present earth. Can you imagine a heavenly high-rise fifteen hundred miles high and fifteen hundred miles square? This is how John described it. In fact, the New Jerusalem will have twelve gates, each one made of a huge pearl and named after a tribe of Israel, and twelve foundations, each one adorned with a different precious gem and named after one of the twelve apostles. The city will be of pure gold, transparent like glass (see Rev. 21:10–21). One of the most wonderful facts about heaven and the new Jerusalem is that there will be no more tears, death, mourning, crying, or pain (21:4). All that will be gone for we will be in God's very presence with new bodies.

One evening after I preached on the New Jerusalem in Revelation 21, a little boy met me at the door with his daddy and said, "Mister, will that building have an elevator?" He knew, of course, that all high-rise buildings have elevators. I said, "Well, how fast can you think from the bottom of that fifteen-hundred-mile-high building to the top?" He thought for a moment or two and then, snapping his fingers, he said, "Just like that." I responded, "That's just how fast you will be able to get from the bottom to the top in your new body." His eyes became huge like saucers as he walked away with a big smile.

THE REWARD OF OUR WORKS

Christ is presently seated at the right Hand of the Father's eternal throne, offering the following invitation to His children: "To him who overcomes I will grant to sit with Me on My throne, as I also overcame and sat down with My Father on His throne" (Rev. 3:21). This possibility leads us to consider the final evaluation of the believer's works, which is mentioned in about one hundred Bible passages,[1] climaxed by Christ's last reminder in the last chapter of the last book: "And behold, I am coming quickly, and My reward is with Me, to give to everyone according to his work" (22:12).

Throughout this study we have emphasized that works have absolutely no part in securing eternal salvation for the sinner. We receive eternal salvation by grace as a gift (Rom. 3:24; 4:5; Eph. 2:8–9), and we shouldn't insult the Giver by trying to pay for His gift, even though it has come at tremendous cost to Him. Augustus Toplady stressed this truth in the words of his gospel song "Rock of Ages": "Nothing in my hand I bring, simply to Thy cross I cling."

But even though we cannot be saved by works (Titus 3:5), believers are to "maintain good works" (3:8) *because* they are saved. Our position in the coming millennial reign of Christ will reflect the way we have used the resources He has given us. What we do in this life will affect our life to come.

I am becoming today by what I do (sanctification salvation)

with what He gave me (justification salvation)

what I will be in the life to come (glorification salvation).

Today is a day of becoming (sanctification salvation);

then is a day of being what I have become (glorification salvation).

Today is a day of change (sanctification salvation);

then is a day of no change (glorification salvation).

No punitive judgment lies ahead for any child of God. Jesus promised forcefully, "Most assuredly, I say to you, he who hears My word and believes in Him who sent Me has everlasting life, and shall not come into judgment, but has passed from death into life" (John 5:24). If a believer in Jesus Christ were ever to be punished for even one sin, God would be unrighteous. Even in our legal system we understand that when a person's sin has been paid for once, that penalty cannot be exacted again. We have been once-for-all redeemed by the priceless, precious blood of Christ (Rom. 3:23–24; 1 Pet. 1:18–19).

How then do we explain 2 Corinthians 5:10, which states that "we must all appear before the judgment seat of Christ, that each one may receive the things done in the body, according to what he has done, whether good or bad"? In what way will each Christian "give account of himself to God" (Rom. 14:12)?

These verses are not referring to punitive judgment. Instead, they are talking about the coming judgment seat of Christ, when He in heaven will evaluate the extent to which His followers have invested the resources God gave them. Jesus put this in graphic form in His parable of the talents (Matt. 25:14–30) and of the minas (Luke 19:11–27). Christ will take a good look at how well we invested our eternal "stock portfolio." Paul stated that as stewards (managers of what belongs to another) we are to be faithful in managing what has been entrusted to us. "It is required in stewards that one be found faithful" (1 Cor. 4:2). The returns of our Christian service will be profit or loss. The word "receive," used in Matthew 25:27; 2 Corinthians 5:10; and Colossians 3:24, is the Greek word *komizō*, which means "to pay back, or to requite." Isn't it amazing that Jesus, having given us the resources, actually wants to reward us for the way we have used them?

We ought to watch carefully for good "investment" opportunities. They may even be found in unlikely circumstances such as when people "revile and persecute you, and say all kinds of evil against you falsely for My sake. Rejoice and be exceedingly glad, for *great is your reward in heaven*" (Matt. 5:11–12, italics added). Do we ever think of persecution as a potential investment in future rewards? Too often we think only in terms of investing money for the Lord's work. William Tyndale made a great investment in the Lord's work by his translating the Bible into English. Because of his work he was imprisoned, strangled to death, and his body burned at the stake. He is now considered "the father of the English Bible." What a capacity he developed for future service in Christ's coming kingdom!

In the Sermon on the Mount Jesus Christ specified how His followers can use their daily circumstances to gain reward in the kingdom. In "the disciples' prayer" the first petition focuses on the coming kingdom ("Your kingdom come," Matt. 6:10), and then Jesus spoke of the need to "lay up for yourselves treasures in heaven" (6:20). After discussing how His disciples should react to persecution (10:16–39), Jesus concluded with words of strong encouragement on rewards (10:40–42). He also spoke of rewards in 16:27; 19:29; 25:21, 23, 40. And, as previously noted, from heaven Jesus Christ urged the churches of Asia Minor to focus on His coming kingdom reign (Rev. 2:5, 7, 10, 17, 23, 25–28; 3:5, 10, 12, 21). These teachings of Jesus about future rewards are a great motivational force for faithful service to Christ.

Paul, too, challenged believers to strive for the "prize" (1 Cor. 9:24–27). He also pointed out the seriousness of potential loss (3:5–15). James, Peter, and John all discussed the place of believers' rewards (James 1:12; 1 Pet. 5:4; 2 Pet. 1:5–11; Rev. 2:10). And various crowns are mentioned (1 Thess. 2:19; 2 Tim. 4:6–8; James 1:12; 1 Pet. 5:4). The writer of the Epistle to the Hebrews wrote of Moses, who was motivated by the prospect of reward (Heb. 11:26), and of others who were tortured and who will "obtain a better resurrection" (12:35).

When Peter asked Jesus what he would receive in return for leaving everything for Him, Christ did not belittle his asking or accuse him of self-seeking. Instead, He said that those who forsake their possessions and family for His sake would receive reward much greater than what they gave up (Matt. 19:27, 29). When we invest what we have for Christ, the remuneration always greatly exceeds the renunciation. Receiving rewards for faithful service and for diligent investments for Christ will be one of the blessings of our glorification in heaven. Having "treasures in heaven" is mentioned in several verses (Matt. 6:19–21; 19:21; Luke 12:32–33; see 1 Tim. 6:17–19).

THE ASSIGNMENT OF POSITIONS OF GLORY

Rewards given to believers will not be for the purpose of honoring Jesus' followers. Instead rewards will enable us to serve Christ and bring *Him* glory in His coming magnificent reign, the climax of all history. We will be involved in various administrative responsibilities in the Millennium. Paul wrote, "Do you not know that the saints will judge the world? . . . Do you not know that we shall judge angels?" (1 Cor. 6:2–3). This stimulated Elsa Raud's imagination concerning the administrative needs in the coming kingdom: "Can we even imagine what a fascinating, diversified future awaits us? Just consider how far-reaching will be the administrative activities of the church. Heavenly realms now unknown to men, stellar spaces whose limits defy astronomers, with these we then shall be well acquainted. Splendid, strong angels, mighty angelic princes shall submit to our authority because we are in Christ Jesus. And when we turn our thoughts to this troubled world, how we rejoice in the prospect that one day we shall have our part in bringing its inhabitants to love their King and Savior who died for them."[2] That is only one small picture of the administrative duties Christ will give believers who have demonstrated themselves worthy of the kingdom.

THE ETERNAL REIGN WITH CHRIST

Earlier we spoke of the fact that every child of God will be glorified (Rom. 8:30), that the body of every believer will be tranformed to be like Jesus' glorious body (Phil. 3:20–21), and that every Christian will reside in the holy city, the New Jerusalem, and be with Jesus Christ forever (John 14:3). Those things are not conditional. But reigning with Christ *is* conditional. Of course, we will all "live together with Him" (1 Thess. 5:10; see also Rom. 6:8; 2 Tim. 2:11); that will be true of all believers. But reigning with Christ is conditioned on faithful service (2 Tim. 2:12; see also Matt. 25:23; 1 Cor. 4:2; 2 Cor. 5:10). This is why Paul wrote, "But I discipline my body and bring it into subjection, lest, when I have preached to others, I myself should become disqualified" (1 Cor. 9:27). Disqualified from what? The prize (9:24–25). Later, as he faced execution, he wrote that because he had "finished the race" and had "kept the faith," he would receive a "crown of righteousness" (2 Tim. 4:7–8).[3]

Paul stated in Romans 8:17 that "if indeed we suffer with Him . . . we [will] also be glorified together." And yet in 8:30 he affirmed that all believers are "glorified." How are we to understand the difference? Dillow answers this question this way:

> In v. 17 the glorification is conditional and only for those who suffer with Christ, but in v. 30 it is unconditional and is for all who are justified. In v. 17 it is a sharing in the glory of Messiah, but in v. 30 it refers to our own glorification. In v. 17 the verb is "be glorified with," and in v. 30 the verb is "glorified." In v. 17 it refers to the wonders of the messianic era, but in v. 30 it refers to our ultimate conformity into the image of Christ at the resurrection of the body. In v. 17 the verb is in a purpose clause implying intent and not necessarily certainty. But in v. 30 it is an indicative implying the certainty of a presently achieved fact. Verse 17 is in a context which stresses

exhortation. It is a challenge to persevere in order that we might share in Christ's glory. But v. 30 is a statement of fact that we have already, in a proleptic and anticipatory sense, entered into that glory.[4]

Romans 8:18 points out that "the glory which shall be revealed in us" far exceeds "the sufferings of this present time." To be worthy of co-rulership with Christ makes our present sufferings all worthwhile. This prospect keeps us from discouragement. "Therefore we do not lose heart. Even though our outward man is perishing, yet the inward man is being renewed day by day. For our light affliction, which is but for a moment, is working for us a far more exceeding and eternal weight of glory, while we do not look at the things which are seen, but at the things which are not seen. For the things which are seen are temporary, but the things which are not seen are eternal" (2 Cor. 4:16–18).

When we are with the Lord in heaven, our salvation from the penalty of sin (justification) and from the power of sin (sanctification) will be complete, for we will then be delivered from the very presence of sin (glorification). We will be glorified—home at last with our precious Savior forever!

APPENDIX A

Will Infants Who Die Go to Heaven?

* This material is taken from Roy B. Zuck, *Precious in His Sight: Childhood and Children in the Bible* (Grand Rapids: Baker, 1996), and is used by permission.

Jesus made some interesting, even startling, statements about children. Included in those comments were his words to the disciples, "The kingdom of heaven [or 'of God'] belongs to such as these" (Matt. 19:14, NASB; Mark 10:14, NASB; Luke 18:16, NASB); or as the New American Standard Bible puts it, "Of such is the kingdom of heaven [or 'of God']." This indicates that adults who are like children in acknowledging their lowly and helpless condition will enter God's kingdom. But the Greek *toiautē* ("of such as these") also indicates that children too are in God's kingdom. And as Luke wrote, this includes infants (Luke 18:15–17). But how do those young children get into the kingdom? Undoubtedly, many infants get there by death. The high infant mortality in many countries of the world now and in past centuries suggests that numerous young children are in heaven. Jesus' statement, however, should not be understood as meaning that all children, regardless of their age, are members of God's kingdom.[1] Other children, who live several years beyond infancy and then receive Christ as their Savior (receiving the kingdom as a child; Mark 10:15; Luke 18:17), go to heaven when they die. Having been regenerated by their faith in Christ, they obviously belong to the kingdom of God (John 3:3). They are among those "little ones who believe in me," as Jesus said (Matt. 18:6).

When the baby boy born illegitimately to David and Bathsheba became ill, David prayed and fasted for his healing, lying in anguish on the ground each night. But a week after the baby became sick, he died (2 Sam. 12:15–18). Then David told his servants, "I will go to him, but he will not return to me" (12:23). This speaks of the finality of death, but it also speaks of David's intense desire to be with his son. Some say David was referring only to his own death but not to his being in conscious fellowship with his son after death.[2] However, there would hardly be any comfort in David's saying he would die too. Instead, this verse suggests that his son was experiencing after death a conscious existence in God's presence, and that David anticipated some day joining him. This fact has been a source of great comfort to many Christian parents whose infants have died. "The idea of meeting his child in the unsconscious grave could not have rationally comforted him; nor could the thought of meeting him in hell have cheered his spirit; but the thought of meeting him in heaven had in itself the power of turning his weeping into joy."[3]

Though the Bible does not explicitly state that deceased infants of *unsaved* parents go to heaven, Jesus' words to the disciples and David's words to his servants may well imply that this is the case. For this reason a number of authors assert that heaven is occupied with many children, perhaps with even more children than adults. In the nineteenth century John Newton wrote that the number of infants in heaven "so greatly exceeds the aggregate of adult believers that, comparatively speaking, the kingdom may be said to consist of little children."[4] Charles Spurgeon wrote, "I rejoice to know that the souls of all infants, as soon as they die, speed their way to paradise. Think what a multitude there is of them!"[5]

How can there be in heaven a countless number of people from every nation, tribe, people and language (Rev. 7:9, NIV)? Surely not every tribe of people around the world has adult believers. Is it not possible, therefore, that a number of tribes will be represented by children who die in infancy? And if this is the case, this would point to the probability that infants of even unbelieving parents go to heaven.

Another argument in support of infants being in heaven is Jesus' words that "Your Father in heaven is not willing that any of these little ones should be lost" (Matt. 18:14, NIV). In view of that fact, "how can it be that little children who are set before [the disciples] as ... patterns for imitation ... should perish?"[6] Since it is the Lord's will that these little ones not perish, it is clear that at death they "go to be among the blessed in that heaven, to the kingdom [to] which ... they belong...."[7]

Almost half a century ago John Linton advocated the idea that there will be no babies in heaven. He argued for this view by saying that since veryone in heaven will have a resurrected body, no one will be resurrected to "the weakness of infancy, or the unwisdom of childhood, but into a full grown man."[8] However, this wrongly assumes that an infant in heaven "still needs to grow to maturity," and that his resurrection would "not be a work of perfection."[9] Is it not possible that infants can be resurrected with perfect bodies and still be infants?

By what means will deceased infants go to heaven? Numerous answers have been given to this question. First, some say all children who die as infants are taken to heaven because of the doctrine of universalism. That is, since everyone will ultimately be saved and no one will be in hell, infants too will naturally be in heaven, even though they had no opportunity to believe.

However, the teaching that all will ultimately be saved runs counter to Bible verses that affirm the eternal damnation of the unsaved (e.g., Matt. 25:46; John 3:16, 18; 3:36; Rev. 20:15). And yet this is not to deny the heavenly home of dead infants. It simply means that universalism is not the basis of their salvation.

Second, some affirm a heavenly destiny for infants because they are born innocent, without sin. Clifford Ingle, a Southern Baptist seminary professor, writes that a child "does not inherit lostness [from Adam]; he chooses it."[10] All persons, Ingle says,

> are born with a tendency toward sin; all are destined to sin. However, the individual is not responsible for the sins of the [human] race or his inherited nature. He becomes an actual sinner in the eyes of God when, as a morally responsible person, he chooses sin and rebels against God. Thus there is a time between birth and moral accountability when the child is not guilty for sin.[11]

John Inchley believes that children are not "in a state of being lost from

God," and that until they deliberately refuse Christ, they belong to him.[12] "We must resist the temptation Marlin Jeschke writes, "to place the human race into only two classes, the saved and the lost. We are required to recognize also a third class, the innocent. . . . "[13] However, this view that children are born innocent and without an inherited sin nature conflicts with Scriptures that teach that everyone enters the world as a sinner. "Even though innocent compared to adults who consciously sin, infants and all who can't believe are under the curse of Adam's sin."[14] "In Adam all die" (1 Cor. 15:22). God told Noah after the flood that he would not bring about another flood of that magnitude "even though every inclination of [man's] heart is evil from childhood" (Gen. 8:21, NIV). Solomon wrote, "Folly is bound up in the heart of a child" (Prov. 22:15, NIV). And David said he was born "sinful at birth" (Ps. 51:5, NIV), and that "even from birth the wicked go astray" (58:3, NIV). As Paul affirmed, "There is no one righteous, not even one" (Rom. 3:10, NIV). All are "under sin" (3:9, NIV) and under God's wrath (John 3:36, NIV), and that includes children.

Everyone is born with a sin nature, inherited from Adam, because all mankind was somehow in Adam when he sinned (Rom. 5:12). His sin plunged the entire human race into a stance of guilt before God, because all sinned "in Adam." Therefore, people sin because they are sinners; it is not that they become sinners by sinning.[15] This means that because all infants come with a sin nature, they are all lost and condemned. To say infants are neutral or innocent with respect to sin, and that they are not sinners until they knowingly commit acts of sin, overlooks these significant Scripture verses about the universality of sin. "A theology of childhood salvation must begin with the point that all people, including children, are sinful and in need of redemption."[16] Therefore, there must be some reason other than sinlessness that accounts for infants being in heaven.

A third explanation is that when infants die they immediately mature and are then given opportunity to place their faith in Christ for salvation. This view, first proposed by Gregory of Nyssa of the fourth century, builds on the conviction that faith is necessary for salvation.[17] Buswell has suggested the unlikely view that immediately before death the intelligence of the infant is enlarged so that the child can accept Christ as Savior.[18]

This view, however, is only conjecture; it has no biblical support. If infants immediately before or after death are given the opportunity to be saved, this suggests that some will go to heaven and others will not. And if this enablement to believe occurs after death, where is the child while he is confronted with the claims of Christ? This view wrongly suggests a neutral state after death, before one's final destiny in heaven or hell.

Fourth, infants who die will be in heaven because they are elected by God. Ulrich Zwingli, the Swiss Reformer, asserted that all children of believing parents are among the elect and, therefore, will be saved, and that probably dying infants of non-Christian parents are also among the elect. Many Reformed theologians held this view. Charles Hodge based the belief that "all who die in infancy are saved" on Romans 5:18–19 NIV, "Consequently, just as the result of one trespass was condemnation for all men, so also the result of one act of righteousness was justification that brings life for all men. For just as through the disobedience of the one man the many were made sinners, so also through the obedience of the one man the many will be made righteous." He also referred to Romans 5:20 NIV, "But where sin increased, grace increased all the more." Warfield also defended the view that all infants who die go to heaven by pointing out that for infants God's electing grace supersedes their inborn sin nature because God has chosen them.[19] The Westminster Confession says, "Elect infants, dying in infancy, are regenerated and saved by Christ through the Spirit."[20] While this statement does not explicitly affirm that all dying infants are elect (the words "elect infants" leave the question open), most Presbyterians would, no doubt, affirm that all infants who die are in fact included among the elect.[21]

Fifth, infants can be saved by the "baptism of desire," that is, if they desired baptism but were unable to obtain it before they died, they would go to heaven. This view was held in the ninth century by Hincmar of Rheims (d. 882).[22] Martin Luther applied the idea of the baptism of desire to Christian parents, saying that their desire for their children's baptism, even if not carried out, guarantees their offspring's salvation. However, how can an infant desire baptism? And how does a parent's mere desire substitute for a child's salvation? Also, this view does not adequately address the question of infants of unsaved parents, who may not desire salvation for their young or may know nothing of salvation and baptism. This suggests that salvation for those infants is not available and that they are lost forever.

A sixth view maintains that all infants who die will be regenerated because they have not willfully rejected Christ.[23] This view follows this line of reasoning: (1) Only those who consciously reject Christ are condemned to hell. (2) Infants cannot knowingly turn from Christ. (3) Therefore, all dying infants will be in heaven, even though they are born sinners and do not exercise faith. The problem with this view is that it makes eternal damnation dependent on a willful refusal to believe in Jesus Christ. If this is the basis of judgment in hell, how can those who never heard of Christ be condemned? Therefore, the basis of the condemnation is not rejection of Christ, but the commitment of sins based on one's inherited sin nature. "In Adam all die" (1 Cor. 15:22; cf. Rom. 5:12). Paul reasoned in Romans 1 that all are under the guilt of sin and the wrath of God because of their sin. Therefore, only God's grace can atone for the sin of infants. This leads to the seventh view, which I prefer over the other views.

A seventh view is that all infants enjoy heavenly bliss not because they are born sinless or because they mature immediately after death so they can exercise faith or because they are elect or had a desire for baptism or salvation or because they did not willingly reject Christ, but because of the redemptive work of Christ on the cross. Like everyone, infants need salvation. And salvation is only through Christ. Therefore, even though infants cannot exercise faith in Him, He can remove their depravity. "If they be saved, it must be entirely by the sovereign mercy and positive operation of God. . . . All redeemed sinners owe their salvation to sovereign grace . . . but the salvation of infants is with peculiar circumstances of [God's] favour."[24] In July 1525, the Anabaptist theologian Balthasar Hübmaier, writing against the Swiss Reformers' practice of infant baptism, stated that while we cannot know for sure on what basis unbaptized infants go to heaven, God no doubt saves them because of His grace.[25] Also, Spurgeon said infants enter heaven "as a matter of free grace with no reference to anything they have done."[26] Downs, Lightner, and Lockyer all concur.[27]

Sanders thinks it is inconsistent to say God saves some (adults) by faith but others (infants) without faith.[28] This objection is answerable by noting that in all cases God's grace provides salvation. Even though infants cannot hear the Word and, therefore, cannot exercise faith (Rom. 10:17), God need not be limited, as Calvin noted, because He works in ways we cannot always perceive, and He can still bestow His grace.[29]

An eighth view is that infants qualify for entrance to heaven by virtue of their having been baptized. Roman Catholicism maintains that infant baptism removes the stain of original sin. "Baptism . . . signifies that by the power of the Holy Ghost all stain and defilement of sin is inwardly washed away, and that the soul is enriched and adorned with the admirable gift of heavenly justification. . . . "[30] The recently published new *Catechism of the Catholic Church* states, "Through Baptism we are freed from sin and reborn as sons of God; we become members of Christ, are incorporated into the Church and made sharers in her mission: Baptism is the sacrament of regeneration through water in the word."[31] Since the sacrament of infant baptism is necessary for salvation, according to Catholicism, infants must be baptized in order for them to qualify for heaven. The logical corollary of this position is that unbaptized infants do not enter heaven. In fact, according to Augustine (A. D. 354–430), "the wrath of God abides on them," they "remain in darkness," and they are eternally doomed, though their punishment is less severe than that of others.[32] As Sanders points out, Augustine's position was the dominant view of the Western church throughout the Middle Ages.[33] Even today this harsh view is held by some Reformed theologians. After more than one hundred people, including a number of young children, died in the bombing of a federal building in Oklahoma City in 1995, Sproul chided Billy Graham for saying in the memorial service that innocent children who died in the bombing are in God's arms in heaven. Sproul wrote that all those who died without having received Christ as Savior, *whether adults or children*," are experiencing . . . anguish and torment in hell."[34] A number of church leaders and theologians, however, believed that unbaptized infants do go to heaven, including Victor, John Wycliffe, the Lollards, and John Calvin.[35]

To soften the severity of the Augustinian position, the Roman Catholic Church developed the idea of Limbo *(limbus infantum)*, a neutral place for infants who die unbaptized. In this place between heaven and hell, children experience neither bliss nor torment.[36] While this is not an official dogma of the Catholic Church, it is not denied either. But, as McCarthy explains, "In discussing the fate of unbaptized infants, modern Catholicism usually entrusts their souls to the mercy of God, making no mention of limbo.... Nonetheless, even today, when a Catholic persists in asking where unbaptzied infants go when they die, the answer usually comes back, 'Limbo.' "[37] No scriptural support can be given for this position, however. As Beasley-Murray wrote, "only an evil doctrine of God and man sets them [children dying before the age of responsibility] among the lost or in limbo...."[38]

Obviously, if baptism is essential for salvation, many infants will not be in heaven. The Roman Catholic position limits salvation unduly, makes salvation obtainable not by faith but by a sacrament or work, [39] and in condemning many infants to limbo obliterates the view that Christ's atoning work removes, by His grace, the guilt of original sin for all infants and others who cannot believe.[40]

APPENDIX B

Repentance and Salvation

*This material is taken from Robert N. Wilkin, *Confident in Christ: Living by Faith Really Works* (Irving, Tex.: Grace Evangelical Society, 1999), and is used by permission.

In the gospel debate repentance is a hot topic. One of the most famous questions in the Bible is "What must I do to be saved?" (Acts 16:30). The correct answer to that question is a matter of life and death, eternal life and eternal death.

Must a person repent in order to be saved? If the answer is yes, then what specifically is repentance? If the answer is no, then what *is* the purpose of repentance? Why does God call all men everywhere to repent? (Acts 17:30).

I wrote my doctoral dissertation on this very issue, because it is arguably the single most confusing area regarding the gospel. In this appendix we will consider the meaning and benefits of repentance.

WHAT MUST I DO TO BE SAVED?
THE PLACE OF REPENTANCE IN ETERNAL SALVATION

Paul's answer to the question, "What must I do to be saved?" was simple, straightforward, and clear, "Believe on the Lord Jesus Christ, and you will be saved" (Acts 16:30–31, NKJV). The Lord Jesus and His apostles were united on this point. There is but one condition of eternal salvation, faith in Christ (see, for example, John 3:16–18; 5:24; 6:47; 11:25–27; 20:31; Acts

10:43; Ephesians 2:8–9). Another way of saying this is that there is but one condition of justification before God, faith in Christ (see, for example, Romans 3:28; 4:1–8; Galatians 2:16; 3:6–16). Justification is by faith alone, *sola fide* as the Reformers put it so succinctly in Latin.

Since eternal salvation is by faith alone, what is the role of repentance in eternal salvation? There are three options:

1. Repentance is a condition of eternal salvation since it is a synonym for faith in Christ. Thus, "He who believes in Me has everlasting life" is identical to "He who repents has everlasting life."
2. Repentance is a condition of eternal salvation since it is a necessary precursor to faith in Christ. Thus one cannot believe in Christ until he first repents; that is, until he first recognizes his sinfulness and need of a Savior.
3. Repentance is not a condition of eternal salvation and is neither a synonym for faith in Christ nor a necessary precursor to faith in Christ.

If we can determine what repentance is, then it will be clear which of these three possibilities is indeed correct. Let's turn now to the meaning of repentance.

WHAT IS REPENTANCE?

The meaning of words is determined by examining their usage. Thus to determine the meaning of repentance, we need to look at some of the fifty-eight New Testament uses of *repent* and *repentance*.

Jesus said to a Jewish audience, "The men of Nineveh will rise up in the judgment with this generation and condemn it, because they repented at the preaching of Jonah; and indeed a greater than Jonah is here" (Matthew 12:41, NKJV).

Jesus was here rebuking the people of Israel, most of whom failed to repent even at the preaching of the Son of God! The men of Nineveh repented centuries earlier under the preaching of a much lesser prophet than Jesus. Jonah was a reluctant prophet who didn't want the Ninevites to repent.

What the Lord Jesus means by repentance here is evident when we look at the repentance of the Ninevites. In response to Jonah's proclamation of coming judgment, all of the people of Nineveh fasted and put on sackcloth (Jonah 3:5) and "turned from their evil ways" (Jonah 3:10, NIV). The repentance of the Ninevites was not faith in Christ, nor was it a necessary precursor to faith in Christ. They decided to turn from their sins because they hoped to escape the destruction of their city and the widespread loss of lives which Jonah had proclaimed: "Who can tell if God will turn and relent, and turn away His fierce anger, so that we may not perish?" (Jonah 3:9, NKJV).

The apostle John wrote prophetically about what will happen in the coming Tribulation, "And they did not repent of their murders or their sorceries or their sexual immorality or their thefts" (Revelation 9:21, NKJV). Once again, repentance is not faith in Christ or a necessary precursor to that, but it is a decision to turn from one's sinful ways, which the people in question did not do, in spite of the terrible Tribulational judgments they were experiencing.

Jesus taught the apostles about repentance when He said, "If your brother sins against you, rebuke him; and if he repents, forgive him. And if he sins against you seven times in a day, and seven times in a day returns to you, saying, 'I repent,' you shall forgive him" (Luke 17:3–4, NKJV). Again, repentance here is neither faith in Christ, nor a necessary precursor to faith in Christ, it is a decision to turn from one's sins.

All fifty-eight New Testament references to repentance bear this out. In each case repentance is a decision to turn from one's sins. It is never a synonym for faith in Christ or a necessary precursor to faith.

FURTHER EVIDENCE THAT REPENTANCE ISN'T FAITH OR A NECESSARY PRECURSOR TO FAITH

Since repentance isn't in John's Gospel, it isn't a condition. The word *repentance* isn't found in John's Gospel. Yet the Fourth Gospel is the only book in all of Scripture whose stated purpose is evangelistic, that is, to tell unbelievers what they must do to have eternal life (John 20:31). Therefore, it is extremely telling that the words *repent (metanoeō)* and *repentance (metanoia)* do not occur there. This shows that repentance is *not* a synonym for faith in Christ and that it is *not* a necessary precursor to faith in Christ. If either were the case, *the* book on evangelism would have said so.

The apostle John had to exert considerable effort to avoid any reference to repentance, since he heard both John the Baptist and the Lord Jesus preach repentance. John was careful to include various synonyms for faith, yet he never mentioned repentance. If repentance were a condition of eternal life, John would have said so. That he doesn't proves that it isn't.

Some object that this is an argument from silence. However, it is really an argument *about* silence. Let's say that a retired colonel who served under General Patton in World War II wrote a book about the greatest generals of the twentieth century and yet he never mentioned General Patton in his book. Wouldn't an obvious conclusion be that this writer did not consider General Patton to be one of the greatest generals of the twentieth century. In fact, wouldn't it be a certain conclusion?

So, too, when John is writing to tell people what they must do to have eternal life, and he doesn't even mention repentance, a subject he was very familiar with, and one he was even commanded by our Lord to proclaim (Luke 24:47), it is certain that repentance isn't a condition of eternal life.

Since repentance isn't in the Book of Galatians, it isn't a condition. The Book of Galatians is Paul's defense of his gospel. He repeatedly mentions that faith in Christ is the only condition of justification. He never once mentions repentance. Surely if repentance was a necessary precursor to faith in Christ, or a synonym for faith in Christ, Paul would have indicated this in his defense of his gospel.

The belated repentance of believers in Ephesus shows it isn't a condition. Ephesus was a city known for its occult practices. When the seven sons of Sceva, the Jewish chief priest, tried to exorcise a demon using those practices by substituting the name of Jesus for the normal secret appellations they would have used, the evil spirit attacked them (Acts 19:14–16). When the report of the incident got out, fear fell upon all the inhabitants of Ephesus, including the believers there. Note how *the believers* responded, "And many *who had believed* came confessing and telling their deeds. Also, many of those who had practiced magic brought their books together and burned them in the sight of all. And they counted up the value of them, and it totaled fifty thousand pieces of silver" (Acts 19:18–19), emphasis added).

The ones confessing their deeds and burning their magic books were those "who had believed." Past tense. Paul ministered and led people to faith in Christ in Ephesus for two years (Acts 19:10). Thus, those who repented had been Christians for up to two years before they gave up their magic books! Few sins are more grievous than occultism. Yet these people came to faith in Christ without giving up their occult practices and books first! Clearly their repentance followed their faith and regeneration.[1]

COMMONLY ASKED QUESTIONS ABOUT REPENTANCE

Didn't Jesus say that those who don't repent will perish? Yes, He did. In Luke 13:3, 5, He said, "Unless you repent you will all likewise perish." However, the word *perish* does not always refer to eternal condemnation (as it does, for example, in John 3:16). In many contexts it refers to temporal judgment and death.[2] That is surely the case here, as the context makes crystal clear.

Notice the word *likewise* in the statement by the Lord. The occasion for Jesus' remark was that some "told Him about the Galileans whose blood Pilate had mingled with their sacrifices" (Luke 13:1). In other words, Pilate killed some worshippers. In Luke 13:3, 5, "perishing" refers to physical destruction and death. And, in fact, Israel did not repent, and during the Jewish Wars (66–70 A.D.) the nation was destroyed and many in the nation died.

Doesn't the Parable of the Prodigal Son teach that repentance is necessary for eternal salvation? Well, many understand it in precisely that way. Yet the context suggests a completely different understanding. A fact most fail to take into account is that the prodigal was a son of his father before he went to the far country, when he was in the far country, and when he returned from the far country. He didn't become a son of his father when he repented.

Since the father in the parable surely represents God, the son illustrates a child of God who has strayed and who needs to repent to get back in fellowship with God. Whenever a believer is out of fellowship, God waits with open arms to take him back, if he but comes to his senses.

Doesn't the Great Commission in Luke include the preaching of repentance? Yes. Jesus told His followers "that repentance and remission of sins should be preached in His name to all nations, beginning at Jerusalem" (Luke 24:47, NKJV). However, we must remember the Great Commission was not merely a commission to evangelize. It was also a commmission to disciple those who believe. In fact, in some expressions of the Great Commission the Lord only spoke of discipleship.

In Matthew 28:18–20 the Lord told the disciples to make disciples by baptizing them and teaching them to observe all that He had taught them. We don't conclude from that, do we, that baptism and instruction in discipleship are conditions of eternal life? In the same way, the Great Commission in Luke concerns discipleship. Repentance is indeed a condition of fellowship with God and of the forgiveness associated with that fellowship (see Luke 5:32; 15:4–32). We know from 1 John 1:9 as well that believers need ongoing fellowship forgiveness from God.

Didn't Paul say that repentance leads to salvation? Yes, he did. In 2 Corinthians 7:10 Paul wrote, "Godly sorrow produces repentance leading to salvation." However, we must observe the context to see what type of "salvation" or deliverance is in view. Paul was speaking of the deliverance *of believers* from temporal judgment, not of the deliverance of unbelievers from eternal judgment. Those whom Paul was addressing were "beloved" (verse 1, NKJV). He wrote them a previous letter rebuking them for tolerating blatant sin in their midst. Paul said, "Even if I made you sorry with my letter, I do not regret it." Why? Because "your sorrow led to repentance . . . that you might suffer loss from us in nothing. For godly sorrow produces repentance leading to salvation, not to be regretted; but the sorrow of the world produces death" (2 Corinthians 7:8–10, NKJV).

Paul's point is that if a person is sorry for his sins, but doesn't repent, he is on the path of death. God judges unrepentant sin. Sorrow for sin won't win any release from the punishment. However, the person who is both sorry for his sin and repents is on the path of life. God delivers him from ongoing temporal judgment, just as He delivered the Ninevites from judgment when they repented.

Didn't both John the Baptist and Jesus say, "Repent, for the kingdom of heaven is at hand"? Yes, they did. Compare Matthew 3:2, NKJV and 4:17,

NKJV. However, it is wrong to conclude that what they meant was that in order for an individual to enter God's kingdom, he or she must repent.

John the Baptist and Jesus were preaching to national Israel. They were calling the entire nation to repent in light of the nearness of the kingdom.

God has given only one condition for individuals to enter God's kingdom, faith in Christ. However, He has given *two conditions* for the kingdom to come to the nation of Israel: faith in Christ and repentance. Jesus stated both of these conditions in Mark 1:15 NKJV, "Repent, and believe in the gospel."

At the end of the Tribulation the only Jews who will be alive will be repentant believers. If Israel had responded to the preaching of Jesus and John the Baptist, then the kingdom could have come to national Israel then, rather than later.

Isn't the change-of-mind view clear on the gospel? This view defines repentance as a change of mind, not as a decision to turn from one's sins. It suggests that repentance is sometimes given in Scripture as a condition of eternal salvation and that there the change of mind in view is a change of mind about Christ. In other words, in this understanding repentance is sometimes a synonym for faith in Christ.

As one who held the change-of-mind view for a long time, I certainly agree that it is a view that maintains the clarity of the gospel. Many Free Grace people hold that view and find great comfort in it.

However, as I reflect on the way I presented the gospel when I held that view, I realize that I didn't bring up repentance. I told people that in order to have eternal life they simply had to believe in Christ. The only time I would discuss repentance with someone when witnessing would be when he or she brought it up.

I suspect this is the case for most Free Grace people who hold the change-of-mind view. If believing in Christ is the sole condition, it makes sense to tell people to believe.

I realized even when I held the change-of-mind view that there was a risk in even admitting to someone that they had to repent to have eternal life. Most people think of repentance as a decision to turn from one's sins. Thus when I would say that repentance is indeed a condition, they could reject my definition of repentance (as being clearly contradicted by the context), and yet accept my statement that repentance is required.

While the change-of-mind view is not contrary to the gospel, it is contrary to Scripture in the sense that it is not taught in the Bible. The Lord used His Word to cause me to abandon that view. And, for that reason I now encourage others to change their minds about repentance as well.

WHY, THEN, THE CALLS TO REPENTANCE?

If the calls to repentance were not calls to eternal salvation, what were they calls to? There are, as we have seen above, four reasons why people, individually and nationally, should repent.

For believers and unbelievers to escape temporal judgment. As we have already seen, the Ninevites escaped temporal judgment because they repented at the preaching of Jonah. Both believers and unbelievers are wise to repent so that they escape judgment in this life. This is true not only individually, but nationally as well.

For Israel to receive the kingdom. When John the Baptist and Jesus said, "Repent, for the kingdom of heaven is at hand" (Matthew 3:2; 4:17, NKJV), they weren't telling individuals present that they had to repent to have eternal salvation. Individuals are guaranteed eternal life simply on the basis of faith in Christ. Actually, Jesus and His forerunner were calling *the nation* to turn back to the Lord so that the kingdom might come to Israel at that time.

Both the Old and New Testaments say that the Messiah will not set up His kingdom until the nation has come to faith in the Messiah *and* turned from its wicked ways. While individuals are guaranteed participation in the coming kingdom just by believing in Christ, the national participation of Israel in that kingdom requires both faith *and* repentance. Jesus told the nation, "Repent, and believe in the gospel" (Mark 1:15, NKJV). Jesus called for more than believing the gospel. If believing the gospel is sufficient for justification, and it is, then the Lord was clearly calling for more than justification here. He was calling for justification *and* sanctification. Faith and repentance.

During the Tribulation, the nation of Israel will indeed do both of these things. It will come to faith in the Messiah and it will turn from its wicked ways. The coming of the millennial kingdom will follow Israel's repentance and faith.

For believers to return to fellowship with God. If a believer turns his back on God and fails to confess his known sins (1 John 1:9, NKJV), his fellowship with God is broken. In order to restore that fellowship a believer must repent (Luke 15:11–32, NKJV). While there is but one condition of eternal salvation, there are two conditions of restoring fellowship with God, faith and repentance.[3] The calls to repentance are invitations to renewed fellowship with God, not proclamations of the gospel.

For unbelievers to get right with God. While repentance is not a condition of eternal salvation, God is indeed a rewarder of those who diligently seek Him (Hebrews 11:6). Let's say that an unbelieving couple has two small children who have never been to church. It's been years since the parents prayed, read the Bible, or went to church. Now they decide for the good of the family to get right with God. They start going to church, reading the Bible to their kids, and praying together as a family. Does this guarantee the family's eternal salvation? No. However, it makes them more likely to hear and believe the message that will save them.

Cornelius was a God-fearing Gentile who, before he came to faith in Christ, diligently sought God through prayer and the giving of alms. And, while those things are not conditions of eternal life, they did get God's attention. He sent an angel to tell him, "Your prayers and your alms have come up for a memorial before God. Now send men to Joppa, and send for Simon . . . He will tell you what you must do [to be saved]" (Acts 10:4–6, NKJV; compare Acts 11:14 NKJV, "[Simon] will tell you words by which you and all your household will be saved"). When Peter came, he led Cornelius to faith in Christ and eternal salvation (Acts 10:43–48, NKJV). There is no doubt in the Acts 10 account that Cornelius' prayers and alms motivated God to bring him the message of how to be saved.

Make no mistake about what I'm saying here. The only condition of eternal life is faith in Christ. However, repentance may make a person more receptive to the gospel and may incline God to bring the gospel to that person.

Sadly there are many who repent of their sins, yet who never come to faith in Christ. The reason for this, I believe, is that they are not actually seeking God. Though they may not realize it, they are seeking the praise and approval of man.

I was such a person for years. I tried so hard to be good enough to be saved. This was repentance, but it was self-righteous repentance. I was like Paul's fellow Jews who had a zeal for God, but not according to knowledge (Romans 10:1). I was seeking the praise and approval of the religious club to which I belonged. I thought their approval guaranteed entrance to heaven.

However, God in His grace sent someone to challenge me to reconsider my view of the gospel. Shortly after that I came to faith in Christ. Was there something in my heart that indicated to God that I was genuinely seeking Him? I don't know. However, I know that I have eternal life because I have believed in Jesus Christ for it, not because of any repenting I did before or after my spiritual birth.

If an unbeliever decides to turn from his sins in order to get right with God, then he will be more open to the gospel. If he is sincerely seeking to get right with God, his repentance will ultimately result in his coming to hear and believe the gospel of grace.

HOW DID WE EVER GET IN THIS MESS?

Why all this confusion over repentance? Ultimately it goes back at least to the rabbis who taught that people had to turn from their sins to enter God's kingdom (Luke 18:9–14). Soon after the deaths of the apostles, the second-century church leaders picked up that idea, contrary to the gospel of the apostles, and made it a cardinal doctrine of the Church.

During the latter part of the second century, the Church taught that a person could go to a priest only once in his life, to confess his sins and be granted forgiveness by means of doing prescribed penance. However, this led people to put off repentance until their deathbeds. The church changed the doctrine to allow multiple confessions and penance. Eventually people could even buy advanced penances, receiving forgiveness for sins not yet committed. These were called indulgences.

The Reformers responded to such abuses and said that salvation is *sola fide*, by faith alone. However, their followers have taken this cry and managed to find a place for repentance as well. They say either that true faith *includes* repentance, or that it necessarily *results in* repentance. Either way, they say that no one can get into heaven without repenting.

The bottom-line reason for this mess is that the way is narrow that leads to life and the way is broad that leads to destruction (Matthew 7:13–14, NKJV). The vast majority of people both within and outside of Christendom are seeking to gain entrance to God's kingdom by their works. No matter how well intentioned, no one can be born again by works. Only by believing in Christ for eternal life can anyone be regenerated.

WHAT'S THE SOLUTION?

The solution is simple: Don't confuse justification and sanctification. Tell unbelievers that if they simply believe in Christ they will at that moment have eternal life. That is justification by faith alone. Tell believers to repent of their sins in order to escape temporal judgment and to be in fellowship with God. That is progressive sanctification.

If an unbeliever asks if he must give up his sinful ways to have eternal salvation, tell him no. The only condition is faith in Christ. Tell him, however, that sin never pays, for the believer or the unbeliever, and that he should turn from his sinful ways whether or not he is convinced that Jesus gives eternal life to all who merely believe in Him for it. The passing pleasure of sin is far outweighed by its long-term pain. Just ask any alcoholic or drug addict, or any member of their family.

Paul's answer to the question, "What must I do to be saved?" was, "Believe on the Lord Jesus Christ, and you will be saved" (Acts 16:30–31, NKJV). If repentance is the condition, then Paul got it wrong! That is, of course, absurd. The only condition is to believe in Christ. Believe. Not repent. Not believe plus repent. Just believe. It's that simple.

ENDNOTES

INTRODUCTION

1. Charles C. Ryrie, *Basic Theology* (Wheaton, Ill.: Victor, 1986), 277.
2. For the story behind the writing of this hymn see Ernest K. Emurian, *Living Stories of Famous Hymns* (Grand Rapids: Baker, 1955), 20–23. He relates that the author of these words, John Newton (1725–1807), was born to a devout mother who dedicated him to the Christian ministry as a baby. At four years of age he could recite passages from the Westminster Catechism and the children's hymns of Isaac Watts. But his mother died when he was six. At eleven he went to sea with his sailor father, and at seventeen he joined the British Royal Navy, giving up his early religious training and becoming an atheist. He embarked on a career of blatant wickedness and eventually became a ship's captain engaged in the slave trade. During a violent storm at sea on March 10, 1748, which threatened to engulf the ship, his conscience was awakened as he faced imminent death, and he cried out to God for salvation. The next ten years brought spiritual thirst and transformation of life, resulting in his becoming a minister in the Church of England for almost fifty years until his death in 1802. This hymn, written in Newton's early fifties, reflects the fascinating story of his life. His epitaph, which he wrote

himself, reads as follows: "John Newton, Clerk, once an infidel and libertine, was, by the rich mercy of our Lord and Savior, Jesus Christ, preserved, restored, pardoned and appointed to preach the faith he had long labored to destroy, near sixteen years at Olney in Bucks, and twenty-eight years in this Church" (ibid., 23).

3. Guy H. King, *Joy Way* (London: Marshall, Morgan, & Scott, 1992), 86.

CHAPTER 1—WHAT DOES SALVATION MEAN?

1. John Hartley, *"yāsha,"* in *Theological Wordbook of the Old Testament*, ed. R. Laird Harris, Gleason L. Archer, Jr., and Bruce K. Waltke (Chicago: Moody, 1980), 1:414.
2. I am indebted to my colleague, Kem Oberholtzer, for the suggested graphics in this diagram.
3. W. Robert Cook, "Systematic Theology in Outline Form" (class notes, Western Seminary, Portland, Oreg., 1989).
4. Donald Grey Barnhouse, "Why God Saved You," *Eternity* (February 1958): 26.
5. Ryrie, *Basic Theology,* 277.
6. Lewis Sperry Chafer, *Systematic Theology* (Dallas: Dallas Seminary Press, 1948; reprint, 8 vols. in 4, Grand Rapids: Kregel, 1993), 3:7.
7. Ibid.
8. W. E Vine, *Vine's Expository Dictionary of New Testament Words* (Nashville: Nelson, 1985), 367.
9. We sometimes hear that our salvation is a "costly gift," implying that it will cost the recipient greatly. Not so! People who say this need to note the dictionary definition of a gift: "something that is bestowed voluntarily and without compensation." Paul wrote that we are "justified *freely* [literally, 'as a gift'] by His grace through the redemption that is in Christ Jesus" (Rom. 3:24, italics added). The last invitation in the Bible says, "And let him who thirsts come. Whoever desires let him take of the water of life *freely*" (Rev.21:17, italics added).
10. Chafer, *Systematic Theology,* 3:8.

CHAPTER 2—WHO CAN PROVIDE SALVATION?

1. For a thorough study of the person and work of Christ see John A. Witmer, *Immanuel—Jesus Christ: Cornerstone of Our Faith*, Swindoll Leadership Library (Nashville: Word, 1998).

2. J. I. Packer, *Knowing God* (Downers Grove, Ill.: InterVarsity, 1973), 20–22.

3. This verse was the inspiration for Charles Sheldon's classic work *In His Steps* (Chicago: Advance, 1899).

4. The imperfect tense of the verb "to be" (*eimi*) expresses continuous timeless existence.

5. The preposition "with" (*pros*) is literally "toward," showing fellowship between God the Father and God the Son. Also the word "God" (*theon*) is preceded by the untranslated definite article (*ton*), thus indicating a reference to God the Father.

6. "The last portion of 1:1 is the major point of contention. It reads in the Greek *theos ēn ho logos*, or literally, 'the Word was God.' God, or *theos*, occurs in this verse without the Greek article *ho*, so that some have contended that the lack of the article in the Greek text should cause the statement to be translated 'the Word was a god.' The best understanding for the translation, however, as recognized by Greek scholars, is that since *theos* is a predicate and precedes the noun *logos* and a verb, it is natural for it to occur here without the article. Greek scholars are agreed that the verse should be translated as it regularly is in modern and ancient translations, clearly affirming that Jesus is indeed God" (Earl D. Radmacher, ed., *The Nelson Study Bible* [Nashville: Nelson, 1997], 1756).

7. See the significant account of their giving in 2 Corinthians 8:1–5.

8. It is a worthwhile exercise to contrast the thoughts and actions of Christ in John 13:1–5.

9. Jacobus J. Mueller, *The Epistles of Paul to the Philippians and to Philemon* (Grand Rapids: Eerdmans, 1955), 79–80 (italics added).

10. J. B. Phillips, *The New Testament in Modern English* (New York: Macmillan, 1960), 412.

11. A helpful corrective would be "emptied Himself *because* of love."

12. Mueller, *The Epistles of Paul to the Philippians and to Philemon*, 82.
13. Ryrie, *Basic Theology*, 250.
14. Addison H. Leitch, *Interpreting Basic Theology* (New York: Channel, 1961), 81–82.

CHAPTER 3—SALVATION—FROM ETERNITY TO ETERNITY

1. Charles Ryrie suggests that the word "design" is helpful because it brings into view the concept of an architect. "God is the Architect of a plan which does include all things but includes them in a variety of relationships. Architects' plans are detailed. So is God's plan. In the process of constructing a building, experts can predict that so many workers will be injured and some may even lose their lives. Such grim statistics are included in the planning of the building, yet we would not hold the architect responsible for the injuries and deaths (assuming proper safety measures). Carelessness, indifference to rules, even violation of safety restrictions are usually the causes of accidents. But whose fault are they? The individuals who are careless or indifferent. So God's plan has been designed so that the responsibility for sin lies with the individual even though God knowingly included sin in His plan" (*Basic Theology*, 312).

2. G. C. Berkouwer, professor of systematic theology at the Free University of Amsterdam, wrote, "No doctrine has evoked more intense debates. . . . Sharp reactions have been aroused, but not the Christian doctrine of Election so much as caricatures of it are to blame. . . . Such reactions are very understandable, for the biblical doctrine of Election has at times been presented as though it were a parallel to the Islamic doctrine of election. . . . We must recognize that a more serious error can hardly be conceived than the substitution of fatalism for the biblical portrayal of the electing God. . . . Many people have difficulty with the doctrine of Election because they have encountered the doctrine only in its caricatured form. . . . In the Bible, however, Election is set within a wholly different context than that of perplexity, uncertainty, or resignation. It is always set to the tune of a doxology. . . . This is neither anxiety nor resignation in the face

of arbitrary sovereignty. It is amazement at the ways of divine Grace. ... And he who comes to see that his salvation is not of his works but of God's grace stands before Divine Election and therein finds peace" ("Election and Doctrinal Reaction," *Christianity Today*, 10 April 1961, 10–13).

3. "When we consider the high destiny defined, 'to be conformed to the image of His Son,' there is exhibited not only the dignity of this ordination but also the greatness of the love from which the appointment flows. God's love is not passive emotion; it is active volition and it moves determinatively to nothing less than the highest goal conceivable for his adopted children, conformity to the image of the only-begotten Son" (John Murray, *The Epistle to the Romans*, New International Commentary on the New Testament [Grand Rapids: Eerdmans, 1959], 318).

4. Each of the verbs in this series (foreknew, predestined, called, justified, glorified) is in the past tense. All of them are viewed as completed acts. This shows that God sees the end from the beginning.

5. See these sources on the lostness of those who have never heard of Christ: William V. Crockett and James G. Sigountos, eds., *Through No Fault of Their Own?* (Grand Rapids: Baker, 1991); Robert McQuilken, *The Great Omission* (Grand Rapids: Baker, 1984), 39–53; and John Piper, *Let the Nations Be Glad!* (Grand Rapids: Baker, 1993), 115–57.

6. To a world that believed in many gods, the name of the true and living God was significant.

7. The Lord made this promise to a pagan, Abram, and then proceeded to provide for all the vicissitudes of the trip to bring him to the point of belief that was reckoned to him for righteousness.

8. William E. Booth-Clibborn was my pastor when I was a small boy. He was a son of Catherine Booth-Clibborn, the daughter of General William Booth, who founded the Salvation Army.

9. See also Chafer, *Systematic Theology*, 3:36–43.

10. "His perfection consisted in the retention of his integrity, in the face of every kind of assault on his integrity, and thereby the establishment of

his integrity" (Fritz Rienecker, *A Linguistic Key to the Greek New Testament*, ed. Cleon L. Rogers, Jr. [Grand Rapids: Zondervan, 1980], 679).

11. In a marvelous work Johnston M. Cheney wove together the four Gospels into a consecutive account without adding or leaving out one word. This work was originally published as *The Life of Christ in Stereo* (Portland, Oreg.: Western Baptist Seminary Press, 1969), and later as *The Greatest Story,* but more recently as *The Story of the Greatest Life.*

12. Robert Lightner noted, "One minute infraction of the Law by Christ would have disqualified Him as the sin bearer. Like the priest under the Levitical system, He would have had to provide a sacrifice for Himself before He could have offered one for sinners. Furthermore, He would have had to repeat the sacrifice continually as those priests did" (*Sin, the Savior, and Salvation* [Nashville: Nelson, 1991], 98).

13. "Because of the simile, too much should not be made of this statement, although, in cases of extreme stress, it is physiologically possible for the human body to sweat blood" (Paul L. Maier, *In the Fullness of Time: A Historian Looks at Christmas, Easter, and the Early Church* [San Francisco: Harper, 1991], 131).

14. Louis A. Barbieri, "Matthew," in *The Bible Knowledge Commentary, New Testament,* ed. John F. Walvoord and Roy B. Zuck (Wheaton, Ill.: Victor, 1983), 27.

15. Leitch, *Interpreting Basic Theology,* 80–81.

16. Ibid., 81.

17. S. Craig Glickman, *Knowing Christ* (Chicago: Moody, 1980), 41.

18. G. A. Turner, "Christ, Temptation of," in *Zondervan Pictorial Encyclopedia of the Bible,* ed. Merrill C. Tenney (Grand Rapids: Zondervan, 1975), 1:801.

19. Paul Enns, *The Moody Handbook of Theology* (Chicago: Moody, 1989), 237–38 (italics his).

20. Chafer, *Systematic Theology,* 5:78.

21. The essence of death is separation, not annihilation. The degree or nature of that separation must be determined by the context. Separation of the body from the immaterial part of man is physical death (Gen. 35:18). Separation of the sinner from God is spiritual death

(Eph. 2:1, 5). Separation of the sinner permanently from God's presence is eternal death (Rev. 20:13–15; 21:8). Christ's death had both physical and spiritual implications, but in a moment of separation He bore infinitely the sins of the entire human race.

22. Floyd Hamilton, *The Basics of Christian Faith*, rev. ed. (New York: Harper and Row, 1964), 160. Peter Stoner wrote that if we take only forty-eight of those prophecies of Christ's first advent, the possibility "that any one man [could have] fulfilled all 48 prophecies [would] be one in 10^{157}" (*Science Speaks* [Chicago: Moody, 1963], 109). That's the numeral ten followed by 157 zeros!

23. A type is "an Old Testament person, event, or thing having historical reality and designed by God to prefigure (foreshadow) in a preparatory way a real person, event, or thing so designated in the New Testament and that corresponds to and fulfills (heightens) the type" (Roy B. Zuck, *Basic Bible Interpretation* [Wheaton, Ill.: Victor, 1991], 176).

24. Leon Morris, *The Atonement: Its Meaning and Significance* (Downers Grove, Ill.: InterVarsity, 1983), 68.

25. The veil (*katapetasma*, a term not applied to any other curtain) was the inner curtain which divided the Holy Place from the Most Holy Place in the tabernacle. Someone has noted that the veil was so thick that it could not be pulled apart with a team of oxen at each end. But God didn't take any chances with misinterpretation as to who did it, so He tore it from top to bottom rather than from bottom to top.

26. Ibid., 84.

27. For further study of types and symbols, see Zuck, *Basic Bible Interpretation*, 169–93.

28. Max Lucado, *No Wonder They Call Him the Savior* (Sisters, Oreg.: Multnomah, 1986), 47–48.

29. Ibid., 48.

30. Wayne Grudem, *Systematic Theology* (Grand Rapids: Zondervan, 1994), 576.

31. Chafer, *Systematic Theology*, 3:51–52.

32. "It's a bit ironic that the burial of Jesus should be conducted, not by

those who boasted they would never leave, but by two members of the Sanhedrin—two representatives of the religious group that killed the Messiah" (*No Wonder They Call Him the Savior*, 102).

33. This one word in the Greek, *tetelestai*, is in the perfect tense, which indicates that His redemptive work had been brought to completion. He did not say, "I am finished," but "It is finished."

34. This doctrine is developed more fully in Witmer, *Immanuel*, 109–16.

35. George Eldon Ladd, *I Believe in the Resurrection of Jesus* (Grand Rapids: Eerdmans, 1975), 42.

36. George E. Ladd, "The Resurrection of Christ," in *Christian Faith and Modern Theology*, ed. Carl F. H. Henry (New York: Channel, 1964), 263.

CHAPTER 4—WHAT DOES JESUS DO FOR SINNERS?

1. H. Riesenfeld, "*hyper*," in *Theological Dictionary of the New Testament*, ed. Gerhard Kittel and Gerhard Friedrich, trans. Geoffrey W. Bromiley (Grand Rapids: Eerdmans, 1985), 8:508–13.

2. Robert P. Lightner, *The Death Christ Died* (Schaumberg, Ill.: Regular Baptist, 1967), 24 (italics his).

3. For these and other views on the atonement see Enns, *The Moody Handbook of Theology*, 322.

4. R. Laird Harris, "*gā'al*," in *Theological Wordbook of the Old Testament*, 1:144.

5. John D. Currid, *Ancient Egypt and the Old Testament* (Grand Rapids: Baker, 1997), 108–9.

6. J. Vernon McGee gave a chapter to each of these in his book *Ruth: The Romance of Redemption*, 2d ed. (Wheaton: Van Kampen, 1954).

7. Ibid., 80.

8. In December 1876, after a Christmas holiday with his family in Rome, Pennsylvania, Philip Bliss and his wife were traveling by train to Chicago for an engagement the following Sunday in Moody's Tabernacle. As the train crossed a ravine approaching Ashtabula, Ohio, the cast-iron bridge gave way. Seven cars plunged into the icy river-

bed, and burst into flames. Bliss survived the fall and escaped through a window, but he returned to the wreckage in a desperate attempt to rescue his wife and both perished in the fire. Among the personal papers in his trunk, which was not damaged, was this beautiful song of redemption. See William J. Reynolds, *Songs of Glory* (Grand Rapids: Baker, 1995), 127, 250.

9. Leon Morris, *The Apostolic Preaching of the Cross*, 3d ed. (Grand Rapids: Eerdmans, 1965), 174.

10. Ibid.

11. Ibid.

12. "The heathen worshiped capricious gods. The worshipers could never guess what the gods would be up to next. They could never tell when their gods would be angry or what it was that annoyed them. The Hebrews were not in doubt. They knew that one thing and one thing alone aroused God's anger, and that was sin" (Morris, *The Atonement: Its Meaning and Significance*, 154).

13. Roger Nicole, "The Nature of Redemption," in *Christian Faith and Modern Theology*, 196.

CHAPTER 5—WHAT DOES JESUS DO FOR SAINTS?

1. L. Berkhof, *Systematic Theology* (Grand Rapids: Eerdmans, 1953), 615.

2. A. H. Strong, *Systematic Theology* (Philadelphia: Judson, 1907), 876.

3. William A. Pope, *A Compendium of Christian Theology* (New York: Phillips and Hunt, 1882), 3:174.

4. Oswald T. Allis, *Prophecy and the Church* (Philadelphia: Presbyterian and Reformed, 1945), 39.

5. Matthew Henry, *Matthew Henry's Commentary on the whole Bible* (New York: Revell, n.d.), 6:675.

6. Ryrie, *Basic Theology*, 308.

7. Kenneth Wuest, *Romans in the Greek New Testament* (Grand Rapids: Eerdmans, 1956), 98.

8. A. T. Robertson, *Word Pictures in the New Testament* (Nashville: Broadman, 1932), 6:209.

9. G. Abbott-Smith, *A Manual Greek Lexicon of the New Testament* (Edinburgh: Clark, 1936), 341.
10. Philip Schaff, *History of the Christian Church* (1910; reprint, Grand Rapids: Eerdmans, 1967), 2:254.
11. Wendell Miller, *Forgiveness: The Power and the Puzzles* (Warsaw, Ind.: ClearBrook, 1994), 23.
12. Zane C. Hodges, "1 John," in *The Bible Knowledge Commentary, New Testament*, 885 (italics his).
13. Miller, *Forgiveness: The Power and the Puzzles*, 29.

CHAPTER 6—WHAT IS COMMON GRACE?

1. Cook, "Systematic Theology in Outline Form," 395.
2. L. Berkhof, *Systematic Theology* (Grand Rapids: Eerdmans, 1953), 432.
3. Paul Brand and Philip Yancey, *Fearfully and Wonderfully Made* (Grand Rapids: Zondervan, 1980).
4. I had the privilege of serving as a theological mentor to Dr. Walter Dyke for the last thirteen years of his life as he pursued the application of Romans 1:20 to both nature and Scripture. His work *Biblicosm* was published posthumously in 1994 by Barclay Press in Newberg, Oregon.
5. John Calvin, quoted in L. Berkhof, *Systematic Theology*, 441.
6. Of interest is the fact that these three were representatives of the three branches of humanity. The Ethiopian, Saul, and Cornelius were, respectively, descendants of Ham, Shem, and Japheth.
7. Missionary Don Richardson found among cannibals a number of what he calls "redemptive analogies" (*Peace Child* [Glendale, Calif.: Regal, 1974]).
8. Tacitus, quoted by Will Durant, *Caesar and Christ*, vol. 3 of *The Story of Civilization* (New York: Simon and Schuster, 1944), 281.
9. Ibid., 283–84.
10. Ibid., 670–71.
11. *The World Book Encyclopedia* (Chicago: Field Enterprises Educational Corp., 1975), 15:708.

12. James Patterson and Peter Kim, *The Day America Told the Truth* (New York: Prentice Hall, 1991).

CHAPTER 7—HOW DOES GOD CONVICT SINNERS OF THEIR SIN?

1. Romans 10:9–10 shows the contrast between initial salvation (justification) and continuing salvation (sanctification). The tendency in our day is to reduce salvation to justification, but that is not the case in Scripture. Belief alone brings righteousness (justification salvation), but belief and confession (and much more) bring sanctification. This is in keeping with the past, present, and future tenses of salvation.
2. Robertson, *Word Pictures in the New Testament*, 5:252.
3. Many Bible versions translate the Greek phrase by the words "in the Holy Spirit" and other times translate it "by the Holy Spirit." It seems preferable, however, to be consistent and to translate it each time as "in the Holy Spirit."
4. Robert Famighetti, ed., *The World Almanac and Book of Facts 1999* (Mahway, N.J.: World Almanac, 1998), 590.
5. Rick Wood, "Christianity Waning or Growing?" *Mission Frontiers* (January–February 1993): 25 (italics his).
6. R. Larry Moyer, *Free and Clear* (Grand Rapids: Kregel, 1997), 19.
7. Zane Hodges, "God's Role in Conversion," *Grace Evangelical Society News* (July–August 1993): 1.
8. In the light of the fact that Lydia heard ("listened intently") to messengers (Paul, Silas, Luke, Timothy), it is interesting that "the Lord opened her heart to heed *the things spoken by Paul*" (Acts 16:14, italics added). Robertson suggests, "She rightly perceived that Paul was the foremost one of the group. He had personal magnetism and power of intellect that the Spirit of God used to win the heart of this remarkable woman to Christ" (*Word Pictures in the New Testament*, 3:252). Is it possible that the reason the Holy Spirit used Paul's words to make His case for Christ is because his words were the simplest and the clearest?

9. Hodges, "God's Role in Conversion," 4 (italics his).

CHAPTER 8—WHAT IS REGENERATION?

1. Susannah Spurgeon and Joseph Harrold, comps., *The Early Years: 1834–1859*, rev. ed., vol. 1 of *C. H. Spurgeon Autobiography* (London: Banner of Truth, 1962), 72.
2. When Peter wrote in 1 Peter 1:3; 23, of being born again, he used *anagennaō*, a verb that combines *anōthen* and *gennaō*. Six times John used *gennaō* to speak of the new birth, which, he said, is "of God" (1 John 2:29; 3:9; 4:7; 5:1, 4, 18).
3. Ronald Shea, "Regeneration and Eternal Life" (unpublished paper, 1998 [italics his]).
4. I. Howard Marshall, *The Epistles of John*, New International Commentary on the New Testament (Grand Rapids: Eerdmans, 1978), 180. If a believer does not sin *habitually* because God's seed remains in Him (3:9), then, as Marshall adds, "It is hard to see why God preserves him from some sins, but not from all sins. We must, therefore, wonder whether an important point of interpretation can be made to rest on what has been called a grammatical subtlety."
5. C. H. Dodd, *The Johannine Epistles* (New York: Harper, 1946), 79.
6. Hodges, "1 John," 895.
7. Of the 117 times *menō* is used in the New Testament, more than half (67) are in John's writings (40 in John, 23 in 1 John, and 3 in 2 John, and 1 in Revelation).

CHAPTER 9—WHAT IS FAITH?

1. Spurgeon and Harrold, *The Early Years: 1834–1859*.
2. Adapted from Dorothy Smoker, "The Matchless Pearl," a tract published by Good News Publishers, Wheaton, Illinois. Used by permission.
3. James Montgomery Boice, *Christ's Call to Discipleship* (Chicago: Moody, 1986), 112, 114 (italics his).
4. John F. MacArthur, Jr., *The Gospel according to Jesus* (Grand Rapids: Zondervan, 1988), 106.

5. Ibid.

6. Abbott-Smith, *A Manual Greek Lexicon of the New Testament*, 184.

7. In contrast to the six usages (discounting parallels) of *euangelion* by the Gospel writers, there are sixty occurrences of the noun and twenty-one of the verb *euangelizô* in the writings of Paul.

8. Paul was preeminently the apostle of *grace*. Of the more than one hundred occurrences of *grace* in the New Testament, almost all of them are from Paul's pen. He considered himself "chief" of sinners (1 Tim. 1:15) to whom "the grace of our Lord was exceedingly abundant" (1:14). "To me," he said, "who am less than the least of all the saints, this grace was given, that I should preach among the Gentiles the unsearchable riches of Christ" (Eph. 2:8; see also 1 Cor. 15:9–10).

9. *The American Heritage Dictionary* (Boston: Houghton Mifflin, 1982), 558.

10. Arthur Farstad, "The Words of the Gospel: Believe/Faith," *Grace Evangelical Society News* (June 1991): 1 (italics his).

11. *American Heritage Dictionary*, 169, 486.

12. John MacArthur, *James* (Chicago: Moody, 1998), 16–17, 120–42. See also Earl D. Radmacher, "First Response to 'Faith According to the Apostle James,' by John F. MacArthur, Jr.," *Journal of the Evangelical Theological Society* 33 (March 1990): 37; and Roy B. Zuck, "Review of *James*, by John MacArthur, Jr.," *Bibliotheca Sacra* 156 (October–December 1999): 498–500.

13. Radmacher, "First Response to 'Faith According to the Apostle James,'" 38 (italics added).

14. Joseph C. Dillow, *The Reign of the Servant Kings* (Hayesville, N.C.: Schoettle, 1992), 276 (italics his).

15. Charles C. Bing, "The Condition for Salvation in John's Gospel," *Journal of the Grace Evangelical Society* 9 (Spring, 1996): 26.

16. MacArthur, *The Gospel according to Jesus*, 46.

17. Dillow, *The Reign of the Servant Kings*, 277.

18. MacArthur, *The Gospel according to Jesus*, 49.

19. F. F. Bruce, *The Gospel of John* (Grand Rapids: Eerdmans, 1992), 119.

20. Hodges, "Assurance: Of the Essence of Saving Faith," *Journal of the Grace Evangelical Society* 10 (Spring 1997): 6–7 (italics his).

CHAPTER 10—WHAT ARE REPENTANCE AND JUSTIFICATION?

1. This section is based on material from David Anderson, "Repentance Is for All Men" (paper presented at the Grace Evangelical Society Pastors Conference, Dallas, Texas, 30 March 1989).
2. John Calvin, *Institutes of the Christian Religion* (Philadelphia: Presbyterian Board of Christian Education, n.d.), 3.3.1.
3. Charles H. Spurgeon, "Faith and Regeneration," in *Spurgeon's Expository Encyclopedia* (Grand Rapids: Baker, 1989), 7:139; and A. H. Strong, *Systematic Theology*, 12th ed. (Philadelphia: Judson, 1949).
4. Some Reformed theologians respond that these three occur at the same moment and therefore the order may be logical rather than temporal. However, a number of Reformed theologians do stress the fact that regeneration comes first (because the unsaved, being spiritually dead, are unable to exercise faith until they are regenerated). So their view comes across as suggesting a temporal sequence.
5. Millard J. Erickson, *Christian Theology* (Grand Rapids: Baker, 1989), 932–46); and Bruce Demarest, *The Cross and Salvation* (Wheaton, Ill.: Crossway, 1997), 33.
6. Cook, "Systematic Theology in Outline Form," 411.
7. Moyer, *Free and Clear*, 92.
8. For discussion of this truth see Earl D. Radmacher, *You and Your Thoughts: The Power of Right Thinking* (Wheaton, Ill.: Tyndale, 1977).
9. The accuracy of this conclusion can be seen by comparing Peter's preaching on the same subject, "remission of sins," in Acts 10:43, where the only condition for receiving remission of sins is "whoever believes in Him." Baptism is not "in order to" receive remission of sins, but "because" remission of sins has been received. (Another place where the Greek preposition *eis* means "because," not "in order to," is Matthew 12:41.) Water baptism should be among the first steps of obedience for a new Christian, as demonstrated by Cornelius and his household (Acts 10:47–48).

Stanley D. Toussaint presents another plausible way to view Acts 2:38. He observes that the works "and be baptized, every one of you, in the name of Jesus Christ," are parenthetical. The verb "repent" is plural and so is the pronoun "your" in the clause "unto the remission of your sins" (literal translation). Therefore the verb "repent" goes with (results in) the forgiveness of sins. The command "be baptized" is singular and so it is set off from the rest of the sentence. Luke 24:47 and Acts 5:31 affirm that forgiveness results from repentance (or from faith, as in 10:43), not from water baptism ("Acts," in *The Bible Knowledge Commentary, New Testament*, 359).

10. Norman L. Mitchell, "You Are What You Think," *Ministry* (May 1982): 27.

11. Anderson, "Repentance Is for All Men," 11–12.

12. Calvin, *Institutes of the Christian Religion*, 3.3.5.

13. Chafer, *Systematic Theology*, 3:377–78.

14. Lorman Petersen, "The Nature of Justification," in *Christian Faith and Modern Theology*, 350.

15. The word group of justification includes the adjective *dikaios* (eighty-one times), the noun *dikaiosynē* (ninety-two times), the verb *dikaioō* (thirty-nine times), the noun *dikaiōma* (ten times), the adverb *dikaiōs* (five times), and the noun *dikaiōsis* (twice).

16. Morris, *The Apostolic Preaching of the Cross*, 233.

17. "Catholicism teaches that justification is a gradual process through life; faith is only the initial act. They speak of 'infused grace.' Rome has not changed her views through the years" (Petersen, "The Nature of Justification," 365).

18. Morris, *The Apostolic Preaching of the Cross*, 259–60.

19. Ibid., 283–84. Also Frederic Godet says, "As to *dikaioō* (to justify) there is not an example in the whole of classic literature where it signifies: *to make just*" (*Romans* [Edinburgh: Clark, 1993; reprint, Grand Rapids: Zondervan, 1969], 1:157, [italics his]).

CHAPTER 11—WHY IS SANCTIFICATION SALVATION NEEDED?

1. Of course, even at the moment of justification we are sanctified in the sense of being set apart to God. Hebrews 10:10 uses "sanctified"

in this way. For a full discussion of the doctrine of sanctification see Henry W. Holloman, *The Forgotten Blessing: Rediscovering the Transforming Power of Sanctification*, Swindoll Leadership Library (Nashville: Word, 1999).

2. Earl D. Radmacher, "The Interpretation and Application of Separation in 2 Corinthians 6:14–7:1" (Th.M. thesis, Dallas Theological Seminary, 1959), 102–4.

3. For more information on the identity of those unbelievers in Corinth see William J. Webb, "Who Are the Unbelievers (a[pistoi) in 2 Corinthians 6:14?" *Bibliotheca Sacra* 149 (January–March 1992): 27–44.

4. John Calvin, *Commentary on the Epistles of Paul the Apostle to the Corinthians* (Grand Rapids: Eerdmans, 1948), 260.

5. Kenneth S. Wuest, *Galatians in the New Testament* (Grand Rapids: Eerdmans, 1956), 49.

6. Roy L. Laurin, *Where Life Endures* (Wheaton, Ill.: Van Kampen, 1954), 143 (italics his).

7. Arthur W. Pink, *An Exposition from Hebrews* (Grand Rapids: Baker, 1954), 421.

8. Isaac Watts emphasized this point in his hymn, "Am I a Soldier of the Cross?" As he prepared his sermon each week, Isaac Watts frequently wrote a hymn for the congregation to sing at the conclusion of the message. This hymn followed a sermon on "Holy Fortitude." When Watts was a child, his father and family were severely persecuted. William J. Reynolds writes, "Isaac was born in 1674 to parents who were Dissenters, people whose religious affiliation was outside the Church of England, the state church. His father, a deacon at the Above Bar Congregational Church in Southampton, was arrested several times and imprisoned in St. Michael's prison. When Isaac was an infant, his mother would sit on a stone opposite the jail and nurse her baby while visiting her husband. Dissenters (such as Congregationalists, Presbyterians, Baptists, and Quakers) often experienced persecution in the seventeenth century. The Act of Uniformity in 1662 expelled all dissenting clergy from their pulpits. In 1664 another law forbade religious meetings not in accordance with the state church. In 1667 a law forbade dissenting clergymen

from coming closer than five miles to places where they had preached" (*Songs of Glory* [Grand Rapids: Baker, 1990], 24–25).

9. For more information on the relationship between the Scriptures and the Holy Spirit, see Roy B. Zuck, *Spirit-Filled Teaching: The Power of the Holy Spirit in Your Ministry*, Swindoll Leadership Library (Nashville: Word, 1998), 73–77, 146.

10. On the vital place of the church and churches see my book *The Nature of the Church* (Hayesville, N.C.: Schoettle, 1996).

11. I believe that some dispensationalists do themselves a disservice by designating the present dispensation as the dispensation of grace, because God's grace is not limited to this age. Dispensationalists, along with all other evangelicals, recognize that there was grace in the Old Testament. What is indeed new, however, is the church, the body of Christ, which had its birth at Pentecost. Therefore it seems more appropriate to call the present era the dispensation of the church.

12. Alexis de Tocqueville, quoted in Robert Bellah, *Habits of the Heart: Individualism and Commitment in American Life* (New York: Harper, 1985).

13. Ted Peters, quoted in William J. Petersen, "The Future of Religion— A Consumer Product, Packaged and Purchased" *Evangelical Newsletter*, 14 November 1980, 3.

14. Ibid.

15. Ibid.

16. Ibid.

17. See Dillow, *The Reign of the Servant Kings*, 585–605, for a full chapter on these partakers (*metachoi*).

18. "Rangers' 'Elite' Tag Is Hard-Won," *USA Today*, 24 February 1995, 3A.

CHAPTER 12—WHAT ARE SOME EVIDENCES OF SANCTIFICATION SALVATION?

1. See 1 Corinthians 3:16; 5:6; 6:2, 3, 9, 15, 16, 19; 9:13, 24.

2. W. E. Vine, *Vine's Complete Expository Dictionary of Old and New Testament Words* (Nashville: Nelson, 1996), 130.

3. W. Arndt, "A Royal Priesthood, 1 Pet. 2:9," *Concordia Theological Monthly* 19 (April 1948): 241–42.

4. J. Alexander Findlay, *A Portrait of Peter* (New York: Abindgon, 1935), 174.

5. Chafer, *Systematic Theology*, 4:65–68.

6. One can see that this is a pattern for prayer rather than a formula, by noting the introductory words in Matthew 6:9. Jesus told them *how* they should pray, rather than *what* they should pray.

7. For more on prayer see Paul A. Cedar, *A Life of Prayer*, Swindoll Leadership Library (Nashville: Word, 1998).

8. John Calvin, *Commentary on the Epistles of Paul the Apostle to the Corinthians*, trans. John Pringle (Grand Rapids: Baker, 1979), 121.

9. Abbott-Smith, *A Manual Greek Lexicon of the New Testament*, 46.

CHAPTER 13—WHAT ARE OTHER EVIDENCES OF SANCTIFICATION SALVATION?

1. Abbott-Smith, *A Manual Greek Lexicon of the New Testament*, 313.

2. Arnold Bittlinger, *Gifts and Ministries* (Grand Rapids: Eerdmans, 1973), 9.

3. Vine, *Vine's Complete Expository Dictionary of Old and New Testament Words*, 424.

4. Ibid.

5. Cook, "Systematic Theology in Outline Form," 440.

6. Hodges, "1 John," 884.

7. Zane Hodges, *The Epistle of James* (Irving, Tex.: Grace Evangelical Society, 1994), 71 (italics his).

8. Ibid. (italics his).

9. Thankfully evangelicals are increasingly recognizing the importance of emphasizing discipleship as Christian growth. Evidence of this worldwide concern is the First International Consultation on Discipleship, held in Eastbourne, England, September 21–24, 1999. For information see "Make Disciples, Not Just Converts," *Christianity Today*, 25 October, 1999, 28–29. To read the Consultation's Joint Statement on Discipleship visit www.Global-Discipleship.org.

CHAPTER 14—HOW DO SPIRITUAL GIFTS RELATE TO SANCTIFICATION SALVATION?

1. Earl D. Radmacher, "The Jack of All Trades Syndrome," *Moody Monthly* (March 1971): 41–43.

2. Some Bible students say "pastors" and "teachers" refer to one ministry, based on a principle in Greek grammar known as the Granville-Sharp rule. This rule states that two nouns refer to the same thing if they are connected by the Greek conjunction *kai* ("and") and the definite article "the" occurs before the first noun but not before the second noun. However, the Granville-Sharp rule applies only when these constructions have singular nouns, not when they have plural nouns as in Ephesians 4:11 (Daniel B. Wallace, *Greek Grammar Beyond the Basics: An Exegetical Syntax of the New Testament* [Grand Rapids: Zondervan, 1996], 284). So it seems better to see pastors and teachers as two separate functions (though, of course, pastors should engage in teaching, and teachers should have pastors' hearts).

3. Michael Griffiths, *Grace-Gifts* (Grand Rapids: Eerdmans, 1979), 76 (italics his).

4. An exception to this is the sign gifts (1 Cor. 14:20–22), which are miraculously bestowed. In the gift of tongues, for example, the recipient was able to utter the language of unbelieving Jews he encountered, without having learned that language.

5. The absence of a Greek article before "prophecy" and before "ministry" distinguishes *them* as categories in contrast to the following five specific examples (each with a Greek article) of these two categories. This is also seen in 1 Corinthians 14:3, in which "exhortation" is subsumed under "prophecy" as a specific example. In other verses prophecy is used in the sense of preaching (for example, 12:10).

6. "Speaking in tongues," introduced on the Day of Pentecost, was the supernatural ability to speak a known language not native to or learned by the speaker. Its purpose was to be a supernatural sign to unbelieving Jews (1 Cor. 14:21–25), showing them that God was at work. Whenever it was used in the Book of Acts (chapters 2, 8, 10, 19), Jews were always present. Israel's rejection of the Messiah led to

God's judgment. With the destruction of Jerusalem, dispersion of the nation, and God turning to the Gentiles as His mediatorial people (Rom. 11), the sign gift of tongues speaking had fulfilled its purpose of judgment and had ceased to exist (1 Cor. 13:8).

What is called "speaking in tongues" today does not meet the criteria of tongues-speaking to be followed by the first-century church. Ecstatic utterances were common in Paul's day as well as today. In 1 Corinthians 14 Paul was confronting this counterfeit of biblical tongues-speaking.

7.   Tongues were given not for believers but as a sign of judgment on Israel (1 Cor. 14:22), and as a confirmation that the message of the gospel was from God (2 Cor. 12:12; Heb. 2:4). Some Christians, however, say tongues-speaking is for self-edification, and they base this on 1 Corinthians 14:4, "He who speaks in a tongue edifies himself." But this verse is not stating a purpose for tongues; it is reporting that carnal Christians in Corinth were seeking to edify themselves (see 12:31), whereas spiritual gifts were given for edification of others, not oneself. First Corinthians 14 shows that the Corinthians were using a counterfeit of tongues, namely, ecstatic utterences practiced in the "mystery" (secret) religions of that day. (See H. Wayne House, "Tongues and the Mystery Religions of Corinth," *Bibliotheca Sacra* 140 [April–June 1983]: 134–50.) Several contrasts should be noted between counterfeit tongues-speaking and the genuine practice.

Counterfeit Tongues-Speaking	Biblical Tongues-Speaking
The speaker seeks to edify himself (1 Cor. 14:4)	The speaker edifies others (when his speaking is translated; 1 Cor. 14:4, 13).
The speaker "does not speak to me" (14:2)	The speaker speaks of "the wonderful works of God" (Acts 2:11) to people of other nationalities (2:6–11)
"No one understands him" (14:2)	"Everyone heard them speak in his own language" (2:6).

Counterfeit Tongues-Speaking (Cont'd)	Biblical Tongues-Speaking (Cont'd)
The speaker "in the spirit [literally, 'in spirit,' that is, 'in his own spirit,' or 'to himself']" (14:2), with no benefit to others.	The speakers who prophesy speak in the language of the listeners so that it benefited them (1 Cor. 14:3).
Ecstatic utterances cause unsaved people to think the speakers are insane (14:23).	Speaking a foreign language when others who don't know the language are present, benefits the hearers only if it is interpreted (14:5).

Why, then, did Paul say tongues-speaking was not to be forbidden? Because it would be relevant to Jewish unbelievers at least until A.D. 70, when Jerusalem would be destroyed and the Jews dispersed.

8. For more on spiritual gifts see Tim Blanchard, *A Practical Guide to Finding and Using Your Spiritual Gifts* (Wheaton, Ill.: Tyndale, 1979); Joseph Dillow, *Speaking in Tongues* (Grand Rapids: Zondervan, 1975); Robert G. Gromacki, *The Modern Tongues Movement* (Hartley, N.J.: Presbyterian and Reformed, 1973); Robert Gromacki, *The Holy Spirit,* Swindoll Leadership Library (Nashville: Word, 1999), 205–36, and John F. Walvoord, *The Holy Spirit,* rev. ed. (Grand Rapids: Zondervan, 1958), 168–88.

CHAPTER 15—IS THE BELIEVER'S SALVATION SECURE?

1. Charles C. Ryrie, *So Great Salvation* (Wheaton, Ill.: Victor, 1989), 137.
2. Berkhof, *Systematic Theology,* 545–46.
3. A. W. Pink, *Eternal Security* (Grand Rapids: Guardian, 1974), 15.
4. MacArthur, *The Gospel according to Jesus,* 98 (italics his).
5. Ryrie, *So Great Salvation,* 137.
6. Sir Robert Anderson, *The Coming Prince* (London: Hodder & Stoughton, 1881; reprint, Grand Rapids: Kregel, 1975), 119–29.
7. See J. Dwight Pentecost, "Daniel," in *The Bible Knowledge Commentary, Old Testament,* ed. John F. Walvoord and Roy B. Zuck (Wheaton, Ill.: Victor, 1985), 1362–64.

8. Ryrie, *Basic Theology*, 330.
9. Chafer, *Systematic Theology*, 6:316.
10. "Fallen vines were lifted (J[ohn] 12:2, *airei*, from *airō*, 'to lift,' not from *aireō*, 'to catch, take away,' as in all Eng. Versions) into position with meticulous care and allowed to heal" (R. K. Harrison, "Vine," in *International Standard Bible Encyclopedia*, 4 [1986], 986). Others who take this view that *airō* means "lifts up," not "takes away" or "cuts off," include Gary W. Derickson, "Viticulture and John 15:1–69," *Bibliotheca Sacra* 153 (January–March 1996); 34–52 (Derickson has a master's degree in viticulture); James M. Boice, *Gospel of John* (Grand Rapids: Zondervan, 1978), 4:228; and A. W. Pink, *Exposition of the Gospel of John* (Cleveland: Bible Truth, 1929), 3:337.
11. John G. Mitchell, *An Everlasting Love* (Portland, Oreg.: Multnomah, 1982), 286–87.
12. Gary W. Derickson, a horticulturist and Bible college teacher, explains that in caring for grapevines, fruit-bearing branches are cleaned in the spring, and wood not attached to the vine are burned in the fall. He points out that this action in the spring is behind Jesus' words in John 15:2, and the action in the fall lies behind His words in 15:6. Fruitless branches picture believers out of fellowship with the Lord, whose useless works are burned (15:6; see also 1 Cor. 3:11–15) at the judgment seat of Christ ("Viticulture and John 15:1–6," 34–52).
13. Those who have this life "shall never see death" (John 8:51), "shall never taste death" (8:52), "shall never die" (11:26), and "shall never perish " (10:28).
14. Mitchell, *An Everlasting Love*, 201.
15. Marcus Rainsford, *Our Lord Prays for His Own* (Chicago: Moody, 1958), 35.
16. Chafer, *Systematic Theology*, 3:325.
17. Ibid.
18. Cook, "Systematic Theology in Outline Form," 447.
19. Parallel to this is the miraculous conception of Christ by the Holy Spirit in Mary. In Matthew 1:2–15 *gennaō* is translated "begot" thirty-six times when naming the male source of the seed, but the thirty-seventh use of *gennaō* refers to Mary with no mention of a human contributor. That is because Christ was "begotten" by the

Holy Spirit. Similarly believers are miraculously begotten by the Holy Spirit. So in 1:16 *gennaō* is translated "was born," not "begot": "Mary, of whom was born Jesus who is called Christ."

20. Chafer, *Systematic Theology*, 3:335.

21. I believe the phrase "baptism in the Spirit" is more accurate than "baptism by the Spirit" for two reasons. First, this work is referred to seven times in the New Testament and in four of the occasions, Christ is the Agent of the baptism (Matt. 3:11; Mark 1:8; Luke 3:16; John 1:33). In Acts 1:5 He said He would baptize in the Spirit, a work that would take place after His ascension. Acts 11:15 refers back to its first occurrence on the Day of Pentecost. And 1 Corinthians 12:13 states that Christ, not the Holy Spirit, is the Agent of this baptizing work. This is certainly appropriate as Christ's first act after His exaltation as Head (Eph. 4:15) of the new entity, the body of Christ. Second, the Greek preposition *en* normally means "in." So it seems logical to think of this as the work of Christ in which He places all believers at the moment of salvation in the sphere (care and protection) of the Holy Spirit, thus forming the body of Christ (His church). Thus Christ is the Baptizer and the Holy Spirit is the Protector.

22. Vine, *Vine's Expository Dictionary of New Testament Words*, 331. See also Eldon G. Woodcock, "The Seal of the Holy Spirit," *Bibliotheca Sacra* 155 (April–June 1998): 139–63.

CHAPTER 16—HOW CAN A BELIEVER HAVE ASSURANCE OF SALVATION?

1. More than a decade ago I participated in a major theological colloquium on the subject of faith. In the question-and-answer session at the conclusion of the colloquium, someone asked one of the presenters, "How long would I need to examine myself to know if I am saved?" After considerable delay, the speaker answered, "For the rest of your life." Then the questioner asked, "When will I know for sure that I am saved (that is, justified)?" The speaker said, "Not until you die!" This too is confusing, is without biblical basis, and removes the possibility of assurance.

2. Boice, *Christ's Call to Discipleship*, 112–14 (italics his).

3. Ibid., 41.

4. In Matthew 16:25–26 some translations unfortunately switch from "life" in one verse to "soul" in the other: "Whoever desires to save his *life* will lose it" (16:25), and "for what is a man profited if he gains the whole world, and loses his own *soul*" (16:26, italics added). This change leaves the impression that two different things are spoken of. But actually both words translate the same Greek word *psychē*, and refer to the stewardship of life in this earthly sojourn.

5. "The parallel structure and rhythmic character (compare 2:11–13) make it likely that they are an extract from a liturgical hymn, probably familiar to Timothy and the community (see 1 Tim. 3:16 for the similar use of a hymn)" (J. N. D. Kelly, *A Commentary on the Pastoral Epistles* [Grand Rapids: Baker, 1981], 179).

6. Bob Wilkin, "If We Endure, We Will Reign with Him," *Grace in Focus* (January/February 1996): 2 (italics his).

7. Zane C. Hodges, *Grace in Eclipse* (Dallas, Tex.: Redencion Viva, 1987), 68.

8. Cal Thomas, "Lions vs. Pastor Lamb," *World*, 26 July/2 August, 1997, 19.

9. The word for "reign" in 2 Timothy 2:12 is *symbasileuō*, which means "to rule as a king with someone" (Walter Bauer, William F. Arndt, and F. Wilbur Gingrich, *A Greek-English Lexicon of the New Testament and Other Early Christian Literature*, 2d ed., rev. F. Wilbur Gingrich and Frederick W. Danker [Chicago: University of Chicago Press, 1979], 785).

10. Abbott-Smith, *A Manual Greek Lexicon of the New Testament*, 59.

11. Zane C. Hodges, "Assurance of Salvation," *Journal of the Grace Evangelical Society* 3 (Autumn 1990): 8 (italics his).

12. L. Berkhof, *The History of Christian Doctrines* (Grand Rapids: Eerdmans, 1937), 222 (italics added).

13. Bruce, *The Gospel of John*, 394.

14. The purpose of 1 John, as already noted, is not to give assurance of salvation. Its purpose, instead, is to inform believers how to have fellowship with God. The purpose for the epistle is given in the prologue (1 John 1:1–4): to encourage believers to have "fellowship" with the apostolic circle and, beyond that, "fellowship . . . with the

Father and with His Son Jesus Christ" (1:3). However, in 5:13 John did address the subject of assurance. But in that verse the phrase "these things I have written to you" ought to be taken as a reference to the material immediately preceding it, not to the entire epistle. This, in fact, is how this phrase is used elsewhere in the epistle (2:1 refers to 1:5–10; and 2:26 refers to 2:18–25). So here 5:13 refers to 5:9–12.

15. Zane C. Hodges, "Assurance Is of the Essence of Saving Faith" (paper presented at the Grace Evangelical Society Pastors Conference, Irving, Tex., 1997). Hodges also wrote, "When the NT writers speak of eternal salvation they always use the language of John and Paul. That kind of language should be allowed to sink into our hearts most deeply: The *believer* has eternal life; the one who does *not* work but *believes* is justified; salvation is by *grace* through *faith* and is *not* by works of righteousness, which we have done.... It is inconceivable, in the light of this Scriptural teaching and terminology, that an experience so utterly divorced from our performance *must be verified* by our performance.... No. Good works can never be a fundamental ground of assurance. It is logically and theologically absurd to claim that a salvation which is *apart from* works, is not recognizable *except by* works. God's word teaches no such thing" ("Assurance of Salvation," 10–11, italics his).

16. Paul wrote a similar statement: "I know whom I have believed and am persuaded that He is able to keep what I have committed to Him until that Day" (2 Tim. 1:12). To believe is to be persuaded.

17. John is the only one of the four Gospel writers who used *menō* in a figurative sense. First John 5:9–13 is a summary statement, given near the end of the epistle, in order to keep the objective requirement of belief in Christ distinct from the more subjective requirements for fellowship with Christ.

18. *Webster's Ninth New College Dictionary* (Springfield, Mass.: Merriam-Webster, 1987), 44.

19. "This word means a. 'to stay in a place,' figuratively 'to remain in a sphere,' b. 'to stand against opposition,' 'to hold out,' 'to stand fast,' c. 'to stay still,' and d. 'to remain,' 'to endure,' 'to stay in force'" (Friedrich

Hauck, "*menō*," in *Theological Dictionary of the New Testament*, 4 [1967], 581).

20. Dillow, *The Reign of the Servant Kings*, 407–8 (italics his).
21. Robertson, *Word Pictures in the New Testament*, 5:259.
22. It is significant that in the Upper Room Discourse Jesus referred to "sin" only in connection with the unregenerate (15:22, 24; 16:8–9) and not in relation to the disciples. But in 1 John sin is mentioned twenty-one times, and always in relation to the disciples.
23. This "we" is the same "we" mentioned in 1:5, so that the apostle was applying this truth to himself and his fellow apostles as well.
24. Zane C. Hodges, "Confession and Unknown Sin," *Grace Evangelical Society News* (September 1991), 1 (italics his).
25. Hodges, "1 John," 894 (italics his).

CHAPTER 17—WHAT IS GLORIFICATION?

1. This number was given to me by Dr. Richard Strauss, the late senior pastor of Emmanuel Faith Community Church in Escondido, California. Because few pastors have preached on this subject of eternal rewards, I said one time to him, "Have you ever preached a series on rewards?" His answer was like most: "Well, it seems kind of self-serving. I think we ought to serve out of love for Christ." "Well, if it is self-serving," I responded, "how do we account for the numerous admonitions from Christ urging us to work for reward?" I gave him a copy of Joseph Dillow's book, *The Reign of the Servant Kings*, and it so revolutionized his thinking that later Dr. Strauss preached a series of fourteen outstanding messages on the subject.
2. Elsa Raud, *Introduction to Prophecy* (Findlay, Ohio: Dunham, 1960), 156.
3. Some Bible students hold the view that *all* believers will *reign* with Christ. I believe, however, that while all believers will be with Christ in the Millennium, reigning as His co-regents depends on their meeting the conditions set forth in verses such as Romans 8:17; 1 Corinthians 4:2; 9:27; and 2 Timothy 2:12.
4. Dillow, *The Reign of the Servant Kings*, 381.

APPENDIX A: WILL INFANTS WHO DIE GO TO HEAVEN?

1. Perry G. Downs, "Child Evangelization," *Journal of Christian Education 3* (1983): 10.

2. John Sanders, *No Other Name* (Grand Rapids: Wm. B. Eerdmans Publishing Co., 1992), 289.

3. R. A. Webb, *The Theology of Infant Salvation* (Clarksville, Tenn.: Presbyterian Committee of Publication, 1907), 20–21.

4. John Newton, *The Works of John Newton*, 3d. ed., 6 vols. (1820; reprint, Edinburgh: Banner of Truth Trust, 1985), 4:552.

5. Charles H. Spurgeon, *Spurgeon at His Best* (Grand Rapids: Baker Book House, 1988), 95.

6. George W. Bethune, "The Favour of God in Christ to Little Children," in *Children in Heaven*, ed. William E. Schenck (Philadelphia: Presbyterian Board of Publication, 1865), 144.

7. Ibid., 145.

8. John Linton, *Concerning Infants in Heaven* (Grand Rapids: Wm. B. Eerdmans Publishing Co., 1949), 68.

9. Ibid., 69.

10. Clifford Ingle, "Children and Conversion," *Sunday School Builder*, March 1989, 9.

11. Clifford Ingle, "Moving in the Right Direction," in *Children and Conversion*, ed. Clifford Ingle (Nashville: Broadman Press, 1970), 153–54.

12. John Inchley, *Kids and the Kingdom* (Wheaton, Ill.: Tyndale House Publishers, 1976), 14, 33.

13. Marlin Jeschke, *Believers Baptism for Children of the Church* (Scottdale, Penn.: Herald Press, 1983), 104.

14. Robert P. Lightner, *Heaven For Those Who Can't Believe* (Schaumburg, Ill.: Regular Baptist Press, 1977), 7–8.

15. Ibid., 8.

16. Downs, "Child Evangelization," 11.

17. George J. Dyer, "The Unbaptized Infant in Eternity," *Chicago Studies 2* (1963): 147. Sanders points out that a number of Roman Catholics affirm this view (*No Other Name*, 198; see Ladislaus Boros, *The*

Mystery of Death, trans. Gregory Bainbridge [New York: Herder & Herder, 1965], 109–11).

18. J. Oliver Buswell, Jr., *A Systematic Theology of the Christian Religion*, 2 vols. (Grand Rpids: Zondervan Publishing House, 1963), 2:162.

19. Benjamin B. Warfield, "The Development of the Doctrine of Infant Salvation," in *Studies in Theology* (New York: Oxford University Press, 1932), 438.

20. Westminster Confession, chap. 10, sec. 3.

21. For example, Thomas Smyth, "Opinions on Infant Salvation," in *Children in Heaven*, 34; and Roger Nicole, cited by Ronald H. Nash, in *What about Those Who Have Never Heard?* ed. John Sanders (Downers Grove, Ill.: InterVarsity Press, 1995), 119–20.

22. Warfield, *Studies in Theology*, 415.

23. Neal Punt, *What's Good about the Good News?* (Chicago: Northland, 1988), chap. 11.

24. David McConoughy, "Are Infants Saved?" in *Children in Heaven*, 60.

25. Balthasar Hübmaier, *On the Christian Baptism of Believers*, in William R. Estep, ed., *Anabaptist Beginnings (1523–1533): A Source Book* (Nieuwkoop: D. De Graaf, 1976), 93.

26. Charles H. Spurgeon, *Come Ye Children* (reprint, Warrenton, Mo.: Child Evangelism Fellowship, n.d.), 39.

27. Downs, "Child Evangelization," 11; Lightner, *Heaven for Those Who Can't Believe*, 14–15; Herbert Lockyer, *All the Children of the Bible* (Grand Rapids: Zondervan Publishing House, 1970), 97.

28. Sanders, *No Other Name*, 304.

29. John Calvin, *Institutes of the Christian Religion*, trans. John T. McNeill, 2 vols. (Philadelphia: Westminster Press, 1960), 4.16.17; 4.16.19.

30. *Catechism of the Council of Trent*, 144, cited by J. C. Macaulay, *The Bible and the Roman Chuch* (Chicago: Moody Press, 1949), 81. Also see Günter Koch, "Baptism," in *Handbook of Catholic Theology*, ed. Wolfgang Beinert and Francis Schüsler Florenza (New York: Crossroad Publishing Co., 1995), 43.

31. *Catechism of the Catholic Church* (New Hope, N.Y.: St. Martin de Porres Community, 1994), 1213.

32. Augustine *On the Merits and Forgiveness of Sins and on the Baptism*

of Infants 1.21, 28, 33–35, in Philip Schaff, ed., *A Select Library of the Nicene and Post-Nicene Fathers of the Christian Church* (New York: Charles Scribner's Sons, 1908), 5:22–23, 25, 28–29. A more harsh view on the woe of infants was held by Fulgenticus (d. 533), Alcimis Avitus (d. 525), and Gregory the Great (d. 604), according to Warfield ("The Polemics of Infant Baptism," in *Studies in Theology,* 413).

33. Sanders, *No Other Name,* 292. According to the Roman Catholic Catechism of the Council of Trent, "Infants, unless regenerated unto God through the grace of baptism, whether their parents be Christian or infidel, are born to eternal misery and perdition."

34. R. C. Sproul, Jr., "Comfort Ye My People," *World,* May 6, 1995, 26. He did admit, though, that "we cannot say for sure what happens to young children who die" (ibid.).

35. Calvin wrote that "infants are not excluded from the kingdom of heaven, who happen to die before they have had the privilege of baptism" (*Institutes of the Christian Religion,* 4.15.22).

36. Josef Finkenzeller, "Limbo," in *Handbook of Catholic Theology,* 433–35; Zachary Hayes, "Limbo," in *The Modern Catholic Encyclopedia* (Collegeville, Minn.: Liturgical Press, 1994), 511; and P. J. Hill, "Limbo," in *New Catholic Encyclopedia,* 18 vols. (New York: McGraw-Hill Book Co., 1967), 8:762–63, 765.

37. James G. McCarthy, *The Gospel According to Rome* (Eugene, Oreg.: Harvest House Publishers, 1995), 27.

38. George R. Beasley-Murray, *Baptism in the New Testament* (New York: St. Martin's Press, 1962), 343.

39. The Fifth Session of the Roman Catholic Council of Trent (1545–1565) states, "If anyone denies that by the grace of our Lord Jesus Christ, which is through Baptism [sic], the guilt of original sin is remitted . . . let him be anathema." See T. M. DeFerrari, "Baptism (Theology of)," in *New Catholic Encyclopedia,* 2:63.

40. After examining this problem of unbaptized infants, the Roman Catholic author, George Dyer, wonders if they might possibly be in heaven instead of limbo. "Is there any possibility, they [the unbaptized infants' parents] will ask, that the child is in heaven? We must say that the evidence to the contrary is not clear or so compelling

that it would force us to deny them all hope of the child's salvation"
("The Unbaptized Infant in Eternity," 153).

APPENDIX B: REPENTANCE AND SALVATION

1. See Charles C. Ryrie, *Balancing the Christian Life* (Chicago: Moody Press, 1969), 171–72, for a more detailed discussion of the importance of this passage to evangelism.
2. This is true as well in 2 Peter 3:9, "The Lord is . . . not willing that any should perish, but that all should come to repentance." That isn't talking about eternal condemnation. The only other use of the word *perish* in Second Peter occurs three verses earlier and there it unequivocally refers to the physical death which occurred when God sent a worldwide flood upon Noah's generation: "The world that then existed perished, being flooded with water" (2 Peter 3:6).
3. Of course, as John makes clear in his First Epistle, for the believer who is already in fellowship with God, the conditions are faith and *openness* before God (i.e., confessing our sins, 1 John 1:9). John doesn't even speak of repentance in First John because his readers were already in fellowship with God (see 2:12–14). Repentance is the condition for believers out of fellowship with God to get back in fellowship.

BIBLIOGRAPHY

Aldrich, Roy. *Holding Fast to Grace*. Findlay, Ohio: Dunham Publishing Co., n.d.

Chafer, Lewis Sperry. *Major Bible Themes*. Revised by John F. Walvoord. Grand Rapids: Zondervan Publishing House, 1974.

————. *Systematic Theology*. Dallas: Dallas Seminary Press, 1948. Reprint, 8 vols. in 4, Grand Rapids: Kregel Publications, 1993.

Demarest, Bruce. *The Cross of Salvation*. Wheaton, Ill.: Crossway Books, 1997.

Dillow, Joseph C. *The Reign of the Servant Kings: A Study of Eternal Security and the Final Significance of Man*. Hayesville, N.C.: Schoettle Publishing Co., 1992.

Dodson, Kenneth F. *The Prize of the Up-Calling*. Hayesville, N.C.: Schoettle Publishing Co., 1989.

Enns, Paul. *The Moody Handbook of Theology*. Chicago: Moody Press, 1989.

Epp, Theodore H. *Present Labor and Future Rewards*. Lincoln, Neb.: Back to the Bible Publications, 1960.

Govett, Robert. *Reward according to Works*. Hayesville, N.C.: Schoettle Publishing Co., 1989.

Gromacki, Robert. *The Holy Spirit*. Swindoll Leadership Library. Nashville: Word Publishing, 1999.

Hodges, Zane C. *Grace in Eclipse*. Dallas, Tex.: Redencion Viva, 1987.

———. *Absolutely Free*. Dallas, Tex.: Redencion Viva, 1989.

Hoekema, Anthony A. *The Bible and the Future*. Grand Rapids: Wm. B. Eerdmans Publishing Co., 1979.

———. *Saved by Grace*. Grand Rapids: Wm. B. Eerdmans Publishing Co., 1989.

Holloman, Henry W. *The Forgotten Blessing: Rediscovering the Transforming Power of Sanctification*. Swindoll Leadership Library. Nashville: Word Publishing, 1999.

Kendall, R. T. *Calvin and English Calvinism to 1649*. Oxford, U.K.: Oxford University Press, 1979.

———. *Once Saved Always Saved*. London: Hodder and Stoughton, 1984.

Kroll, Woodrow Michael. *It Will Be Worth It: A Study in the Believer's Rewards*. Neptune, N.J.: Loizeaux Brothers, 1977.

Leafe, G. Harry. *Running to Win: A Positive Biblical Approach to Rewards and Inheritance*. Houston: Scriptel Publishers, 1992.

Lightner, Robert P. *Sin, the Savior, and Salvation*. Nashville: Thomas Nelson Publishers, 1991.

Lucado, Max. *No Wonder They Call Him the Savior*. Sisters, Oreg.: Multnomah Press, 1986.

Lutzer, Erwin W. *Your Eternal Reward*. Chicago: Moody Press, 1998.

Mauro, Philip. *God's Pilgrims: Their Dangers, Their Resources, Their Rewards*. Hayesville, N.C.: Schoettle Publishing Co., n.d.

Morris, Leon. *The Apostolic Preaching of the Cross.* 3d ed. Grand Rapids: Wm. B. Eerdmans Publishing Co., 1965.

———. *The Atonement: Its Meaning and Significance.* Downers Grove, Ill.: InterVarsity Press, 1983.

Moyer, R. Larry. *Free and Clear: Understanding and Communicating God's Offer of Eternal Life.* Grand Rapids: Kregel Publications, 1997.

Neighbor, R. E. *If By Any Means. . . .* Hayesville, N.C.: Schoettle Publishing Co., 1985.

Ryrie, Charles C. *The Grace of God.* Chicago: Moody Press, 1956.

———. *Basic Theology.* Wheaton, Ill.: Victor Books, 1986.

———. *So Great Salvation.* Wheaton, Ill.: Victor Books, 1989.

Stanley, Charles. *The Power of the Cross.* Nashville: Thomas Nelson Publishers, 1998.

Wilkin, Robert N. *Confident in Christ: Living by Faith Really Works.* Irving, Tex.: Grace Evangelical Society, 1999.

SCRIPTURE INDEX

Luke

2:52	40
3:16	199, 270
4:13	38
5:32	242
6:35	84
8:5	100
8:11–12	122
8:12	100
8:14	109
9:23–26	204
9:23–27	205
11:1–4	163
12:32–33	225
13:1/3/5	241
15:4–32	242
15:11–32	245
17:3–4	239
18:9–14	246
18:15–17	229
18:16/17	229
18:33	44
19:10	25
19:11–27	170, 224
22:31–32/44	37
23:46	48
24:25–26	30
24:27	16, 30
24:44	31
24:46–47	133
24:47	240, 242, 263

John

1:1	19, 40, 251
1:1–14	15, 33
1:9	81
1:11	116
1:11–12	92
1:12	7, 107, 108, 139, 205
1:13	107, 108, 110
1:14	19, 56, 198
1:18	18, 150
1:29	25, 31, 42

1:33	199, 270
2:1–12	124
2:19	44
2:25	23
3	123
3:1	121
3:2	123
3:3	107, 121, 198, 229
3:5	107, 121
3:7	107
3:13–16	110
3:14	121
3:14–15/15–16	122
3:16	6, 7, 11, 12, 119, 123, 192, 205, 212, 213, 231, 241
3:16–17	113
3:16–18	237
3:18	122, 231
3:18–19	92
3:36	122, 231, 232
4	123
4:10/19/28–29	123
4:34	167
4:39/41–42	123
4:46–54	124
4:50/53	124
5:9/16	124
5:24	7, 212, 218, 223, 237
5:26	12
5:28	126
5:38–47	124
5:40	92
6:6	38
6:28/29/41	125
6:47	125, 237
6:64/66/68–69	125
7:1/30/31	125
7:37	91
8:12	174
8:30–32	213
8:31	214

8:31–32	149
8:44	56, 100
8:46	37, 96
8:51/52	270
8:58	18, 40, 125
9:14/16	126
9:17	125
9:35–38	126
10:10	6, 12, 110, 207
10:10–11	110
10:11	12
10:17–18	43, 45
10:28	194, 270
10:28–29	110, 192
10:29	195
11:25	49
11:25–27	237
11:26	270
11:26b	127
11:37	126
11:41–42	195
12:2	269
12:11/25–27	126
12:27–28	102
12:31	18, 102
12:42	121
12:42–43	164
13:1–5	251
13:2	217
13:27	38, 217
13:35	11, 175, 214
13:37	54, 206
14:1–4	206
14:2	221
14:3	221, 226
14:7	15
14:9	18
14:15–17	198
14:16	71, 93
14:16–17	94, 199
14:17	93, 94, 95
14:18	199
14:25	198

SUBJECT INDEX

Gospel of Belief, 159
Gospel of John, as "Gospel of belief,"
159–61
Government, as common grace, 84–87
Grace
acrostic, 9
"cheap" grace, 121–22
common grace, 79–90
meaning of word, 79
saving grace, 105
sinner as object of grace, 13
vs. Law, 63–66, 67.
See also Faith; Salvation
Graham, Billy, 235
Great White Throne judgment, 173.
See also Unsaved
Gregory of Nyssa, 232
Grudem, Wayne, 44
Gutenberg, Johannes, 86–87

—H—

Hartley, John, 3
"He Rescued Me," xiii–xiv
Heathens, 145–49.
See also Unsaved
"Heaven Came Down and Glory Filled
My Soul," 143
Hebrews, Book of, and
Old Testament, 41–43.
See also Israel
Hell, 13. *See also* Unsaved
Hendricks, Howard, 144
High priest in Israel, 42, 60. *See also* Jesus
Christ, as High Priest
Hinson, W.B., 195
Hodge, Charles, 210, 233
Hodges, Zane, xi, 74, 100, 101, 109,
126–27, 174–75, 216
Holy Spirit
and effectual call to salvation, 105–7
and eternal security of
believer, 198–201
as Advocate, 94–95
as Helper, 93

as Paraclete, 95
convicting sinners, 92–102
His work of regeneration, 198
indwelling the church, 199–200
protecting believers, 198–200
restraining sin, 90
role in sanctification, 150–51
sealing believers, 200–201.
See also God
Hübmaier, Balthasar, 234

—I—

Incarnation, 19–25.
See also Jesus Christ
Inchley, John, 231
Indulgences, 246
Infant salvation, 229–36
baptism, 235–36
Jesus's statements on children, 230
Limbo, 235–36
Roman Catholic views, 235
Ingersoll, Robert, 81
Ingle, Clifford, 231
Israel, 242–43, 244

—J—

Jehovah's Witnesses, 19
Jeremiah, 84–85
Jeschke, Marlin, 232
Jesus Christ, actions for sinners
propitiation for sinners, 58–60
reconciling sinners with God, 60–62
redeeming sinners, 55–58
substitute for sinners, 53–55.
See also Jesus Christ, believer's
relationship to Him; Salvation
Jesus Christ, believer's
relationship to Him
assurance of salvation by
believing, 121–28, 211–12
eternal security of believer, 194–98
fellowship with Christ, 175–76,
212–18
knowing Christ, 15–17.

Selected titles from the
Swindoll Leadership Library

COLOR OUTSIDE THE LINES
Dr. Howard G. Hendricks

All of us yearn to be creative, but few of us feel we truly are. In this fun-to-read, energy-packed volume of the Swindoll Leadership Series, Hendricks proposes a nine-step process for unleashing an exciting spark of creativity and innovation in our lives and ministry. Includes numerous creative approaches to problem solving.

EFFECTIVE CHURCH GROWTH STRATEGIES
Dr. Joseph Wall and Dr. Gene Getz

Effective Church Growth Strategies outlines the biblical foundations necessary for raising healthy churches. Wall and Getz examine the groundwork essential for church growth, qualities of biblically healthy churches, methods for planting a new church, and steps for numerical and spiritual growth. The authors' study of Scripture, history, and culture will spark a new vision for today's church leaders.

EFFECTIVE PASTORING
Dr. Bill Lawrence

In *Effective Pastoring*, Dr. Bill Lawrence examines what it means to be a pastor in the 21st century. Lawrence discusses often-overlooked issues, writing transparently about the struggles of the pastor, the purpose and practice of servant leadership, and the roles and relationships crucial to pastoring. In doing so, he offers a revealing look beneath the "how to" to the "how to be" for pastors.

EMPOWERED LEADERS
Dr. Hans Finzel

Is leadership really about the rewards, excitement and exhilaration? Or the responsibilities, frustrations and exhausting nights? Dr. Hans Finzel takes readers on a journey into the lives of the Bible's great leaders, unearthing powerful principles for effective leadership in any situation.

END TIMES
Dr. John F. Walvoord

Long regarded as one of the top prophecy experts, Dr. John F. Walvoord now explores world events in light of biblical prophecy. Dealing with every area of biblical prophecy, this is the definitive work on the end times for all church leaders.

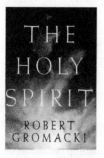

THE HOLY SPIRIT
Dr. Robert Gromacki

In *The Holy Spirit*, Dr. Robert Gromacki examines the personality, deity, symbols, and gifts of the Holy Spirit, while tracing the ministry of the Spirit throughout the Old Testament, the Gospel Era, the life of Christ, the Book of Acts, and the lives of modern believers.

HUMANITY AND SIN
Dr. Robert A. Pyne

Sin may seem like an outdated concept these days, but its consequences remain as destructive as ever. Dr. Robert A. Pyne explores sin's overarching effect on creation and our world today. Learn about the creation of humankind, mankind's sinful nature, and God's plan for the fallen world.

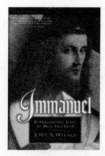

IMMANUEL
Dr. John A. Witmer

Dr. John A. Witmer presents the almighty Son of God as a living, breathing, incarnate man. He shows us a full picture of the Christ in four distinct phases: the Son of God before He became man, the divine suffering man on Earth, the glorified and ascended Christ, and the coming King.

A LIFE OF PRAYER
Dr. Paul Cedar

Dr. Paul Cedar explores prayer through three primary concepts, showing us how to consider, cultivate, and continue a lifestyle of prayer. This volume helps readers recognize the unlimited potential and the awesome purpose of prayer.

MINISTERING TO TODAY'S ADULTS
Dr. Kenn Gangel

After forty years of research and experience, Dr. Kenn Gangel knows what it takes to reach adults for Christ. In an easy-to-understand and apply style, Gangel offers proven systematic strategies for building dynamic adult ministries in the local church.

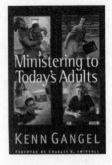

MORAL DILEMMAS
J. Kerby Anderson

J. Kerby Anderson presents a penetrating volume of solid, practical answers to some of the most perplexing issues facing our society today—issues such as abortion, euthanasia, cloning, capital punishment, genetic engineering, and the environment.

THE NEW TESTAMENT EXPLORER
Mark Bailey and Tom Constable

The New Testament Explorer provides a concise, on-target map for traveling through the New Testament. The reader is guided through the New Testament, providing an up-close and to-the-point examination of each paragraph of Scripture and the theological implications of the truths revealed. A great tool for teachers and pastors alike, this book comes equipped with outlines, narrative discussions, and applicable truths for teaching and for living.

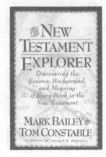

SALVATION
Earl D. Radmacher

God's ultimate gift to His children is salvation. In this volume, Earl Radmacher offers an in-depth look at the most fundamental element of the Christian faith. From defining the essentials of salvation to explaining the result of Christ's sacrifice, this book walks readers through the spiritual meaning, motives, application, and eternal result of God's work of salvation in our lives.

SPIRIT-FILLED TEACHING
Dr. Roy B. Zuck

Acclaimed teacher Roy B. Zuck reveals how teachers can tap into the power of divine energy to fulfill their calling and use their gifts at a deeper level. By applying these timeless, spirit-focused principles, teachers will learn how to teach more effectively and inspire students to live out God's word.

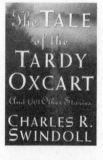

TALE OF THE TARDY OXCART AND 1501 OTHER STORIES
Dr. Charles R. Swindoll

In *The Tale of the Tardy Oxcart*, Charles Swindoll shares from his life-long collection of his and others' personal stories, sermons, and anecdotes. 1501 various illustrations are arranged by subjects alphabetically for quick-and-easy access. A perfect resource for all pastors and speakers.

WOMEN AND THE CHURCH
Dr. Lucy Mabery-Foster

Women and the Church provides an overview of the historical, biblical, and cultural perspectives on the unique roles and gifts women bring to the church, while exploring what it takes to minister to women today. Important insight for any leader seeking to understand how to more effectively minister to women and build women's ministries in the local church.